BRIAN H EDWARDS

D1362803

Grace–
amazing Grace

DayOne

© Day One Publications 2003
First printed 2003

ISBN 1 903087 55-4

9 781903 087558

British Library Cataloguing in Publication Data available

Published by Day One Publications
Day One Publications P O Box 66, Leominster, HR6 0XB
Tel: 01568 613 740
Fax: 01568 611 473
email—sales@dayone.co.uk
web site—www.dayone.co.uk
North American—e-mail-sales@dayonebookstore.com
North American web site—www.dayonebookstore.com

Designed by Steve Devane and printed by CPD

Contents

1 AMAZING GRACE   **4**

2 UNIVERSAL GRACE   **19**

3 SOVEREIGN GRACE   **42**

4 THE GRACE OF LAW   **61**

5 JUSTIFYING GRACE   **87**

6 INCARNATE GRACE   **109**

7 INVINCIBLE GRACE   **129**

8 FORGIVING GRACE   **147**

9 ETERNAL GRACE   **175**

10 PURPOSEFUL GRACE   **193**

11 SUFFICIENT GRACE   **213**

12 COMMUNITY GRACE   **241**

13 SANCTIFYING GRACE   **260**

14 THE GRACE OF PRAYER   **280**

15 REJECTED GRACE   **297**

16 ULTIMATE GRACE   **314**

INDEX OF SCRIPTURE REFERENCES   **339**

Amazing Grace

'The immeasurable riches of his grace in kindness towards us in Christ Jesus' Ephesians 2:7

Grace is one of the most beautiful words in our language and the supreme description of God. It is greater than the words salvation, justification, sanctification or glorification; it is far greater than peace or joy, forgiveness or reconciliation. Grace encompasses all the great truths of Christianity, for without grace they would have no meaning—they could never be part of our Christian language. Grace conceives every hope offered to the human race, and gives birth to all the benefits of the Christian faith. Grace is not love, it conceives love; it is not mercy, it gives birth to mercy. Grace is the creator of both love and mercy in action.

Grace is the creator of faith. It cocoons the gospel as the heavens envelop planet Earth; it sustains trust as air sustains life; it is the energy of evangelism as the heart is to the body; it is the controller of hope as the mind is to action. Grace is uncreated and eternal, for wherever God is, there is grace. Grace is not simply what God does, it is what God is. Grace is the ultimate expression of God and the most attractive of all his perfections: for Christ came from the Father 'full of grace and truth' and from his grace 'we have all received grace upon grace'. Grace is the twin of truth, and both are expressed supremely in Christ.

Without grace, God would not be known, and without God, grace would have no meaning. God is always all that he is; but we can never know all that he is, and we cannot see anything that he is for long. But there is one glory of God's character that is always visible—and that is grace. Grace is the universal evidence of God all around us; it is also the unseen hand on the helm of world affairs. Few have eyes to see it, but grace does not have to be seen to be believed and it does not have to be believed to be seen. Nor does grace have to be seen to be real. Grace is enjoyed even when men curse it, but it is celebrated best when they embrace it. When men choose to ignore God's love or rebel against his word, the fact that he withholds his judgement is due to grace; when he allows bad men to prosper and good men to suffer that too is the result of grace.

Simply to define the word grace as God's undeserved mercy towards a sinner is to probe its meaning as deeply as a pond skater penetrates the water. Grace is not merely God's attitude towards undeserving rebels, it is ultimately and above all *God giving himself* to us and for us—as the Man on a cross.

Grace in the Old Testament

When the apostle Paul wrote of: 'The immeasurable riches of his grace in kindness toward us in Christ Jesus', he wrote as a Jew who had been converted to Christ; he therefore possessed a far greater understanding of the history of the word 'grace' than any Greek or Roman. There were two words in Paul's Hebrew Old Testament that approached the idea of grace. One was the word *hesed*, which was a two-way word. On the one hand it could refer to God's resolute love towards us: 'The *steadfast love* of the LORD never ceases; his mercies never come to an end; they are new every morning; great is your faithfulness' (Lamentations 3:22–23). Whilst on the other hand it could refer to our loyal love to each other or to God himself: 'I desire *steadfast love* and not sacrifice' (Hosea 6:6).

Grace does not have to be seen to be believed and it does not have to be believed to be seen

Some have argued that the meaning of this word is not so much God's unmerited mercy, but his loyalty to his covenant with Israel. Certainly it carries this meaning, but to restrict it to that ignores the fact that when it is used of the relationship between men and women it clearly refers to acts of free kindness where no obligation was at stake. God's loyalty to his covenant with his chosen people is on the basis that it was a covenant born out of his own undeserved love alone. For this reason, the word most commonly used in the New Testament to translate *hesed* is the word 'mercy'. In the Old Testament, the noun of this word *hesed* is used thirty-

Chapter 1

two times—twenty-five in the Psalms alone—and it refers to the 'holy ones' or 'saints' who have received the mercy of God. Mercy is the child of grace.

The other Old Testament Hebrew word that approaches the idea of grace is the word *hanan*. It meant 'favour', and was always a one-way response from a superior to an inferior. This word could be used of our relationship to each other, but it was never used of our response to God. The first use of it in the Bible is found when we are told that, 'Noah found *favour* in the eyes of the Lord' (Genesis 6:8). David used it as a verb: 'Turn to me and *be gracious* to me' (Psalm 25:16), and again, '*Be gracious* to me O LORD, for I am in distress' (Psalm 31:9). Of the fifty-six occasions where it is used as a verb in the Old Testament, forty-one refer to God's way of behaving. As a noun it is a common word for the favour of a superior person, but as an adjective, all thirteen occasions found in the Old Testament refer to God.

God used both *hanan* and *hesed* to describe his own matchless character to Moses: 'And the LORD passed before him and proclaimed, "The LORD, the LORD, a God merciful and *gracious*, slow to anger, and abounding in *steadfast love* and faithfulness, keeping *steadfast love* for thousands, forgiving iniquity and transgression and sin"' (Exodus 34:6–7). This was a description never forgotten, and again and again God's people drew comfort from it (see for example: Numbers 14:18–19; Nehemiah 9:17; Psalm 85:10–11; 103:8; 145:8; Joel 2:13; Jonah 4:2). Both *hanan* and *hesed* are found in David's great psalm of sorrow: 'Have *mercy* upon me, O God, according to your *steadfast love*' (Psalm 51:1). David clearly understood mercy to be the result of God's steadfast love. Mercy is always the child of grace.

To appreciate the depth of this grace we must understand the character of God. He is majestically powerful, magnificently holy, inconceivably wise and fearfully just. And that is exactly where the problem of the human race lies. In the light of this awesome and supreme God we are helpless and hopeless; or as Paul describes our condition: 'Having no hope and without God in the world' (Ephesians 2:12).

Grace was revealed when God planned good for this fallen world; but he did not design this good immediately after the human race fell into sin—he designed it long before then. Though it came to birth when God first responded to Adam after the Fall, it was conceived long before. Whenever God speaks and whatever he says, it is evidence of his grace; whenever God acts and whatever he does, that too is always grace. Whether God warns or promises, condemns or acquits, it is grace. The first record of grace after the Fall is found in the words: 'The LORD God called to the man and said to him, "Where are you?"' (Genesis 3:9). God did not have to call—he knew exactly where Adam was; and Adam did not want God to call—he was in hiding. That voice was God's undeserved initiative—that is grace. He condescended to speak to a rebel. God judged Adam's sin but provided at once for his restoration—and that is all grace.

The law of God in the Old Testament, for all its rigorous demands and severe punishments, was an expression of God's grace; this is precisely why Paul concludes that the law is 'holy, righteous and good' (Romans 7:12). Paul's reasoning is that through the law we recognise sin as 'sinful beyond measure' (v 13), and only when we acknowledge the reality of sin will we be ready to receive the grace of forgiveness and reconciliation. It is therefore a perversion to talk of 'law *or* grace' as if the two were mutually exclusive; we will not even find the phrase 'law *and* grace' in the Bible. Instead, we should always think of 'the grace of law'; *Paul summarises the whole of the gospel in four words, 'By grace ... through faith'* because law is grace. For this reason we may speak of 'law and gospel', for both the law—which in the words of William Tyndale 'asks and requires', and the gospel—which Tyndale claimed 'pardons and forgives', are expressions of grace. Whenever God gave his people laws, he provided salvation through the offering of a sacrifice. That is grace. In God's covenant, wherever there was law there was also gospel. In the New Testament, the good news of Jesus Christ is called, 'The word of his grace' (Acts 14:3) and 'The gospel of the grace of God' (Acts 20:24). For his part, Paul summarises the whole of the gospel in four words, 'By grace ... through faith' (Ephesians 2:8).

John MacRea was brought up on the far west coast of the Scottish

Highlands at the end of the eighteenth century. As a shepherd in the wild mountains, MacRae was careless about his soul until God's grace broke into his heart. When she heard of his conversion, an old lady in his area commented, 'If John MacRae has become a new man, surely the latter day glory is not far off!' MacRae became a preacher in 1830 and for more than forty years he preached powerfully across the Western Isles and Highlands of Scotland. Shortly before his death he wrote a letter to his daughter Jane and in it he included his view of grace: 'What a meaning there is in that word 'grace' for such as I am. It contains everything necessary for the salvation of the sinner, leaping over mountains of aggravated rebellion, infinite in its absolute freeness. What I need is to realise this in its power and glory.' One hundred and thirty years on we need the same realisation.

Grace and the Gospels

The word 'grace' (*charis* in the Greek) never appears in the Gospels of Matthew or Mark, though its meaning is constantly in view. Luke, a close companion of Paul for many years, only uses the word to describe Mary's relationship with God, 'you have found *favour*' (1:30) and our Lord's with his heavenly father, 'Jesus increased … in *favour* with God and man' (2:40, 52; the word 'gracious' is used in 4:22). However, stories illustrating grace abound. The parables of the wedding garment, the prodigal son, and the invitation to the marriage feast are each illustrations of the true meaning of grace. But such parables as the rich man and Lazarus or the unmerciful servant are no less illustrations of grace. It is not claiming too much to conclude that all the parables of Christ illustrate grace and all his works and words are beautiful pictures of grace. We do not deserve that God should communicate with us at all; the fact that he spoke so generously through his Son is nothing other than grace.

John in his Gospel develops the word and conspicuously introduces us to grace in a phrase that has produced a field-day for commentators. John 1:14–17 reads, 'The Word became flesh and dwelt among us, and we have seen his glory, glory as of the only Son from the Father, full of grace and truth … And from his fullness we have all received, grace upon grace. For the law was given through Moses; grace and truth came through Jesus Christ.'

The little word here translated *upon* in the phrase 'grace *upon* grace', when it is used as a comparison or contrast as it is here, carries the idea of something that comes as a replacement. In other words, whilst we had grace and truth before Christ—through the law and priesthood given by Moses—it is through Jesus Christ himself that we receive the *fullness* of both grace and truth (v 14). Grace in the Old Testament has been exchanged—replaced—for the fullness of grace in Christ. That is the meaning of 'grace upon grace'. The difference is as great as between this sad and suffering world, and the new heavens and new earth that God will create at the end of time.

This then is what John the Apostle is saying: The glory of Christ, which reflected that of his Father and shone through his earthly life, was the *fullness* of grace and truth. It is a grace that has replaced the grace of the law of Moses. Both truth and grace came through Moses, but both have found their fullest expression in Jesus Christ. This, incidentally, helps us to understand Matthew 5:17, 'Do not think that I have come to abolish the Law or the Prophets; I have not come to abolish them but to fulfil them.' We will return to this in the chapter on the grace of law.

The glory of Christ, which reflected that of his Father and shone through his earthly life, was the fullness of grace and truth

John 1:14–17 is the only place where the Apostle John uses the word *charis* in his Gospel—just four times in four verses—but it is a brilliant introduction to the word and a fitting preface to the way Paul employs it. Dr Donald Guthrie rightly observed that, 'The mission of Jesus was a supreme revelation of the God of grace.'

Grace for Paul and his colleagues

For the apostle Paul, grace was his favourite word—and with very good reason. The achievements of Paul were colossal. His dramatic conversion and then his firm loyalty to the gospel under pressure must have been an incredible encouragement to the first Christian communities. Added to this he was the man who spearheaded the first unevangelized fields mission and planted churches right across Asia Minor and into Greece. His planned vision to encircle the Roman Empire with gospel churches, which appears to be woven into Romans 15, remains a challenge for us even today. His deliberate and efficient action to organise the young churches into vital training centres is still our model for evangelism. From these centres Christians, with Christ as the Lord of their lives, would go out to evangelise the world. And of course it is Paul who by the power and influence of the Holy Spirit has given us so many of those valuable teaching letters in our Bible.

But Paul had not always been a Christian, even though he had always been very religious. He himself tells us that as a well educated Pharisee he was proud whilst pretending to be humble, a lawbreaker whilst teaching the law to others, and a blasphemer whilst claiming to serve the true God. In addition he was a persecutor and destroyer of the church whilst believing that he belonged to the only true church; and he was an ignorant and violent man, whilst he thought he possessed the wisdom of God, believed in the only true God and lived to please God. And none of his pretending or claims to self-righteousness remotely excused him for any of his actions.

Then one day, shortly after the death and resurrection of Jesus Christ, this proud and zealous Jew called Saul from the city of Tarsus, was dramatically converted by the one he so bitterly hated. His life was radically changed; and in the light of this it is not surprising that Paul loved to tell his story. He does this twice in Acts when he is on trial, and there are frequent references in his letters to the revolution of his life after that encounter on the road to Damascus. Paul looked for a word that would adequately sum-up what God had done for him.

In five striking phrases Paul revealed the progression of his thinking when he looked at himself in the light of what he once was. Somewhere around the year AD 57 Paul wrote a letter that we know as 1 Corinthians; he was writing from Ephesus and in this letter he claimed, 'I am the least of the apostles' (1 Corinthians 15:9). A little later to the same church he confessed, 'I am nothing' (2 Corinthians 12:11). Five years later whilst under house arrest in Rome he declared, 'I am the very least of all the saints' (Ephesians 3:8), and in the same year, but now writing from a Roman prison cell, he admitted, 'I am the foremost (of sinners)' (1 Timothy 1:15). Finally, two years later in AD 64—the year of the great fire in Rome started by the Emperor Nero to create a brown-field site for urban redevelopment—Paul wrote, 'I am not ashamed' (2 Timothy 1:12).

What do these five 'I am' phrases of Paul have in common? We may conclude that they are each Paul's personal put-down, because twice he says, 'I am the least', once he claims, 'I am nothing', and once: 'I am the worst'. But then he writes, 'I am not ashamed', which is hardly self-deprecating. So the common denominator cannot be a belittling of himself.

Whenever Paul confessed his own great sin and failure or his abundant hope for his ultimate security, it is always firmly in the context of this magnificent word 'grace'

The key that is common to these five phrases is contained in a word that appears close by in the context of each of them. At 1 Corinthians 15:10 Paul wrote, 'by the *grace* of God I am what I am'; in 2 Corinthians 12:9 he reflects on God's promise: 'My *grace* is sufficient'; in Ephesians 3:8, he declared, 'this *grace* was given (to me) to preach to the Gentiles'; in 1 Timothy 1:14, Paul added that 'the *grace* of our Lord overflowed for me'; and finally in 2 Timothy 1:9, he concluded that he had been saved not because of works, 'but because of (God's) own purpose and *grace*'. In other words, whenever Paul confessed his own great sin and failure or his abundant hope for his ultimate security, it is always firmly in the context of this magnificent word 'grace'.

Paul came to love that word, and as a noun he used it almost one hundred times in his correspondence—twenty times alone in his letter to the Christians at Rome and eleven times to the Ephesians. In every sense he would have been lost without it. He begins and closes each one of his letters with a salutation including the word grace: Romans 1:7, 'Grace and peace to you', and he signs off in Romans 16:20, 'The grace of our Lord Jesus Christ be with you.' Similarly in 1 Corinthians 1:3, 'Grace to you and peace', and finally in 16:23, 'The grace of the Lord Jesus be with you'. Yet again in 2 Corinthians 1:2, 'Grace to you and peace' and he concludes with the well-used, 'The grace of our Lord Jesus Christ and the love of God and the fellowship of the Holy Spirit be with you all' (13:14). Paul follows the same pattern in his epistles to the Galatians, Ephesians, Colossians and Thessalonians.

Writing to Timothy, Paul varies the greeting only slightly by adding a third word, 'Grace, mercy and peace' (1 Timothy 1:2 and 2 Timothy 1:2)— but then, Timothy was a pastor in Ephesus and Paul presumably thought he needed 'mercy' more than most! Titus in Crete, missed out on the mercy, but not on grace (Titus 1:4). Both these young pastors were left with a message to pass on to their churches, because the last phrase in each letter is plural and means—as he spelt out to Titus—'Grace be with you *all*' (Titus 3:15). The only exception to Paul's otherwise invariable pattern is found in the letter to the Hebrews (on the well-attested assumption that Paul is the author of this book also); but there is no greeting at all in this book and the word 'grace' does not appear until 2:9. However, from there on we have some rich uses of the word in Hebrews, and at least the apostle closes with his usual signature: 'Grace be with all of you' (13:25).

Even Peter picked up on this greeting and included it in his two letters, 'Grace and peace be multiplied to you' (1 Peter 1:2 and 2 Peter 1:2). He then weaves grace into his conclusions in 1 Peter 5:12 and 2 Peter 3:18. The fact that John, who used it so sparingly in his Gospel, also includes 'Grace, mercy and peace' as his greeting in 2 John 3, and begins and ends his letters to the churches with grace (Revelation 1:4 and 22:21), implies either that this had become a standard greeting in the early church or else John had been reading a lot of Paul! Jude is an odd man out by greeting his readers with, 'Mercy, peace and love' (Jude 2); but even he does not overlook the word 'grace' altogether (v 4). James nearly skips grace completely but squeezes it into just one part of his letter in 4:6 where he borrows from Proverbs 3:34 and paraphrases with 'God opposes the proud but gives grace to the humble.'

New words for old

Today, we may greet our friends with the meaningless, 'Hi!' In the first century a common greeting was the Greek word *chairo*, meaning 'joy'; but for thousands of years the Hebrew greeting among the Jews had been *shalom*, 'peace'. The Greek equivalent of the Hebrew word for peace was *eirene*—from which we get our word 'irenic' (peaceable). Paul changed the Greek salutation to *charis* ('grace') and combined it with the Jewish greeting to make up his own: 'Grace and peace' (*charis kai eirene*). *Charis* was a well-used word in the first century, and generally it referred to the favour shown by a superior to an inferior, the deserving to the undeserving. In the Acts of the Apostles the early church found 'favour with all the people' (Acts 2:47), and the Roman Governors, Felix and Festus, showed favour to the Jews (Acts 24:27 and 25:3, 9). The word was also used of the response of the one who received this favour, so that 'thanks to the gods' (*Charis tois theois*) was a common expression. In fact, Paul used it in this way himself in Romans 6:17 'Thanks be to God ...', and in 1 Timothy 1:12 'I thank ... Christ Jesus our Lord ...' and 2 Timothy 1:3 'I thank God whom I serve ...' In each place the word 'thank' translates the word *charis*.

Paul was a master of language, and one of his great pleasures was to give old words new meanings. There were so many facts about the Christian faith that were unfamiliar to converted pagans—and even to converted Jews—so, rather than coin a brand new word, Paul often preferred to take an old one and give it new value. For example, when the Christians were smarting under the accusation of being *atheos*—the word meant 'without god' because they had rejected the Roman and Greek pantheon of pagan gods—Paul re-coined the word in order to encourage the young Christians at Ephesus. He tells them that when they were all very religious in the city, worshipping Diana of the Ephesians, they were in reality *atheos*—without God. But they are no longer the atheists, and it is the pagans who are *atheos* (Ephesians 2:1).

Paul does exactly the same with the word *charis*. He takes it out of the commonplace and clothes it with a wonderful new meaning. From the condescending, patronising favour of a superior, Paul turns *charis* into the most expressive word in our Christian language. So much did Paul love this word that often he could not leave it to stand on its own but felt that he must adorn it with adjectives or adverbs. He writes of 'much more grace', 'abundant grace', 'superabundant grace', 'abounding grace', 'reigning grace', 'exceeding grace', 'exceeding abundant grace', 'glorious grace', 'sufficient grace' and even, 'incomparable riches of grace'.

For Paul, grace was the only way to explain his salvation, it was the key to all his benefits in the Christian life, it was the single-word summary of his message to the world and the only guarantee that the One who had found him would never lose him. God's choice of his people is 'of grace', we are justified freely 'by grace' and saved 'by grace', we have access to God 'through grace' and all spiritual gifts come to us 'according to grace'.

For Paul, grace was ... the single-word summary of his message to the world and the only guarantee that the One who had found him would never lose him

Paul seems to have made a conscious decision to commandeer this word grace in order to express God's response to us. He never once soils it by using it to describe our response to God. On just two occasions in his letters Paul allows himself the use of the word *charis* to describe our relationship to each other. In 2 Corinthians 8:6–7 he writes of the 'act of grace' when he refers to the church's giving, and in Colossians 4:6 he urges that our speech should always be 'gracious'—although even these have a clear God-ward dimension. Beyond this, the word belongs to God. If every other word was denied him, grace is the one Paul would retain to explain the very heart of his gospel. If you asked him how sinners could be rescued from themselves, from Satan and from hell, he would reply simply, 'By grace'; and if you enquired on what ground this could be, he would respond, 'Jesus Christ and him crucified'.

Grace is perfect, all-embracing and costly, because grace is expressed ultimately in Jesus Christ who is, in himself, the fullness of grace.

Though grace is ubiquitous—it is everywhere—it is recognised by only a few, embraced by even fewer, and understood fully by none. Grace is often a mystery, a puzzle. There is an enigma about grace. It is present above the mindless destruction and passionate hatred of men; it is there in our shattered plans, frustrated expectations, and broken hearts; and it is to be found even in the dull grind of our daily routine. Can grace really be present here on earth always and everywhere? Yes, because the absence of grace is hell.

Though grace is ...

everywhere—it is

recognised by only a

few, embraced by even

fewer, and understood

fully by none

For Saul of Tarsus there was nothing more wonderfully reassuring than to receive grace, and there was nothing more dreadful than to come close to it and then to 'fall away from grace'. The most glorious experience known to Paul was to be embraced by grace—and the most terrifying possibility was to reject it.

John Newton was born in 1725 in Wapping, one mile down river from the Tower of London, and he died eighty-two years later barely one mile away in the City. His life in between is well summed up by his own epitaph written on a plain marble slab that can be found in the parish church of St Mary Woolnoth in the City of London. Part of it reads:

John Newton
once an infidel and libertine
a servant of slaves in Africa
was
by the rich mercy of our Lord and Saviour
Jesus Christ
preserved, restored, pardoned
and appointed to preach the faith
he had longed laboured to destroy.

Abandoning his mother's Christian faith, the young Newton became an arrogant unbeliever. Having rejected God and his conscience, he considered that he was free to live as he pleased—and he did! As a blaspheming, drunken, promiscuous sailor, he filled up his teenage years until, herded onto a warship and pressed into His Majesty's service at the age of nineteen, he refined his anti-Christ philosophy and dragged others with him. Eventually Newton turned up in West Africa as a slave trader and sunk so low that he became the pity and scorn of slaves himself.

In March 1748 John Newton was on his way back to England when a violent storm smashed into the little ship *Greyhound* and for weeks the crew nursed their shattered boat across the Atlantic, expecting a choking grave with every shift of wind. In his terror Newton called out to God for help and his prayer was heard. After days of remorseless battering by the ocean and his conscience, John yielded to the claims of Christ, believed the promises of God's word, and received his first hope of forgiveness. Somewhere on board the broken ship Newton found a little book of sermons, and one in particular he read over and over again, it was based on the words of John the Baptist recorded in John 1:29, 'Behold the Lamb of God which taketh away the sin of the world'. The Easter sermon was entitled, 'The merits of Christ's passion', and in it he read these words: 'We can think and talk of Christ dying for our sins and yet live in them. We can hear of his being accused and condemned and yet not condemn nor so much as accuse ourselves for our sin. We can read over the whole history of our Saviour's passion with dry eyes, and be no more troubled at it than if we had been in no way concerned in it.' As the shivering, starving sailor read those words he knew they were so true of him. He had for too long responded to the death of Christ exactly like that. Newton read on and learned that Christ had come to take away sin, 'Not only for some particular sins but sin in general, sin as sin … the strength as well as the guilt of our sin, our inclination to it, as well as our obligation to punishment for it.'

Just four weeks after the terrifying storm that almost sank Newton's hope of salvation, the broken *Greyhound* struggled into Lough Swilly, one of the northernmost points of Ireland. The date was 8 April 1748, which in that year was Good Friday—a neat coincidence for the man who had been reading an Easter sermon. Less than two hours after they had anchored in the comparative shelter of the bay, a gale blew at sea with such a force that the ship would certainly have been broken to pieces had it still been beyond the Lough.

John, who was born in the rough waterfront village of Wapping and whose formal education amounted to just two years at an inferior school, found in Christ alone the grace of God. And Saul, who grew up as a graduate in the university city of Tarsus close to the wild frontier of the Roman Empire, had long before found exactly the same. These two men, seventeen hundred years apart, had both experienced the meaning of grace, and each had begun an adventure in which their life would explore and enjoy the incredible wealth of amazing grace. For this reason, since John of Wapping and Saul of Tarsus have so much in common, we will return often in this book to the life of John to illustrate the teaching of Paul. Years later John Newton turned his experience into what has become one of the most popular hymns of the Christian church. It was written for his congregation at Olney in Buckinghamshire to sing on New Year's morning 1773 and was based upon the text for his sermon from 1 Chronicles 17:16–17.

> AMAZING GRACE—HOW SWEET THE SOUND—
> that saved a wretch like me!
> I once was lost, but now am found;
> was blind, but now I see.
>
> 2 God's grace first taught my heart to fear,
> his grace my fears relieved;
> how precious did that grace appear
> the hour I first believed!
>
> 3 Through many dangers, toils and snares
> I have already come;
> his grace has brought me safe this far
> and grace will lead me home.

4 The Lord has promised good to me,
his word my hope secures;
my shield and great reward is he
as long as life endures.

5 And when this mortal life is past
and earthly days shall cease,
I shall possess with Christ at last
eternal joy and peace.

6 The earth will soon dissolve like snow,
the sun no longer shine;
but God, who called me here below,
will be for ever mine.

JOHN NEWTON 1725–1807
Praise! 772

Universal grace

'He himself gives to all mankind life and breath and everything' Acts 17:25

It is not only the Christian who can declare with the psalmist, 'God does not deal with us according to our sins, nor repay us according to our iniquities' (Psalm 103:10), the whole world should be singing from the same hymn sheet. The God of supreme order, perfect beauty, unbridled wisdom and unlimited power, has not dealt with our fragile, ugly and rebellious world as it deserves. Ever since the rebellion of the human race in sin, the whole universe—and our planet Earth in particular—is filled with the evidence of God's grace, his undeserved love in action. This is often referred to as 'common grace'—grace shared by all without exception; but that is an unfortunate phrase since 'common' sounds like the grace of the ordinary or commonplace. I prefer to use the term 'universal grace', which more obviously means: grace for all. Universal grace does not mean that all receive the same, but that all receive some. God's grace is more abundant and more obvious to some than others, but none are overlooked altogether. We might even call it 'prodigal grace', or 'lavish grace' because it is scattered so liberally across the globe.

Universal grace does not mean that all receive the same, but that all receive some

When the seraphim in the temple called out: 'Holy, holy, holy is the LORD of hosts; the whole earth is full of his glory' (Isaiah 6:3), from their vantage point they must have enjoyed a large understanding of the universal grace of God. Paul neatly summarised it in his sermon to the people at Athens: 'He himself gives to all mankind life and breath and everything' (Acts 17:25). Our Lord, as always, reduced the same great theology to a plain and simple statement: 'He is kind to the ungrateful and the evil' (Luke 6:35). So, what is this universal grace that everyone born into this world enjoys?

The gift of spiritual life is universal grace

The Apostle John described Christ as the true light coming into the world but then added that this is the light which 'enlightens everyone' (John 1:9). He meant just that. Every human being ever born into this world has an enlightenment that comes from the Creator. The creation story expresses it only slightly differently: 'So God created man in his own image, in the image of God he created him; male and female he created them' (Genesis 1:27). This meant that many of the great attributes—or characteristics—of God were reflected in the human race, such as: wisdom, understanding, appreciation of beauty, compassion, and a sense of eternity.

The preacher in the book of Ecclesiastes tells us that God 'put eternity into man's heart' (3:11). This is precisely why we have never found a people, anywhere in the world, who do not worship. Their worship may be primitive as they honour the moon, or the spirits of their ancestors, or stones or animals; it may even be evil as they offer cruel sacrifices, scourge their own bodies or bitterly persecute all who are not of their religion. But all over the world, people have a sense of God, an awareness of accountability, a belief in life beyond here. Somehow we all know that there is something more. Significantly even in our hard-nosed scientific age of apparent unbelief, the world's bestsellers and blockbuster movies all reflect this. The Narnia stories of C S Lewis, the Middle Earth saga of J R R Tolkein, the magical Harry Potter world of J K Rowling, and even books and films like *The Final Odyssey* and *Star Wars* all speak of something more beyond.

This reveals something very significant. At the Fall into sin by Adam and Eve, God might have sucked the soul out of mankind, he might have withdrawn that gift of 'light'; the light of knowing that there is more beyond. He might have left us all not merely to be atheists—believing that there is no God—but without even the evidence that there is a being called God whom we may choose not to believe in.

In these days of pluralism, we are constantly told that all the world's religions have something to teach us. They certainly have. They teach us that the human soul is not extinct; that it is alive to spiritual reality even though dead towards God. No one is born an atheist—and that is universal grace. Paul shared a common truth at Athens when he declared that God's universal grace is what caused the Athenians to seek God: 'In the hope that they might feel their way towards him and find him' (Acts 17:27). They ended up with a multiplicity of gods, and even one that they called the Unknown God. But at least their worship marked them out distinctly from the animal world. This enlightenment of which John speaks in his Gospel is not the knowledge of salvation in Jesus Christ or even an effective knowledge of the true God, but it is the knowledge that there is a God, and that in this world there is much more than meets the eye—there is more beyond.

Though all religions outside of Jesus Christ are false ways into eternity, at least religion is part of being essentially human. Atheism is subhuman. Religions are a groping darkly after God; a longing to find him, somehow, somewhere; religion is a hand reaching out from the shadows into the unknown. The primitive tribesman worshipping his sticks, stones or ancestors is at least showing his dignity as a human being; he is worshipping—albeit in tragic error. God is not far away, he knows it, he feels it; but in his spiritual blindness he cannot find God. The animal kingdom does not even do that much. Cats and caterpillars do not pray, nor do antelopes and apes. Atheism is not human, on the contrary it is humanity aping the ape—trying to live like the animals, as if there is no God. The 'humanistic atheist' claims that he is merely an intelligent animal; from his perspective this may be right, but from a higher perspective he is therefore more primitive and less human than the idol worshipper; the atheist is not using his superior intelligence to draw the obvious conclusion from the evidence around him. Paul assured the Athenians: 'He is actually not far from each one of us, for "in him we live and move and have our being"' (Acts 17:27–28).

In her book *Leading Little Ones to God*, Marion Schoolland has a beautiful way of explaining this part of universal grace to a small child: 'Some people say there is no God. They do not pray at all. But deep down in their hearts there is that little voice that says, "Yes, there is a God"'. Of course they do not hear an audible voice, and they may never admit to such a voice; but it is that voice that raises such questions as, 'What if?' and 'Perhaps there might just be?' It is this same voice that sends a shiver of uncertainly when death is close: perhaps, after all, there is more beyond.

The evidence of spiritual life in the human race is all part of the universal grace of God. The devil cannot rob anyone of their soul, the worst he can do is deceive it.

Our active conscience is universal grace

In the Old Testament, God gave the revelation of his law to his chosen people, Israel, so that they might be distinguished from all the nations around them and might become the envy of those nations (Deuteronomy 4:5–8). His law was good and it was meant for good; it was not intended to spoil their lives but to increase their joy; and this is precisely why the Psalmist could often reflect on how much he loved and found pleasure in the law of the Lord: 'I find my delight in your commandments, which I love. I will lift up my hands towards your commandments which I love, and I will meditate on your statutes' (Psalm 119:47–48). In fact the Psalmist went further than this and declared that in keeping the law of God he found true freedom, which he called 'a wide place' (Psalm 119:45). For him the law was not a narrow shackle, but a wide path to freedom; true freedom is not freedom to do whatever I want, but freedom to do what God wants me to do and to be what God wants me to be. The law is a tyrant only to the lawbreaker.

The devil cannot rob anyone of their soul, the worst he can do is deceive it

But one problem with the law of God in the Bible is that not everyone has access to it. There were millennia before it was written down in the time of Moses, and in the three and a half millennia since then we still have not ensured that everyone in the world has access to it. So, does this mean that God has left the world without any understanding of right and wrong?

A significant part of the image of God in all men and women is what is called 'conscience'. We may think of this as the awareness that there is right and wrong, good and evil, kindness and wickedness. It is what the eighteenth century German philosopher Immanuel Kant called: the 'categorical imperative'; he saw it as mankind's sense of 'ought'. Paul put it more plainly when he wrote that those who do not have the law 'by nature do what the law requires', and added, 'They show that the work of the law is written on their hearts, while their conscience also bears witness, and their conflicting thoughts accuse or even excuse them' (Romans 2:14–15). But conscience is more than this. Conscience is also that part of the human life that is aware of God and of eternity. In fact it is the awareness of God and eternity—and our accountability to God *in* eternity—that makes conscience a distinctly human thing. Certainly false religions may not express it in this way. They may talk of many gods, rewards and punishments, even reincarnation; but all religions teach somehow of life beyond the grave and of accountability. This is all part of that little voice that says, 'Yes, there is a God'.

God has left us with a clear reference to himself in the dramatic design of creation: 'What can be known about God is plain to (all) ... his invisible attributes, namely his eternal power and divine nature, have been clearly perceived, ever since the creation of the world, in the things that have been made' (Romans 1:19–20). Paul concludes that, tragically, our conscience has become so perverted and spoiled by sin that the great majority of people across the world turn truth into a lie and worship anything other than God himself. But in so doing we are without excuse (v 20).

The catastrophic result is that our whole conscience is affected. The very thing that marks us out from the animal kingdom has now become spoiled. Animals do not have a conscience and therefore are not held morally responsible for their actions. When my dog bites you, the court fines me and orders my dog to be destroyed—not the other way round! But something has happened to the human conscience. In Paul's vivid expression in 1 Timothy 4:2, he claims that our 'consciences are seared'. The word 'cauterise' comes from this word 'seared', but in Paul's day it referred to the branding of a slave with a hot iron. In other words, the conscience of the unbeliever is branded with the beliefs and standards of the society around and not by the law of God.

A few years ago, after preaching at a summer holiday camp, the campers presented me with a most unusual present: it was a beautiful clock that went backwards. I have not yet worked out whether that meant that they enjoyed my ministry so much that they wished it would not end or else …! That clock is still in perfect working order and tells the time accurately— but according to a very warped sense of timekeeping. At least it was more consistent than a clock we once had at church that not only took upon itself to run backwards, but was inconsistently slow as well; no amount of careful calculation could ever arrive at the correct time from that useless item. Everyone has a conscience, and everyone's conscience is in working order; the tragedy is that our conscience too often works to a different rule than God's law. As time passes and we are more and more influenced by the standards of society, like our church clock our conscience becomes less and less reliable. Sadly it often works in reverse—and this is why a man can carry out the most horrendous acts of cruelty and terror and convince himself that what he is doing is right. Occasionally, after a particularly vile murder or act of brutality, the media refer to those responsible as 'animals'. Sadly they are not; if they were, they could not be held responsible for their actions. Men may behave *like* animals but they are never to be thought of as animals. It is the universal grace of conscience that makes cruel human behaviour so appalling.

It is the universal grace of conscience that makes cruel human behaviour so appalling

Paul describes the significance of conscience in Romans 2:14–15, 'When (those) who do not have the law, by nature do what the law requires, they are a law to themselves, even though they do not have the law. They show that the work of the law is written on their hearts, while their conscience also bears witness, and their conflicting thoughts accuse or even excuse them.' Here, precisely, is the conflict of conscience. This is what is often referred to as 'the natural law'—the sense of right and wrong that everyone possesses. Rats and rabbits do not have a conscience but the human race does.

Paul was not teaching his readers in Rome anything new. Even the ancient Greeks referred to this natural law; they called it *nomos agraphos*, which, though it may sound like a hex from Harry Potter's Hogwarts, is Latin for 'law unwritten'. It was, they believed, the only basis for universal standards of right and wrong. Paul's argument is that when their conscience guides them correctly and they obey it, then, unknowingly, they are obeying the moral law of God. This means that even those who have never heard the gospel of Jesus Christ and have no knowledge of the law of God, can still do actions that are good. They are not sinful actions but they are not sufficient to save either. Paul concludes that ultimately, since no one fully obeys even their own conscience, everyone will be found guilty on the Day of Judgement. The good works of the unbeliever are not grace, but they are the evidence of God's grace—his universal grace. It is this conscience that makes many people sensitive to the needs of others and leads to the compassion of famine relief and global disaster aid.

The beauty and design of creation is universal grace

When God completed creation he saw everything that he had made 'and behold, it was very good' (Genesis 1:31). That does not mean that it was the best he could do; it means that it was the best that could ever be done. God does not botch, and he cannot do anything that is less than the most perfect it could ever be. Even Adam's sin could not entirely ruin the wonder of God's creation. There is beauty even in this fallen world, and no one who has ever watched some of the fascinating nature films can doubt this— whatever other conclusions they may draw. So much of creation still reflects the Creator. In Romans 1:20 Paul tells us that, 'God's invisible attributes, namely, his eternal power and divine nature, have been clearly perceived, ever since the creation of the world, in the things that have been made.'

We speak of the 'power' of the snow-capped mountain, the 'awesome majesty' of a vast echoing canyon, the complex 'design' of the laced wings of a butterfly, the deep 'mystery' of the migration of birds, and the 'beauty' of a field carpeted with flowers. These all reflect a God of power and wisdom, who delights in exquisite beauty and intricate design. They are meant to. The very words, 'power, awesome majesty, designer, mystery, beauty' are descriptions of God himself. The thing created will always tell us something about the creator.

It is a tragedy to attribute to blind evolution that which rightly belongs to the wisdom of God. But it is more than a tragedy: it is irrational unbelief in the obvious. The psalmist wisely mocked, 'The fool says in his heart, "There is no God"' (Psalm 14:1). But even such a fool can enjoy God's creation, admire his wisdom, marvel at his design, revel in the kaleidoscope of his colours and shades, glory in the infinite variety of sights and tastes, smells and touch, and stand transfixed before his starry galaxies in the heavens. If the stars came out only once a year the whole world would stay up all night to enjoy the spectacle. It would be the same with the exquisite cacophony of birdsong in the dawn chorus. When the atheist simply exclaims, 'Wow!' he betrays the poverty of his own mind and soul. Instead of 'Wow!' he should worship.

A fallen world could have been colour blind, tasteless and tone deaf. But God poured out the grace of his rich variety of beauty and order

This is all God's universal grace. After the Fall, God could have left us with a world that knew only darkness and pain, the gloom of unrelieved evil, the foul smell, cruel sights and bitter taste of the worst that rebel sinners are capable of. A fallen world could have been colour blind, tasteless and tone deaf. But no, God has limited his judgement, tempered his anger, and poured out the grace of his rich variety of beauty and order on an undeserving world. After the devastation of the universal Flood in the time of Noah, the whole earth could have been left as one vast rain forest, or arid wilderness or bitter snow-scape; instead, we have a diversity of ice and desert, mountain and plain, jungle and scrub, savannah and grassland, wide oceans and rippling streams. That too is universal grace.

And if all this is true of a fallen world that has been ravaged by a terrifying universal Flood not so very long ago, what will the recreated heavens and earth be like in unimaginable breathtaking magnificence?

Creation also enshrines awesome design. If the moon were ten percent nearer the earth than it is, daily huge tides would sweep even the mountains bare. If the myriad of stars and planets did not move in a perfect harmony then none of our mariners and explorers could have navigated around the world. The stars change their position just slightly each night, but every 365 days 6 hours 9 minutes and 9.6 seconds they are back where they started. Even our atomic clocks were originally set by the stars—what is known as sidereal time—and our most sophisticated global positioning devices depend ultimately upon this perfect order in creation. God has even given us a wise pattern of day and night to regulate our work and rest; and wherever you live in the world, in one full year you will have the same amount of daylight and darkness as everyone else. That is all grace. Scientists are just discovering that there is an ordered symmetry about the universe: when one star dies, it appears that another of a similar size takes its place.

In that all-embracing response of God recorded in Job chapters 38 to 41, poor suffering Job is reminded of the grace of God in the whole of creation. God surveyed his control of the natural world from the planets to the earth, from the stars to the sea, from the mountains to the mines, from the animals that act wisely to those that act stupidly, from the powerful to the weak, from the seasons to the sunshine and the storms, and above the poetry of this passage stands the opening text, 'Where were you when I laid the foundation of the earth?' (Job 38:4).

One great thunder cloud can contain up to a quarter of a million tons of water; and when we read of one inch of rain falling in the space of an hour or so, that represents around 100 tons of water per acre. Aren't we glad that it falls in the form of rain droplets and not a mighty 100 ton splodge?

Even our scientists and engineers are continually learning from the world of God's design. Millions of lives have been saved by the use of the antibiotic penicillin. But Sir Alexander Fleming discovered its value by accidentally observing the common mould *penicillium notatum* in action in a laboratory dish. All who practise medicine know that we can never imitate the healing of a wound. We may assist or hinder it, but healing is another mark of grace.

The Bombardier Beetle has for some time been a good ally of those who demonstrate design in creation. This little insect can combine and eject from its tail gun onto any unsuspecting predator, two powerfully explosive chemicals—hydroquinone and hydrogen peroxide—in perfect balance and with pinpoint accuracy and incredible speed. There are engineers today studying the precision built nozzle of the Bombardier Beetle's rear gun to find a possible solution to the problem of how to reignite the burners of aircraft jet engines that fail at high altitudes. Whether the beetle gives up its secret remains to be seen.

The dolphin has a remarkable ability to streamline the flow of water over its body virtually to eliminate drag. Submarine engineers discovered that the secret was not in a perfectly smooth skin as we might imagine, but a skin with small indentations that keyed-in the boundary layer of air that it pulled down from the surface, thus holding it close to the body and reducing drag. The engineers copied this, making very small indentations to roughen the surface of the submarine hull. A more obvious example of the same principle is the dimpled golf ball!

A large oak tree that stands twice the height of a house weighs an estimated four tons (roughly the equivalent of four family cars). How does it stay up in a high wind since not many trees bury their roots much more than three or four feet into the ground? The answer lies in the fact that the structure of wood is very light and, weight for weight, the tensile or pulling strength of wood is four or five times the strength of some of the best of our modern steel. Engineers are currently learning from the way tree roots spread and anchor into the ground to discover more efficient ways of keeping our tall buildings standing.

And thinking of strength, the pulling strength of the spider's web, if you compare its strength-to-weight ratio to the strongest steels, has never been beaten. To spin a man-made spider silk is what the scientific journal *Materials World* (July 2002) has described as 'a holy grail for materials scientists'. But Nexia Biotechnologies Inc. is on the verge of discovering that holy grail. By injecting an engineered segment of spider DNA into the egg of a goat they expect very shortly to produce a spider silk that will, in the first instance, be used for fishing lines and micro sutures for eye operations. In collaboration with the US army they will then move on to the production of body armour made of spider silk!

In the last few years, as a result of the work of Sir James Lighthill, we have begun to understand the movement of the wings of butterflies and moths. It is known as the 'clap and fling principle'. They clap their wings at the top and as the wings spread out they cause two vortices of air which increases the lift. This is why insects can fly using wings that, according to our best calculations, should not be able to lift them off the ground. In both America and the UK scientists are at work in this area today with the hope of increasing the flight efficiency—not of butterflies and moths who already have it all perfectly sussed—but of our clumsy, cumbersome, mechanical aeroplanes. And still scientists cannot tell us how the bumble bee flies since its body weight and apparent wing size and structure imply that it could never take off, let alone manoeuvre delicately around the flowers in your garden. In a similar way, the hummingbird—with a heart beat of 20 per second, a wing beat of 200 per second and the ability to fly forward, backward or hover—makes a cross between a modern supersonic fighter, a jump jet and a helicopter look positively prehistoric.

When the human race uses its God-given intelligence it will never cease to learn from the God-given creation

When the human race uses its God-given intelligence it will never cease to learn from the God-given creation. That is universal grace. We must be unashamed to declare with the Psalmist: 'You have multiplied, O Lord my God, your wondrous deeds and your thoughts toward us; none can compare with you! I will proclaim and tell of them, yet they are more than can be told' (Psalm 40:5). And again: 'Wonderful are your works; my soul knows it very well' (Psalm 139:14). But more than this, what all the incredible complexity and design in the natural order tells us is of a God who 'measured the waters in the hollow of his hand and marked off the heavens with a span, enclosed the dust of the earth in a measure and weighed the mountains in scales and the hills in a balance'

(Isaiah 40:12–14). The inevitable conclusion, as the Old Testament prophet sees it, is that no one 'taught him knowledge or showed him the way of understanding.' Paul agreed that God's wisdom and knowledge are both unsearchable and inscrutable (Romans 11:33). If we do not at least learn this much from the design of creation then we are fools and utterly without excuse.

The kindness of God's provision is universal grace

In his kindness to the 'ungrateful and evil' God allows them to enjoy the warmth of the sun, the gently refreshing rain, the cooling breeze, the abundance of his harvest and the pleasure of his colours, sounds, tastes and smells. As our Lord himself simply expressed it: 'He makes his sun rise on the evil and on the good, and sends rain on the just and on the unjust' (Matthew 5:45).

Abundance it most certainly is. There is more than sufficient food and water on this earth to fill every hungry mouth and satisfy every thirsty child. And though the world could survive on a basketful of different fruits and vegetables, God has given us truck loads of variety instead. We could enjoy the pleasure of a handful of different species of colourful birds and fish and interesting animals, or a few dozen scented flowers, pretty shrubs and magnificent trees. But instead, God created an almost inexhaustible variety of species—an estimated 9,000 different sorts of birds, 20,000 of trees, 200,000 of flowers, and over 300,000 of beetles alone (that amounts to one third of all types of insects!). We are only now beginning to understand the enormity of this diversity and still there is more to discover.

The psalmist claimed, 'The LORD is good to all, and his mercy is over all that he has made' and as a consequence, all his created works should give thanks to him (Psalm 145:9–10). After all, the whole world is dependent upon God for food and it is by his provision of the cycle of life and growth and the seasons of the year that he 'satisfies the desire of every living thing' (vs 5–16). Millions may not recognise this—and because of the selfishness of a fallen human race millions are denied the benefit of it— but it will be part of the sentence of final judgement to be made aware of what has been staring us in the face for a whole lifetime. We have no excuse for not having wide eyes for God's open hand. It is little wonder that Paul could conclude when writing to Timothy: 'Everything created by God is good' (1 Timothy 4:4).

You may object, 'But it's not all like that. What of the searing heat of the desert, the lashing tropical storm and the freezing Arctic ice flow?' That is a reminder that all is not well with the world because sin has spoiled a perfect creation. It is even grace when things are abnormally out of step with an ordered world. We may well question whether God would really create a cruel burning desert or a howling Arctic waste and then call it 'very good'? The truth is that he didn't. These are the harsh legacies of sin which God has left to show that all is not well. Everything that is not as it should be is a reminder not only that everything is not as it was, but that everything is not as it ultimately will be.

Everything that is not as it should be is a reminder not only that everything is not as it was, but that everything is not as it ultimately will be

What when the unexpected happens—when mountains spit fire, the earth cracks open or snow falls in July? This too is a reminder that even in the midst of the beauty and order, creation is still captive to the burden of decay and death (Romans 8:19–22). If we ask how it is possible for a world of such impeccable and detailed design to exhibit such incongruous and deadly disasters, we can only return to the Fall recorded in Genesis 3 for an explanation: when the very beauty that reflects God turns ugly, that too is universal grace. It is a legacy of the Fall through which God reminds us that whilst sin deserves judgement like this, he so often holds back his hand and pours out grace instead.

Fortunately the great majority of the population live outside the prisons in our nation. But prisons are the result of law and order; they are grace in a fallen world. What would happen if all the prisoners were released tonight? Would you feel safer and freer? Prisons serve not only to restrict those who break the law, but they serve as a warning to all of us that, however free and happy we may be at the moment, there is always a penalty for disobedience. So, just when the world is thoughtlessly enjoying the universal grace of a God who has provided generously more than all we need, something, somewhere goes wrong—disastrously wrong. That is a warning. And that too is grace. But you say, people don't listen; suffering in the world only makes them, as the writer Somerset Maugham claimed, 'petty and vindictive'. Sadly that may be true, but when a criminal ignores the warnings of the law, the activity of the courts and the evidence of the prison system, who is at fault? And that leads us directly to another aspect of universal grace.

The unseen providence of God is universal grace

Asaph the psalmist was in a fix. Exactly what his problem was he does not tell us, but it kept him awake at night and made him feel that God had forgotten him. His response was not simply to despair, but to spend some of his time recollecting the goodness of God to his people in the past. His mind went back to the time when God brought the Israelites out of Egypt and safely across the Red Sea on dry land. What impressed him about this story, and the subsequent way that God led them through the wilderness, was that God himself was not seen. This is how he graphically describes it: 'Your way was through the sea, your path through the great waters; yet your footprints were unseen' (Psalm 77:19). Asaph should not have been surprised since that is true for the whole world, all of the time.

God does not often advertise himself because he gives away his benefits for free. Although he is at work constantly in this world, more often than not we do not see how. Christians frequently thank God for unseen safety in the course of a day. In the Old Testament David did: 'You know when I sit down and when I rise up ... You search out my path and my lying down and are acquainted with all my ways ... You hem me in, behind and before, and lay your hand upon me' (Psalm 139:2–5). But whilst that is a specific understanding and encouragement for those who are on the side of God, the reality is also true for everyone in this world. God is not so limited that he knows all about his own people but little or nothing about anyone else.

If the kings and rulers of the nations are in the hand of God (Ezra 6:22), why them alone? No one is beyond the control of God, and for that matter, no one is beyond the protective care of God when he chooses. It is true that the unbeliever has no right to claim such care, but he may nonetheless receive it. The 'lucky escape', 'great good fortune' and 'sheer coincidence' that is arrogantly boasted of by so many, is always the hand of God—though rarely is it seen as such. This is all part of universal grace. What else could the psalmist mean when he declared that God's steadfast love extends to the heavens, his faithfulness to the clouds and that, 'man and beast you save' (Psalm 36:6)? Perhaps this is the context in which we can best understand Paul's claim that God 'is the Saviour of all people, especially of those who believe' (1 Timothy 4:10). There is salvation in the daily experiences of life that is not for eternal welfare but certainly provides more time to think seriously about God.

By comparison with the creativity, aesthetic pleasure and inventive genius of the human race, animals are soulless, mindless and colourless

Imagination and appreciation are universal grace

By comparison with the creativity, aesthetic pleasure and inventive genius of the human race, animals are soulless, mindless and colourless. I am often puzzled that we can be considered close relatives to the chimpanzee when I watch the enthusiasm of the scientist who has discovered one such primate using a stick to dig ants out of a hole in a tree. With all the millions of years he has supposedly had to perfect his art I would have expected him to have got at least as far as a hand drill!

I know that animals are intriguingly adaptable: the arbour bird builds a series of attractive nests for his mate to choose from, and the weaver birds can plait an incredible dome of reeds at the end of a slim branch—but they have all about reached their limit. Man's resourcefulness and creativity is stunning by comparison. A recent survey of bird song in Britain unsurprisingly put the blackbird at the top of the poll; beautiful it certainly is—though there are better—however, his repertoire is seriously limited. The Indian Myna and its relative the European Starling, are versatile mimics in the world of birds, but few of us would wish to spend an evening listening to the twittering of starlings at our local concert hall.

By contrast, the creative art of the human race in colour, music and sculpture—and our ability to appreciate and enjoy such inspired design—is part of our uniqueness and that which marks us off from the animal world. It is all part of God's universal grace in the reflection of his image and likeness in us. We have little evidence that the goat, living high on a breathtakingly beautiful mountain range, or the eagle soaring into a shimmering valley, or the bullock grazing in the lush pasture of a peaceful English village, have any appreciation of the awesome beauty or tranquil calm around them other than its purpose in providing their next meal. One good reason why God created Eve as a 'compatible' companion to Adam was that not one of the animals around him was capable of sharing in Adam's awe and wonder at the beauty of God's perfect creation.

Beyond all this, it is God's universal grace that has given mankind a mind to explore, discover and invent. The discovery of the atom, invention of the silicon chip and our understanding of the human DNA and gene system are just a few of many areas of knowledge that are of immense value to the human race. Sadly, because our conscience is seared by sin, we have abused so much that God has given us, and everything good we find a bad use for. But we cannot blame the Creator for our misappropriation of his grace.

The church in the world is universal grace

When Jesus told his disciples that they were salt and light in this world (Matthew 5:13–16), he set before the church a marker that it should never lose sight of. Sadly, in its two thousand year history the professing Christian church often has lost sight of this great calling. There is no value in trying to excuse some of the terrible acts that point a finger at the so-called church. However, if the church is defined in line with the Bible itself, it would refer to those who are born again by the Spirit, who obey the teaching of Christ and his apostles, and who therefore live in a way that reflects the Master himself. Any religion is entitled to define itself by the life and teaching of its leader—and Christianity must be allowed that right; but every religion will be judged also by the quality of life and influence of its followers—and Christianity cannot duck that responsibility. In the light of this, the Crusades of the eleventh to thirteenth centuries, the Inquisitions of the thirteenth to the nineteenth centuries, the traffic in human slaves from the seventeenth to the nineteenth centuries and some of the negative legacy of colonialism, have no support from the teaching of either Christ or his disciples, nor do they represent the lives of those who are wholly committed to the example of Christ. Those involved in perpetrating historic crimes may have employed the banner of Christ, but their actions separated them from his true family.

Christianity that follows the teaching and example of Christ has always been a powerful force for good in this world

On the contrary, a Christianity that follows the teaching and example of Christ has always been a powerful force for good in this world. It is the Bible that taught justice, the value of life, freedom and compassion; and it is Protestant Christianity in particular that has recognised this and applied it most vigorously. Of course there have been inconsistencies when true Christians have failed to apply the revelation of God in the Bible that they profess to believe, but these are deviations rather than normalities. Because of its two thousand year history, Christianity is bound to be vulnerable. There are renegades in every walk of life. However, when I read the attempts of the Humanist Society to ransack history in order to discredit the Christian faith, I find it sadly amusing. What, we may respond, is the legacy of atheism to the modern world? The regimes inspired by a belief that there is no God—of which there have been and still are many—have an impressive record of genocide and torture over their short one hundred year history.

Chapter 2

If the humanist levels the field by pleading, as I have done for Christianity, that we must exclude those who behave contrary to the teaching of the religion of humanism, then we may ask what its positive achievements have been? How many atheistic missions are scattered in the hard places of the world caring with famine relief, or opening hospitals, dispensaries and leprosariums? How many agricultural projects, literacy programmes, and self help schemes have been initiated by Humanism? Where is the army of young atheists dedicating their lives in tough parts of the world to humanitarian care? And where are the hundreds of missions, inspired by a belief in no God, that are involved in such care? Christians in the United Kingdom alone give in the region of two billion pounds each year to support their caring work. We may ask what the comparable figure for atheistic humanism is.

The overwhelming majority of the world's asylum seekers are clamouring to gain entrance to countries with a Christian history. And from what governments are the majority fleeing? Whilst no nation on earth can be considered a Christian nation in the definition I have given above, there are many nations whose modelling influence for their constitution has been a Protestant Christianity based upon the Bible. On the contrary we may well ask which other nations, where atheism or a non-Christian religion is the controlling influence, provide anything like a model today for freedom, justice and compassion? And which of these countries are confronted with an overwhelming flood of voluntary would-be refugees from fear?

But the salt and light claim of Christ was not directed at nations, rather it referred to the lives of individual Christians in their society. Across the world today, true Christians who take the Bible as their instruction manual are influencing society by their honesty, hard work, compassion and purity. I recently came across a beautiful example of this. At the age of five, Ban Mau was sent by his parents to train as a Buddhist priest. The harsh treatment he received caused him to run away several times, but he was always taken back to the temple. By the age of thirteen he escaped and joined a band of guerrillas attacking the Burmese government; later he enlisted in a mercenary group fighting the communists in Thailand. Finally, wounded by a land mine, he left the army and earned his living by making illegal liquor. Ban Mau began to observe a group of Christians in his village: they lived good lives and worked hard and honestly. They also carried a book that taught about love and compassion to those in need. Eventually he heard the Christian message and decided to follow Christ. Right now, Ban Mau is involved in Bible translation and evangelism. What benefits a society most: a guerrilla, drug dealer and a purveyor of illegal liquor—or a Bible translator?

Stories like this can be multiplied literally millions of times over. If we were not aware of the spiritual dimension of all persecution, it would be a remarkably strange thing why governments of the world choose to hound and destroy the very people who are their most peaceful, law-abiding, honest and hard working citizens. Our Lord expected the lives of his disciples to count in society; their good works would cause others to 'give glory to your Father who is in heaven' (Matthew 5:16).

What benefits a society most: a guerrilla, drug dealer and a purveyor of illegal liquor—or a Bible translator?

It was this expectation of Christ that his church should be salt and light in the world that led Paul to emphasise the importance of the reputation Christians should have in the world. The Corinthians were to be 'letters of recommendation … known and read by all' (2 Corinthians 3:1–2); the Thessalonian Christians were encouraged to 'live properly before outsiders' (1 Thessalonians 4:12); and Timothy was reminded that a Christian leader 'must be well thought of by outsiders' (1 Timothy 3:7). Peter was equally adamant that if Christians are to suffer, it must be because of what they believe and not how they live (1 Peter 4:12–16).

The world will never understand what an immense value Christians are in society. Everybody knows the Judas who lives or works close by them, but he was the only one of twelve—that's eight percent failure. If ninety-two percent of Christians were living as their Master expects them to, and they were all removed from this world, there would be an enormous black hole remaining. It is Christians who so often remind the world of integrity and loyalty at work, who demonstrate the value of love and purity in marriage, who reach out in warmth and compassion to those in fear and anxiety, and who provide for the poor and suffering in the world. All this is God's universal grace to a rebellious world.

The long patience of God's mercy is universal grace

God's universal grace is always intended to bring us to the knowledge of himself. The evidence stares at us every day. To the challenge: 'How can you believe in God with all the pain and evil in the world?' The shortest answer is, 'How can you *not* believe in God with all the joy and beauty in the world?' If God gets the blame for cruelty, of which there is so much, who receives credit for all the kindness, of which there is so much? He allows sin and evil to remind us that all is not well. That is grace. Even the process of growing old is grace. Pain and disease can be understood as grace if we view them as reinforcing our short, uncertain life and preparing us for eternity.

Even the process of

The German philosopher, Friedrich Nietzsche dismissed suffering as 'senseless'.

Somerset Maugham claimed that suffering makes character 'petty and vindictive'.

growing old is grace

Oscar Wilde called it a 'revelation'.

But C S Lewis was wiser than all when he declared suffering to be 'a roadblock on the way to hell'.

Put together the gift of human life, the beauty and design of creation, the kindness of God's provision and the wisdom of his law, and all this is grace. Sadly, the universal grace of God passes over so many; they learn nothing from it. Even when God shows himself to be upright, kind and wise, they go on doing evil. Through the prophet Jeremiah, God identified those who take this grace for granted and attribute it their own wisdom, power, wealth—or we may add, to their good luck: 'Let not the wise man boast in his wisdom, let not the mighty man boast in his might, let not the rich man boast in his riches, but let him who boasts boast in this, that he understands and knows me, that I am the Lord who practices steadfast love, justice and righteousness in the earth. For in these things I delight' (Jeremiah 9:23–24).

As years pass into centuries and centuries into millennia God is waiting patiently, not willing that any should perish, but that all should come to repentance and faith in Jesus Christ. The cross of Christ is God's most powerful witness that something is immensely wrong with this world; something so wrong that only God himself could put it right—and this he did in his Son Jesus Christ. The cross is God's offer to the world. And the promise of Christ to return and recreate the heavens and the earth and make all things new (Revelation 21:1–5) is the only ultimate hope for a universe out of alignment with the Creator's original design. The apostle Peter warned of those who mock the delay in Christ's return and scoff, 'Where is the promise of his coming?' (2 Peter 3:4). But the delay is grace, God is offering more time. The prophet Isaiah set out the tragedy so accurately: 'If favour is shown to the wicked, he does not learn righteousness; in the land of uprightness he deals corruptly and does not see the majesty of the LORD' (Isaiah 26:10).

Despots brutally ill-treat their citizens but God does not immediately take action; the widow and orphan cry for justice and still God remains silent; the cynic blasphemes God and mocks his Creator, and he does the same day after day as if God is not listening; a man steals and kills on Sunday but God does not pay out on Monday; the humanist publishes his arrogant philosophy but the print shop does not burn down, and his books sell well. Does all this point to a disinterested or powerless God? No. It is universal grace. God is waiting, allowing more time for repentance.

Universal grace points only in one direction—towards the God that Peter calls 'The God of all grace' (1 Peter 5:10). Wherever there is grace—patience in the midst of wickedness—it has its origin in God. There is no grace in Satan; he cannot ever be gracious—not even to advance his evil designs. When an atheist or unbeliever, or a zealous follower of a religious cult or false religion, shows mercy or kindness for no other motive than to be merciful or kind, it is always a reflection of the image of God in them. Of course the devil has his nice people and his compassionate warriors, but he is only trading on the image of God in the human race; Paul understood this when he warned that, 'it is no surprise if his servants, also, disguise themselves as servants of righteousness' (2 Corinthians 11:15). Never does Satan promote kindness and compassion for anything other than an evil purpose: which is to delude and deceive men and women into believing that life without God is safe, secure and nice.

Satan never acts out of grace, because he cannot. The word grace has no meaning in his fiendish world. In fact it is the one word he fears most of all because though he can ape so much of God's work—just as the magicians in Egypt copied some of the miracles of Moses—he can never reproduce grace. It would be more possible for an elephant to swim the Atlantic than for Satan to show grace. That beautiful word belongs to God alone.

If the purpose of universal grace is that we might come to the knowledge of God, this means that the purpose of grace is therefore itself grace. And Paul pleaded with the congregation at Rome in case some were strangers to the grace of God: 'Do you presume upon the riches of his kindness and forbearance and patience, not knowing that God's kindness is meant to lead you to repentance?' Apparently Paul did not consider that his gentle pleading was sufficient, for he continued with a stern warning: 'But because of your hard and impenitent heart you are storing up wrath for yourself on the day of wrath when God's righteous judgement will be revealed' (Romans 2:4).

It would be more possible for an elephant to swim the Atlantic than for Satan to show grace

Those who take advantage of God's patience to continue in their unbelief simply stack up more judgement that will inevitably fall—sooner or later. God is rich in his kindness, forbearance and patience. The more time we have, then the more we can discover of his wisdom, power and love. The more we ignore it, then the more judgement grows.

All grace is ultimately in Jesus Christ, and that is why Satan so fears it. There is no true grace anywhere that does not come from and is not defined by, the person of Jesus Christ who is the radiance of the glory of God and the exact character of the reality of God himself (Hebrews 1:3). Grace is a person and not a cold, lifeless theology. It is seen above all in the cross of Christ where the anger of God and the love of God met; and where love conquered wrath. That is grace.

If I may borrow Peter's final greeting: 'I have written briefly to you, exhorting and declaring that this is the true grace of God. Stand firm in it' (1 Peter 5:12).

FOR ALL THE GLORIES OF THE EARTH AND SKY,
for night's soft voice, and morning's silent haze,
for trees that whisper, and for winds that sigh,
we give you praise.

2 For summer sunshine and for cooling showers,
for stars that light the heavens' darkening maze,
for dewdrops sparkling on the newborn flowers,
our hearts would praise.

3 For lightning's flash, and thunder's echoing roar,
for seas that beat upon their endless ways,
for wild waves' anthem on a rock-bound shore,
we offer praise.

4 For mighty mountains and eternal snows,
enduring changeless through the changing days,
for moonlit valleys and for sunset glows,
accept our praise.

5 Yet for Christ's great redeeming work of love,
our souls their highest hymn of thanks would raise,
for free salvation streaming from above,
we render praise.

6 For all the matchless wonders of your grace
seen in that cross on which we humbly gaze,
for peace and pardon to a fallen race,
your name we praise.

MRS G GOLDEN
Copyright control
Praise! 205

Chapter 3

Sovereign grace

'Oh, the depth of the riches and wisdom and knowledge of God! How unsearchable are his judgements and how inscrutable his ways!' Romans 11:33

Tuesday 11 September 2001 was one of the many dates in history on which the world changed course. At precisely 8.45am the Boeing 767 of American Airlines flight 11 was pitilessly flown into the North Tower of the World Trade Centre in New York by al-Qaeda terrorists. Eighteen minutes later a second 767, this time United Airlines flight 175, crashed into the South Tower. The carnage and destruction that followed in New York City, together with American Airlines flight 77 that plunged into the Pentagon almost one and half hours later, is now all part of the dark side of history. Thousands died in the fireball that engulfed and destroyed the 110 storey, quarter mile high towers. In London the *Daily Mail* front page headlines the following morning read simply: 'Apocalypse—NY Sept. 11th 2001'.

As the sickening newscasts flashed across the world, many thought that they were watching a horror movie: the result of a scriptwriter's imagination and a brilliant surreal set arranged by a Spielberg-type director. Soon we would realize that it was all just a vivid film or a bad dream—but it wasn't. It could not really happen—but it did. No one could do such a callously evil thing—but they could. The world, we were told, would never be the same again. Perhaps. But the persistent question was: What kind of world will it look like in the future? Will it really be any different from the past? Would our world democracies led by our political leaders simply 'sort it'? Would we rely upon the intelligence services and Western hardware to 'settle the score'? Would we trust in a political, economic or military response—and that alone?

Or, above all else that we may have to do, would we humbly cry to God for help and ask for his wisdom? Would we look and listen for his voice in

42 Grace—amazing grace

all this? Would we ask if there were any spiritual, and not merely political and military lessons that we should be learning? In short, would God be brought into the situation for better reasons than simply to throw him out of it? Christians, like everyone else, were not only shocked and sickened by the stark reality that human beings could actually plan, let alone carry out such a crime, but they had to answer some painfully hard questions. And for Christians the questions were more urgently in need of answers than for anyone else: Where was God on the morning of Tuesday 11 September? Am I right to feel anger burning in my heart? What is the purpose of such brutal and inhuman carnage? Is there a purpose? How should I pray? What for? Who for? Can I still believe in a God of grace when such terror is unleashed? Should I keep quiet about God and just hope that people don't ask me questions? Or is there something courageously positive that the Christian can say to a grieving and sceptical world?

Can there be such a thing as grace when the worst that men can imagine is planned and executed so incredibly successfully?

Tragic and sickening as September 11 was, it was by no means the worst act of genocide in history. Every year of every century throughout human history has seen cruelty—often on a scale that dwarfs the New York inferno—that most people find hard to believe and even harder to accept. There have been far worse events even in the past century. Millions died in the Nazi death camps, and millions more in that regime's carnage across Europe. The Communist era may have eclipsed even the Nazis' grand achievement, and Pol Pot slaughtered two million of his own people in the killing fields of Cambodia. Across war-torn Africa and battle weary Bosnia, millions more died in horrific cruelty. Has grace worn thin among the sunken mass graves and the stench of rotting corpses? Has the Christian nothing to say in the blackened ghost town where once children laughed and played on their way to school? Must the Christian remain silent?

Although Christians do not glibly pretend to have all the answers, they need to reaffirm boldly and without hesitation some of the great certainties of the Christian faith and then to unpack the significance of this. Can there be such a thing as grace when the worst that men can imagine is planned and executed so incredibly successfully? Let me begin by making four simple but vital statements of Christian conviction:

First, nothing happens anywhere or at anytime without God's knowledge beforehand

There are no surprises with God. He is never waiting for a BBC or CNN news bulletin to keep him informed. He knows everything that happens, everywhere—not at the time but before the time.

Through the prophet Jeremiah, God revealed something of himself to us: 'Am I a God at hand, declares the LORD, and not a God afar off? Can a man hide himself in secret places so that I cannot see him? declares the LORD. Do I not fill heaven and earth? declares the LORD' (23:23–24). The Old Testament psalmist takes us further and personalizes it: 'O LORD you have searched me and known me! You know when I sit down and when I rise up; you discern my thoughts from afar. You search out my path and my lying down and are acquainted with all my ways. Even before a word is on my tongue, behold, O LORD, you know it altogether' (Psalm 139:1–4). The same theme follows into the New Testament: 'No creature is hidden from his sight, but all are naked and exposed to the eyes of him to whom we must give account' (Hebrews 4:13). All thoughts and words are open to God and nothing is planned or carried out in secrecy from him.

Secondly, God plans all events in this universe

This is a tougher claim, but we cannot avoid it unless we make God as helpless in the foreknowledge of events as we are. It is not just that he knows what will happen, but he determines everything that will happen. The issue gets tight at this point. God does not just see what is coming and then decide whether he will stop it from happening or else let it happen. He will sometimes allow evil people to scheme and carry out their plans as part of his greater plans. God never surrenders control, but he often withdraws his hand of protection. The most outstanding example of this is found in the crucifixion of Jesus. Preaching on the day of Pentecost shortly after the death of Christ, Peter declared, 'This Jesus, delivered up according to the definite plan and foreknowledge of God, you crucified and killed by the hands of lawless men' (Acts 2:23). The vicious death of Christ as the result of an illegal court, trumped-up charges, and endorsed by a weak governor, is plainly a matter of history; no one involved can bear any credit. But Peter is aware that behind even this evil action was the 'definite plan' that lay behind the 'foreknowledge of God'. Behind the evil plans of men are the good plans of God—always.

This dual understanding of evil is found frequently in the Bible. Commenting on the Egyptian Pharaoh who cruelly treated the Israelite slaves, God says, 'For this very purpose I have raised you up, that I might show my power in you, and that my name might be proclaimed in all the earth' (Romans 9:17); doubtless it did not appear to the Israelites, who were groaning under the whip of their Egyptian slave drivers, that God was in control. Eight hundred years later Sennacherib of Assyria devastated the land of Judah, marched his terrifying army to the walls of Jerusalem and mocked Hezekiah and his God claiming in his own records that he 'Shut up Hezekiah like a bird in a cage'. In reply, God scorned Sennacherib for his arrogance of behaving as if his successes over the nations and his threats to Jerusalem were all his own doing: 'Have you not heard that I determined it long ago? I planned from days of old what now I bring to pass, that you should turn fortified cities into heaps of ruins ... But I know your sitting down and your going out and coming in, and your raging against me. Because you have raged against me and your complacency has come into my ears, I will put my hook in your nose and my bit in your mouth, and I will turn you back on the way by which you came' (2 Kings 19:25, 27–28). That night Sennacherib saw his entire army decimated under the walls of Jerusalem, and when he returned to his capital Nineveh, he was assassinated by his own sons (vs 35–37).

Behind the evil plans

of men are the good

plans of God—

always

Similarly it may not have appeared to the eyes of Jews in exile in the time of Daniel that God was in control when King Cyrus of Persia came to power; the fact that God referred to him as 'my shepherd, (who) shall fulfill all my purpose' (Isaiah 44:28) was perhaps little comfort to the Jew who struggled to survive in the pagan environment of his Persian exile. But it was true. These three rulers—Pharaoh, Sennacherib and Cyrus—who were separated by one thousand years and as many miles and who reigned as undisputed despots over empires, which were gained and held by the brutal and unforgiving power of the sword, each served God's purpose in the next stage of Israel's story.

Can it be that terrorists capable of callous evil are not merely in the hand of God but are somehow fulfilling his purposes? Yes, it must be. Or else God is as much a helpless victim of evil men as we are. God is not the author of evil or the perpetrator of wickedness, but he plans to use the violence and cruelty of evil men for his own purposes. Nothing is beyond his control. And there is nothing that does not fit into his sovereign plans. Even the most heinous crimes and callous indifference to human suffering is strangely part of God's plan for a fallen world. Nothing is senseless with God. This is equally true of our personal circumstances, and with typical wisdom the Bible reminds us: 'In the day of prosperity be joyful, and in the day of adversity consider: God has made the one as well as the other' (Ecclesiastes 7:14). The Bible never backs away from acknowledging that God has a purpose in everything that he allows to happen in this world: 'The LORD has made everything for its purpose, even the wicked for the day of trouble' (Proverbs 16:4). This does not make God complicit in evil, but it does make him in control of it. Even the cast of a dice is under his command (Proverbs 16:33).

Thirdly, God is therefore in total and supreme control of all events in the world

In the story of the deep suffering of Job, he lost almost everything—his family, property, friends, reputation, health and even the love of his wife—yet in the light of his own misery that followed upon misery and in his despair and agony, he was not afraid to reaffirm that the unseen God is in control of the detail of the whole universe from the moment of creation even to the mystery of his own experience. Job concluded, 'He is wise in heart and mighty in strength—who has hardened himself against him and succeeded?... Who can turn him back? Who will say to him, "What are you doing?"' (Job 9:4,12). We may wonder if the pagan king, Nebuchadnezzar had a sight of this passage in Job when he finally admitted the sovereign power of God who 'does according to his will among the hosts of heaven and among the inhabitants of the earth; and none can stay his hand or say to him. "What have you done?"' (Daniel 4:35). Certainly Paul was aware of Job's triumph when he penned those magnificent words in Romans 11:33–36. That is all sovereign grace.

If our Lord could claim that not even a sparrow falls to the ground without the knowledge of God and, in an even more striking picture, that even the hairs on our head are numbered (Matthew 10:29–30), it is beyond belief that God should be taken by surprise by the actions of cruel terrorists or that he was not the silent listener at all their secret preparations. After terrible atrocities, world leaders will spend hours of intense discussion with senior advisers planning how they can regain the initiative and establish control. All is change: new strategies are called for and new precautions *There is never any crisis management with God* are set in place; new departments are set up and new orders go out across the world. But it is not so with God. Not for one millisecond does he ever lose total control. There is never any crisis management with God.

Some years ago, after a particularly heart-rending disaster in which many school children were engulfed in the choking mud of a landslide, a clergyman registered his response on the radio by claiming, 'This must be one of those occasions when the Almighty made a mistake'. Such an anaemic theology sent a shiver down my spine. That man did not worship the God that I do. His was a pathetically weak and unreliable deity who was a miserable and forlorn victim of the world he had created but apparently was now incapable of controlling. I would far rather worship a God who is in total control and takes ultimate responsibility for all that happens in this world—and then face the issue of whether this makes him the willing spectator of evil—rather than believe in a God who is little more than a cringing sugar daddy in the face of powerful terrorists.

Fourthly, God is wise, purposeful and just in all his plans

Nowhere is this more simply expressed than in this passage in Romans 11:33, 'Oh, the depth of the riches and wisdom and knowledge of God! How unsearchable are his judgements and how inscrutable his ways!' The visible tragedies that God allows and the unknown tragedies that he prevents; the evil that the devil unleashes and the righteousness that is overturned; the good that God gives and the good that he withholds—all these are wise, purposeful and fair.

Samuel Medley was born in 1738 and became a Baptist pastor. When one of his children was tragically killed in an accident, he penned a hymn to express his deep confidence in God. Here is part of it:

> God shall alone the refuge be,
> and comfort of my mind;
> too wise to be mistaken, he,
> too good to be unkind.
>
> 2 In all his holy, sovereign will,
> he is, I daily find,
> too wise to be mistaken, still
> too good to be unkind.
>
> 3 What though I can't his purpose see,
> nor all his footsteps find?
> Too wise to be mistaken, he,
> too good to be unkind.
>
> 4 Hereafter he will make me know,
> and I shall surely find,
> he was too wise to err, and O,
> too good to be unkind!

God's wisdom is too profound for us to understand and his plans are too deep for us to fathom. This is not a retreat into blind faith but the affirmation of trust in the God who is in charge. The alternative to God in total control is not God out of control, but no God at all. He cannot be God if he is not always in command. If for one moment the satanic evil of wicked men gains the upper hand and places God on the defensive then he is no longer God, and the devil rules the universe—and beyond.

The alternative to God in total control is not God out of control, but no God at all

God is always God. Nothing happens without his knowledge beforehand and everything happens as part of his plan. All events are totally under his control, and all his plans are wise, purposeful and just.

How must we respond to personal and national attrocities

We respond with confidence

If we abandon God when disaster strikes, then all hope is gone. We are left with unrestrained evil and blind chance pitted against polite morality and good intentions. The Christian declares God is still in control:

when volcanoes spit fire over a town
when mighty rivers deluge helpless villages
when the earth splits open and cities collapse
when the sun scorches the earth
when hurricanes devastate crops
when armies massacre civilians
when callous terrorists destroy whole communities
when death takes my friends and loved ones
when school kids murder their classmates
when a baby dies in its cot
when my dearest friend dies horribly
when disease wracks my own body
when those I trusted betray me
when my best plans collapse in a chaotic heap

We cannot always explain what is happening or immediately find the purpose in it. But we know who has the explanation and confidently we can pray for him to comfort those who mourn, to heal minds and bodies, and to defeat evil men across the world. Joseph was sold into slavery by his brothers who then lied to their father about his disappearance. Falsely accused of attempted rape in the household of his slave-master he barely escaped with his life and was thrown into prison—his reputation and any hope of release destroyed. It appeared that God had forsaken him. God either did not know of Joseph's desperate condition, or if he knew he did not care—or if he cared then the circumstances were beyond his control. Just how Joseph viewed these events at the time we are not told, though there is enough evidence in the story to save us from guessing; years later when the whole situation had turned around, he could remind his brothers of their intention and conclude, 'You meant evil against me, but God meant it for good' (Genesis 50:20).

That is confidence in sovereign grace.

We respond with compassion

The Christian must never become indifferent to suffering. We see so much pain in our world and our human response mechanism copes by shutting down our anguish. We no longer feel as once we did; we are desensitized to suffering. Terrible things are happening all the time all around us, and then suddenly it hits our soft, protected, democratic freedom. We have been blind and silent to so much suffering in the world, but then it is our turn and we want the whole world to feel for us and with us.

All over the world Christians are brutalised by cruel religious and non-religious groups and governments; churches are destroyed, congregations massacred, women and girls are raped and men are tortured. Every day of the year, far more people die either through deliberate genocide or from preventable hunger and thirst than were killed on September 11, but do we really care? Even Christians have lost the ability to cry over the condition of the widow and orphan. When it is far from our shores it is often far from our minds and terrible things can be done without so much as a whisper of objection. But compassion raises a voice of dissent and demands justice. Compassion is the very heart of God and the life of Christ (Matthew 9:36). Compassion is always a reflection of God's grace.

We respond with constraint

On Sunday 9 September 2001, I preached a sermon on Christian anger! It was part of a series I had been following on the life of Samuel and the lessons for leadership that we can learn from this outstanding man. My text was from 1 Samuel 15:11, 'And Samuel was angry, and he cried to the LORD all night.' I commented that that one phrase revealed an aspect of Samuel's character that is essential for any leader; a leader must at times be angry, because this reveals that he is a man who cares deeply—about God, and about God's law, about righteousness and justice, and about people. A man who is never angry has no convictions. Moses was angry in the valley of the golden calf (Exodus 32:19); Jonathan was angry at the way his father disgraced David, his own best friend (1 Samuel 20:34). In fact, righteous anger is a reflection of God himself; over thirty times in the Old Testament we read of the 'anger of the LORD' and there are almost one hundred more references to his anger and wrath. I reminded my congregation of the anger of Christ in the synagogue at Capernaum: 'He looked round at them with anger, grieved at their hardness of heart' (Mark 3:5). I distinguished between righteous anger (Ephesians 4:26) and the anger that is accompanied by bitterness, wrath, clamour, slander and malice (Ephesians 4:31).

Then, just two days later the terrorists struck! We felt sick and distracted—and angry. We watched some in Palestine dancing and celebrating such inhuman carnage—and we became angrier still. We listened to the response of many around us: bomb all Muslims into oblivion, blast Afghanistan, Iraq and anyone else who sympathised; turn away all asylum seekers, throw all Palestinians out of Israel. But blind and irrational reaction like this is not for the Christian. Those who believe in a God who is in control will pause to reflect and search for a purpose. Our concern is not for revenge but for justice; evil must be justly and righteously opposed. But even beyond this, our concern must be to learn what God may be teaching us. The Christian who believes God has plans will pause to find a purpose.

Finding a purpose

If God is in charge and always has a plan, can we ever discover his purpose? Yes, though never completely. As Paul reminded us: 'How unsearchable are his judgements and how inscrutable his ways!' His wisdom is deep—far beyond our understanding—and that is how we would expect it to be. If we could understand all there is to know about God and his ways he would cease to be God, since he would be small enough to fit into the rational mind of a human being. So, why do such things happen? I have four responses, though there are many more.

FIRST, GOD'S PURPOSE WHEN WICKEDNESS WINS IS TO REVEAL TO US THE CONTRAST BETWEEN THE BADNESS OF EVIL AND THE RIGHTEOUSNESS OF GOOD. All around us in this world, we can see the naked heart of godless irreligion and godless religion. If a man's god rewards him for the perverse cruelty of deliberately blowing up thousands of 'innocent' civilians, of detonating a bomb in a crowded shopping centre or youth club or for the brutal genocide of hundreds of unarmed men, then that man may choose such a god if he wishes. For my part, the God revealed in the life and teaching of Jesus Christ—a God of peace and compassion and selfless love—will be the God I wish to follow. What terrible lies the devil and his agents will promise to those who will kill themselves to massacre others. Yet when they stand before the judgement of God, what agony they will feel in the knowledge of their deception. This stands in deadly contrast to the nations that still hold, however timidly, to the Christian values of justice, freedom, and compassion. This is why, for all our wilful erosion of our Christian moral base, nations with a 'Christian' history are in the forefront of the relief of world famine and poverty.

The reason we can still be shocked by the outrage of mass destruction is that God has given us rules that form part of our way of thinking and therefore our way of life—even though we hardly recognise this any longer. The Ten Commandments and the teaching of Christ in the Gospels still have a greater influence upon many nations than they choose to admit. God has given us a perfect and pure example of this in the life of Jesus Christ, and arrogant violence should remind us of the immense chasm between Christian morality and that of theistic religions or atheistic philosophies. It should also warn us of where we are heading if we abandon the gospel of Jesus Christ.

Whilst it is certain that there are renegades among all philosophies of life that bring discredit to their founders, the contrast between the best that Christianity has offered the world in its two thousand year history and the best that atheism and the world religions have offered is evident for everyone to see. If I may repeat what was said in the previous chapter, the flood of world refugees—both economic and political—pours from nations controlled by atheism and world religions into those with a legacy of Christian values. Terrorism today survives only because of the freedoms enjoyed in nations that believe in the value of life. We may well ask to be given the identity of the governments, whether secular or religious, that in *practice* stand as the best models for justice, freedom of conscience, compassion and the value of life. The answer will, without exception, be those that have a legacy of Christian teaching and values. This is why the world's oppressed are flocking to live in countries with a Christian history. None of this is to pretend that there is such a thing as a Christian nation in the world today or a perfect model of government. There never has been. It is all too obvious that the laws of God and the example and teaching of Christ have been relentlessly rejected by generations in Britain; but it takes many years of ingratitude and unbelief to squander entirely a rich legacy of social conviction.

When God allows wicked men to triumph he is compelling us to think

When God allows wicked men to triumph he is compelling us to think. The contrast between the wickedness of evil and the righteousness of good is intended to jump us out of our comfortable moral coma—that self-contented stupor that smugly believes we are morally superior to others. We should be asking just why we consider some actions to be wrong and others to be right? What, after all, was so very evil about the actions of September 11? Many across the world believe that the destruction of over three thousand lives was a just response to what they consider to be a greater evil. How do we judge whether they are right or wrong, good or evil? By allowing such things to happen, God is forcing us to face such questions, and he is warning us that when we allow his laws to drift and we abandon the restraints that he sets on us for our good, then we are heading in the direction of a miserable moral maze. If we fail to take this lesson to heart when wickedness wins, then we have learnt nothing from sovereign grace.

The tragedy of our western civilization is not our affluent decadence—that is merely a symptom of a far greater problem. The real tragedy is that we have allowed our moral base to be eroded so that we no longer have a clear definition of sin. The existential philosophy that controls so much of our thinking allows for no absolutes and therefore nothing is certainly right or wrong; today we can even talk about 'contradictory truth'—what is right for me may be wrong for you and vice versa. Once we have abandoned the rules that God gave us—and the Ten Commandments are a straightforward starting point—we have little or no hope of ever regaining a clear view of how we judge good and evil. At best, righteousness is simply what the majority like, and at worst it is a matter of national defence.

When wickedness wins, it is God's red alert to evil

If I go on living high when in reality my bank balance is empty, it is nothing other than grace that bounces my cheques and forecloses my account! Similarly, when a nation is running down its stock of morality, it is grace when God allows evil to triumph. He is bouncing our cheque and alerting us to our moral bankruptcy. If we go on spending when we have nothing in our account, who do we blame when our number is called?

SECONDLY, GOD'S PURPOSE WHEN WICKEDNESS WINS IS TO COMPEL US TO ACT AGAINST EVIL.

We take sin so lightly: worldwide slavery, easy abortion, endemic adultery and fast divorce, blasphemous boasting of irreligion, exploitation of the poor, haughty defiance of the moral laws of God: these are all evidence of our selfish unconcern. Every year millions are left to die of hunger and disease in our deserts and wastelands and no action is taken against the nations that allow and often cause it to happen. Governments of the world remain silent at the blatant abuse of human rights in so many countries, simply because it is not in the interests of their national economy to raise a fuss. Then, suddenly, a few thousand die in a New York terrorist outrage and we come alive to injustice; our moral outrage knows no bounds. But we will only unite to defend ourselves, we still have little care for the defenceless millions. When wickedness wins, it is God's red alert to evil.

Christ forbad his followers to fight for his cause. True Christianity may result in suffering, but only because wickedness goes to war against it. There is no such thing as a holy war, whether or not it is religiously dignified with the word crusade or jihad. All war is unholy and evil, and if a religion does not denounce the concept of a 'holy war' then it is undoubtedly guilty in the eyes of God and is a religion to be rejected. Some wars have been necessary in the defence of freedom and justice—though not as many as history would like us to believe—but that does not make them holy. Christianity claims that all war is one of the evil results of a wicked world. To speak of a holy war is as precise as speaking of a holy lie, a holy theft, a holy rape or a holy murder.

To speak of a holy war is as precise as speaking of a holy lie, a holy theft, a holy rape or a holy murder

Our response to wickedness should never be one of merely settling scores. Revenge will simply smash an iron fist where it thinks it will hurt most. Justice, on the other hand, will join forces to defeat evil honourably. If the nations had a mind to, they could destroy international terrorism—but they do not have a mind to, so they will not. A sovereign God gives us a chance; he shocks us into action; he alerts us to a danger that not even the strongest nation can defeat on its own. It is utter selfishness if a nation merely defends its own interests when, together, we could work for global freedom and justice. Is that an impossible dream in a fallen world? Perhaps, but Christians should know how to pray for the impossible. The triumph of evil would be seen as grace if only we allowed it to spur us into just and effective action against all wickedness.

THIRDLY, GOD'S PURPOSE WHEN WICKEDNESS WINS IS TO DISPLAY THE COMPASSION THAT EXISTS IN THE HUMAN RACE.
There is something unique in the response of decent men and women at times of national and international disaster. The tears of sympathy, the letters of condolence, the e-mails and phone calls, even the feeling of outrage. There is a sense of unity in suffering. Whether it is the tiny premature baby gasping for life in the neo-natal incubator, the despairing community huddled in their rags on high ground as the torrent washes their flimsy homes into the raging river, or the dust choked firemen digging desperately at Ground Zero. Communities around the world that care for life, feel pain at the horror of the way people suffer and die.

On September 11 there was sheer unbelief that wicked men could be so pitiless. This response does not turn us all into saints. I am not 'Christianizing' society because of its sudden sympathy and willing charitable response. But what God is showing us is what the human race is capable of. We are not animals who simply run in the face of danger and barely pause to mourn when one of the herd is picked off by a lion. There is love, compassion, protective care, and understanding among us that is unknown in the animal world. That is a positive reminder that we are not animals, but are created in the image and likeness of God.

If a slag tip slides and engulfs a rabbit warren, do those that escape turn and spend days, even weeks, digging to rescue the buried bunnies? I have seen a herd of impala and blue wildebeest stop running the moment an animal is brought down by a cheetah; but instead of turning to charge, which would inevitably have forced the hunter to flee for its life, they simply snorted their breathlessness and resumed their grazing in sight of the big cat enjoying his meal. I know there are some animals that will defend their young at the hazard of their own lives, but when the battle is over and the young is taken, it is all soon forgotten. A cow mourns for its calf for one night only.

Where does the exceptional sympathy of the human race come from? It is nothing less than a reflection of the image of God. We are unique in creation. The reason why at worst the human race can behave more hideously than anything in the animal kingdom and can be repugnantly and totally evil, is because at best we can be beautifully and supremely good. We know how to be loving, kind, and compassionate, and therefore we are all the more guilty when we fail to be that. When God allows wickedness to win he is alerting us to the best, as well as the worst, that we are capable of. That too is sovereign grace.

FOURTHLY, GOD'S PURPOSE WHEN WICKEDNESS WINS IS TO BLOW A TRUMPET OF WARNING AND OFFER A MESSAGE OF HOPE.
In Luke 13 we have on record the response of our Lord to some disasters of his own day. One of them concerned a tower in Siloam that collapsed and killed eighteen people. He drew two applications from their death: first, they did not die because they were more sinful than anyone else, and secondly, their death was a warning that we all die for our sin (vs 4–5). What Jesus was saying was that this disaster, tragic though it was, would prove beneficial only if those who were not destroyed in it would learn from it. It is a warning of a judgement to come—of the ultimate effects of sin unrestrained and unforgiven. We are all sinful in the sight of God, and disasters do not necessarily mark out any community as more sinful than another, but they do remind us all that such tragedies are the inevitable result of a fallen world and they point to a greater and final disaster. Terrible things happen to a community, not necessarily because that community is more sinful than others, but as a warning of the results of wickedness. When God stands back and lets evil have its way, he is warning of the dreadful consequences of sin. In

At worst the human race can behave more hideously than anything in the animal kingdom ... because at best we can be beautifully and supremely good

John's apocalyptic vision in the Bible there is a vivid and poetic reflection of much that we see in our modern world:

'I looked, and behold, there was a great earthquake, and the sun became black as sackcloth, the full moon became like blood, and the stars of the sky fell to the earth as the fig tree sheds its winter fruit when shaken by a gale. The sky vanished like a scroll that is being rolled up, and every mountain and island was removed from its place. Then the kings of the earth and the great ones and the generals and the rich and the powerful, and everyone, slave and free, hid themselves in the caves and among the rocks of the mountains, calling to the mountains and rocks, "Fall on us and hide us from the face of him who is seated on the throne, and from the wrath of the Lamb, for the great day of their wrath has come, and who can stand?"'(Revelation 6:12–14).

Whenever we see or hear of a reflection of this dramatic picture in a modern disaster or outrage, it is a reminder that there is worse to come; it is a trumpet call from God alerting us to the inevitable outcome of sin and evil. And such a trumpet is certainly not giving an uncertain sound. If we will not learn that all is not well with the world, what will we learn? And if it does not convince us that we are not in control of the world we often boastfully assume we have mastered, what will convince us?

But God's trumpet blasts are not only warnings. The very first trumpet call from heaven is recorded in Exodus 19:16 as the Israelites gathered at Sinai to receive the law of God: 'On the morning of the third day there were thunders and lightenings and a thick cloud on the mountain and a very loud trumpet blast, so that all the people in the camp trembled.' The next trumpet call from heaven—and the last—will be heard at the end of time when the dead will rise and Christ will return with his angels in power and glory: 'The trumpet will sound ... and we shall be changed' (1 Corinthians 15:52; 1 Thessalonians 4:16). But every great tragedy is God's interim trumpet call of warning that there is a final day coming—and then a great divide. C S Lewis in his book *The Problem of Pain* expressed this clearly: 'God whispers to us in our pleasures, speaks in our conscience, but shouts in our pains: it is his megaphone to rouse a deaf world.'

But the same trumpet that warns of the law and of judgement will be a different kind of music to those who are waiting for his coming. It is the herald of that glorious, eternal kingdom where no sin and evil exists, but only pure joy and peace in the presence of a holy, just and righteous God and with Jesus Christ our Friend and Saviour. The cross makes all things new. Repentance and forgiveness lead to the promise of heaven. Christ offers new people here and new hope there. Our Lord would say to us today: 'Early on the morning of 11 September 2001, thousands had no idea that they would soon be rushed into eternity. Do you think they died because they were more sinful than most? No, but unless you repent, you also will perish.'

GOD IS OUR REFUGE AND OUR STRENGTH,
our ever-present aid,
and therefore though the earth should move,
we will not be afraid;
though hills are thrown into the sea,
though foaming waters roar,
and though the mighty earthquake moves
the mountains on the shore.

2 A river flows whose streams make glad
the city of our God,
the holy place in which the Lord
most High has his abode;
since God is in the midst of her,
unmoved her walls shall stand,
for God will help at break of day,
when trouble is at hand.

3 The nations rage, and kingdoms fall,
but when his voice is heard
all earthly power shall melt away
before his mighty word.
The LORD of hosts is on our side,
our safety to secure;
the God of Jacob is for us
a refuge strong and sure.

4 O come and see what mighty works
the hand of God has done;
come, see what desolation great
he brings beneath the sun.
To utmost ends of all the earth
he causes wars to cease;
the weapons of the strong destroyed,
he makes a lasting peace.

5 'Be still and know that I am God,
set over all on high;
the humbled nations of the earth
my name shall magnify.'
The LORD of hosts is on our side,
our safety to secure;
the God of Jacob is for us
a refuge strong and sure.

The Psalter 1912, alt.
Praise! 46A © in this version Praise Trust

The grace of law

'The law is holy, and the commandment is holy and righteous and good' Romans 7:12

Across the River Jordan, on the western side of the road towards the setting sun in the land of the Canaanites, were two great hills mounting some fifteen hundred feet above the valley floor. Three and a half thousand years ago Moses gathered the people of Israel together and pointed out these mountains rising from the plain in the western horizon. The land between the two hills provided a natural amphitheatre and it was there that Moses told the people to gather when they entered the Promised Land. Half of the twelve tribes of Israel were to assemble at the hill called Ebal and the other half at the hill called Gerizim. On Ebal they were to build a cairn of stones, cover the stones in plaster and in the plaster write the words of the law of God they had received forty years earlier at Sinai. Beside the cairn they were to build a stone altar on which they would offer sacrifices for the forgiveness of their sin. Wherever there was law, there was the offer of forgiveness. Both the law and forgiveness were grace.

Wherever there was law, there was the offer of forgiveness. Both the law and forgiveness were grace

Then, as six tribes stood on one mountain and six on the other, the Levites on Mount Ebal would declare the judgements that would come if Israel broke the law, and the Levites on Mount Gerizim would declare the blessings that would follow obedience to the law. You will find all this in Deuteronomy chapters 11, 27 and 28, and it was obeyed in full by Joshua: 'There was not a word of all that Moses had commanded that Joshua did not read before all the assembly of Israel, and the women, and the little ones and the sojourners who lived among them' (Joshua 8:35). This law revealed by God to Moses covered every area of the life of Israel and was, 'no empty word for you, but your very life' (Deuteronomy 32:47). God was insistent that all who lived in Israel, including foreigners, women and children, should hear, learn and obey the law of God—and there was a very important reason for this.

The comment in Deuteronomy 1:7 that God ordered the people of Israel to leave Sinai where they had received the law, and go 'to the hill country of the Amorites', may not appear very exciting, but in fact it was highly significant. Like all the tribes in the land of Canaan, the Amorites backed a fair number of gods. Chief among them were El, Baal (or Hadad the storm god) and Dagon; and of course they had to have their goddesses of violence and fertility, like Asherah, Astarte and Anath. Baal took the form of a bull and Asherah a carved pole. Possibly some of these religions practised adult human sacrifice, but certainly many followed the cruel practice of child sacrifice when infants were thrown into the burning arms of Moloch. Every town and city had its gods, temples, sacrifices, priests, priestesses and cult prostitutes.

It is not difficult to imagine the life-style of people who worship like this. Religion always governs the way people live. The gods of these nations did not give moral laws, they did not inspire moral laws and they neither approved nor disapproved moral laws; they were blind, deaf and dumb idols who retained a static disinterest in the way of life of their devotees. And the worst among all the nations were the Amorites. Years later when God wanted to describe just how bad a bad king of Israel was, he referred back to the Amorites. Ahab was one of the most evil kings of Israel and he was described as behaving, 'very abominably by going after idols, as the Amorites had done, whom the LORD cast out before the people of Israel' (1 Kings 21:26). And Manasseh, who if possible was worse than Ahab, did 'more evil than the Amorites' (2 Kings 21:11). The Amorites were a marker for all kinds of cruel and vile sin, and so when God sent his people 'into the hill country of the Amorites', they were heading among the most godless and immoral people imaginable. The gods could not care less, but the God of Israel did care. He was a God who spoke and he was a moral God.

Ebal and Gerizim

Back at Ebal and Gerizim, the Lord promised happiness for obedience and misery for disobedience. There are two laws that govern this: there is a natural law and there is a spiritual law. The natural law is the way God's ordered world works. God's laws cover every area of life, and when we choose to break his rules, sooner or later the curse from Mount Ebal is heard. But there is a spiritual law also. God brings a judgement against law-breakers that is not necessarily the natural result of sin. He may punish in a way that has no obvious connection with the crime.

In Deuteronomy 28 the space given to the warning of punishment is far greater than that given to the blessings for obedience. In our English translation there are fourteen verses recounting the blessings (vs 1–14), but fifty-four that focus on the penalty of disobedience (vs 15–68). Why? Suppose a father promises his son a small treat for good behaviour, then he'll not make too much of it—after all, it is only a *small* treat. But if a whole day outing is planned as a reward for a whole day of good behaviour, then he'll constantly remind his son of the danger of losing the promise and of the importance of obedience. The greater the blessing, the greater the penalty if it is lost. Everyone wants a life of happiness, but few want to take seriously the conditions attached. This was true of Israel three and half millenniums ago, and it is true today. But grace gave the law and the warnings—and the promises attached.

Everyone wants a life of happiness, but few want to take seriously the conditions attached

Conscience and the grace of law

Conscience and law are universal. Conscience tells everyone that there is right and wrong, and every society on earth, however advanced or primitive, however compassionate or cruel, has laws. One of the earliest law lists we possess are the 282 laws of Hammurabi, the sixth king of an old Babylonian dynasty generally reckoned to be around seventeen hundred years before Christ; that would place him a little later than Abraham and a little earlier than Moses. Human laws reflect conscience which is that inbuilt sense of obligation. It is part of our moral make up and is inseparable from our soul. It is what makes us human instead of animal. When Paul wrote, 'Where there is no law there is no transgression' (Romans 4:15), he was not referring to the law of God specifically, but to law generally. His point was that if there is no law—whether of God or man—then there is no understanding of sin, and if there is no sin there will be no punishments. Paul put the same thing a different way when he wrote, 'When Gentiles, who do not have the law, by nature do what the law requires ... They show that the work of the law is written on their hearts' (Romans 2:14–15). Every person's conscience tells them that there is right and wrong.

Although conscience can tell us that there is right and wrong, it can never reliably tell us what is right and wrong

However, although conscience can tell us that there *is* right and wrong, it can never reliably tell us *what* is right and wrong. This is why standards change from generation to generation, from society to society, and from culture to culture. It is also why men can commit depraved and cruel acts and not only convince themselves that they are right, but that they are even pleasing their god. This is because our conscience is spoilt by sin which, as we saw in chapter two, Paul described as 'seared' by sin (1 Timothy 4:2)—the word is used of a branding iron and forms the basis for our word 'cauterise'. We have trampled on God's grace by defying our conscience until it can no longer be relied upon because it is branded with the standards of our fallen society.

This is precisely why God gave the world a revelation of his laws. He began in the Old Testament, and the psalmist declares that God's word is a lamp and a light to guide him through life (Psalm 119:105). This is our only reliable guide, and the principles of God's law revealed in the Old Testament cover every area of life. The law was given chiefly through Moses

3,500 years ago and is found in the books of Exodus to Deuteronomy. For convenience we can divide the laws given by God into two parts, though the Jews themselves never made this distinction. First there was the moral law which covered all human relationships including marriage and sex, social and business relationships, leadership and judges, employers and employees, health and safety, hygiene and employment, property rights, the treatment of animals and even ecology. The Ten Commandments are a summary of this moral law. The second part of the law was the priestly ceremonial which included the detailed religious observances which was God's way of preparing his people for the coming of Christ. The ceremonial law taught people the seriousness of sin by the death of an animal sacrifice; it led them to repentance and then, through the offerings and sacrifices, assured them of forgiveness and reconciliation with God.

The reason why the Israelites made no distinction between the moral and ceremonial law was that there was a vital link between the two. For them the law—all of it—was one undivided piece; to break the ceremonial law was every bit as bad as breaking the moral law. Uzzah bore the same penalty for touching the Ark of God (2 Samuel 6:3–7 cf. 1 Chronicles 13:9-10) as he would have for committing murder or adultery (Leviticus 20:12, 14). The moral law revealed how holy God is and how far short everyone falls. The priestly law revealed how holy God is and how completely anyone can be forgiven. This is the grace of law.

The law and the Christian

How far does the Old Testament law of God apply to the Christian? In the history of the church, the law has been seen by Christians to have three uses: first to convict sinners of sin, secondly to keep the unruly in check, and thirdly to guide Christians in the path of holiness—this last one is what is known as 'the third use of the law'. But above these three uses there are two others that are far more important. The law reveals to the world what a holy, wise and gracious God we worship (Deuteronomy 4:6–8), and it is also our tutor to guard us and lead us to Christ (Galatians 3:24). The Greek word *paidagogos* that Paul uses here in Galatians carried the meaning of tutor in the first century, because the 'child minder' was often the educator as well. These are in fact the chief purposes of the law of God. Above the cruel values surrounding the world's idols, the God of Israel towered as a Creator of supreme purity and righteousness—and one who expected the same from his people.

When we have set aside two opposite positions in the whole debate about the value of the law for the Christian—those who take the view that it has no value at all (antinomian), and those who write law books based upon the Old Testament law (Christian Reconstruction)—the gap between the rest should be fairly small. After all, if the law has any value at all we must learn how best to use it. Paul pointed out that the law is holy, righteous, good and spiritual (Romans 7:12, 14), and he repeated this to Timothy: 'We know that the law is good' (1 Timothy 1:8). He reminded the Christians at Rome that everything written in the Old Testament is intended for us (Romans 15:4), and when he encouraged Timothy to teach the Christians at Ephesus that, 'All Scripture ... is profitable for teaching, for reproof, for correction, and for training in righteousness, that the man of God may be competent, equipped for every good work' it was the whole Old Testament that was in the apostle's mind (2 Timothy 3:16–17).

> For the Christian, the value of the law is not as a big stick with which to be beaten ... but as a friendly guide to pull him back into line

For the Christian, the value of the law is not as a big stick with which to be beaten constantly, but as a friendly guide to pull him back into line when he is tempted to stray. It is no longer his enemy as it once was. This must be what Paul meant when in Romans 7:6 he claimed, 'Now we are released from the law, having died to that which held us captive, so that we serve not under the old written code but in the new life of the Spirit.' It is this spiritual interpretation of the law that the Christian is looking for. Far from dismissing the value and significance of the law, this enhances it; the Christian is able to employ the law in a way that few in the Old Testament could. It is what Paul meant when he encouraged the Galatians—a church severely tempted to return to a strict observance of the Old Testament rule of law—to 'walk by the Spirit' (Galatians 5:16, 25); this was his new 'rule' for them (6:16). This new spiritual life should be compared to the relationship between a husband and wife who have family rules that will be observed in loving regard for each other's benefit—and not to the government official who is overwhelmed by the bureaucratic red tape of officialdom.

However, there is a strange idea put about that in the Old Testament the law was little more than a club to beat the nation with, and that Israel lived in fear of breaking it. Doubtless this would have been true of some, but we have already seen how David loved the law with all his heart. Perhaps also we should learn from Isaiah in his chapter of perfect peace, where 'judgements' refers to the law of God: 'In the path of your judgements O LORD, we wait for you; your name and remembrance are the desire of our soul. My soul yearns for you in the night; my spirit within me earnestly seeks you. For when your judgements are in the earth, the inhabitants of the world learn righteousness' (Isaiah 26:8–9). This example surely gives us a different perspective on the value of the law of God for the true Old Testament Christian.

In case we should ever doubt the value of the law in the life of the Christian, Paul left us examples of how it should be wisely and properly used. The law has a value well beyond hard and vital moral choices that we are confronted with in our society. It will no longer be the dead letter of the law that the Christian slavishly adheres to, but the application of law spiritually understood. This is precisely what Jesus did in his Sermon on the Mount and what Paul constantly did in his letters to the young churches.

A further illustration of Paul's use of the Old Testament, is found when he encouraged the young churches to support financially those working in gospel ministry. He looked to the Old Testament law for support, and focused on Deuteronomy 25:4, 'You shall not muzzle an ox when it is treading out the grain.' Paul's reasoning in 1 Corinthians 9:8–11 is that this passage in the Old Testament law is not only or even primarily about our concern for the welfare of animals—though it is concerned for that—but it has a much wider and more spiritual application. This is a perfect example of a Christian application of Old Testament law. The whole New Testament ethic is an exposition of Old Testament law. When one writer criticises the 'expositions of the Decalogue (that) move from crime to "deeper applications"', he may have forgotten that this is precisely what Paul is doing here and exactly what our Lord did in his Sermon on the Mount.

I do not for one moment overlook those few parts of the law where we find it hard to understand exactly what their application is for us today. But when applied through the filter of the life and ministry of Christ and the life and ministry of the apostles, the Old Testament law is full of instruction. Here are just a handful of examples among many.

The whole New Testament ethic is an exposition of Old Testament law

Leviticus 11 lists all the animals that Israel could eat or must avoid eating; they were known as the 'clean' and 'unclean' animals. Within that record is the instruction that if a housewife discovered that a lizard had fallen into her kneading bowl, she must break the bowl and destroy any food that was left in it (vs 33–34). That may seem a harsh response when she could more easily have washed out the bowl. However, the severity of the law would soon help her to realise that it would be far more sensible never to leave food overnight in an uncovered bowl, and that it would be wiser for her to turn all unused kitchenware upside down. I doubt whether too many bowls were broken in Israelite homes—mothers would train their daughters better than that. Is this frivolous? Not when you consider the millions that have died in history—and are still dying across the world today—from dysentery simply because basic rules of hygiene like this are neglected. Similarly, some of the extravagant washing listed in the law would doubtless have been intended to eradicate the ubiquitous human louse—an insect which causes typhus resulting in more deaths than any other insect-borne disease with the exception of the malarial mosquito.

Deuteronomy 22 is an Old Testament chapter that deals with lost property, neighbourliness, cross-dressing, ecology, health and safety, agriculture and horticulture, marriage relationships, adultery, and rape—are we really suggesting that there is nothing for the Christian or the modern world to learn in a passage like this? Of course we will always be looking for the higher and more spiritual application *as well as* the immediate application. In any discussion on the wise use of the earth's resources, can the Christian learn nothing from the simple check on egg-collecting found in Deuteronomy 22:6–7? If our Victorian forefathers had paid attention to the principles enshrined in Deuteronomy 22:8 then thousands of little children, who were operating unguarded machinery, would not have been so brutally maimed and killed. This is precisely why Jesus told the Pharisees that they should not neglect tithing but should look for the 'weightier matters of the law' (Matthew 23:23). Nothing in the law is irrelevant for the Christian and everything—spiritually understood—is of value. Neither our Lord nor the apostles dealt with all these issues because the foundation was well laid fifteen hundred years earlier.

By meditating on the law day and night ... David had made it a subconscious controller of his life

The Spirit and the law

Does this place us under the burden of insignificant rules and regulations? Not if we allow the Spirit to guide us in interpreting and applying the law. This surely is at least part of the meaning within Jeremiah 31:33. Legalism is the result of an obsession with legal details. When we demand total adherence to the minutiae of the law we have forgotten how our Lord intended us to use it. I am sure that when David in Psalm 119 claimed that he so valued and enjoyed the law of God that he thought about it and stored it up in his mind, he was as close to a Christian experience of the law as it was possible for an Old Testament saint to get. By meditating on the law day and night—and he said it was like honey to his taste—David had made it a subconscious controller of his life.

The good citizen always loves good laws; it is only the law-breaker who hates them. In a similar way to David, the psalmist Asaph could think of nothing more wonderful in this life as a preparation for the next, than the guidance of God in his word leading him to God himself: 'You guide me with your counsel, and afterwards you will receive me to glory. Whom have I in heaven but you? And there is nothing on earth that I desire besides you' (Psalm 73:24–25). The more I understand the whole law of God the more I will know the meaning of loving God and loving my neighbour. Explaining this to a young reader, John Newton claimed that the Christian who uses the law in this way 'acquires an habitual, spiritual taste of what is right or wrong.' That is precisely the purpose of the grace of law.

I first learned to drive in an old Land Rover, and the rules for changing gear were extremely hard to remember—I had to double de-clutch both up and down the gears. My instructor told me to take my right foot off the accelerator and at the same time depress the clutch with my left foot; then I must slip the gear into neutral and release the clutch just as I gave a short burst on the accelerator to increase the engine revs. Immediately I must de-clutch once more, push the gear lever into second gear and lift my left foot from the clutch pedal at the same time as depressing the accelerator. And I must do all this so fast that I do not lose engine speed. That was the rule. But it was so very hard to remember. At first I crashed gears and stalled the engine so many times. But now I can do all that in a second and without thinking. The rule has become part of my subconscious life when driving. I don't even say to myself: 'Now I must double de-clutch. Right foot off the accelerator …' This is exactly what the Psalmist meant in Psalm 119:45 when he wrote, 'I will walk about in freedom for I have sought out your precepts' (*New International Version*). God's laws had become part of his mind-set.

If the world of automobiles is not your scene, let me take an illustration from the world of music. When we are learning to play the piano, one of the most important points is to look carefully where we place our fingers on the keyboard. Similarly we have to pay attention to the notes on the sheet music in front of us; we must observe carefully whether a note is above, on or below the line and whether the note is black or white and whether it has a tail or not—it all makes a lot of difference. At first this is painfully slow and tedious. We make many mistakes and the concentration is enormous. I compare this to the way the Israelites used the Old Testament law. It was detailed and laborious and often it must have proved tedious and irritating—but it was all vitally necessary. In the course of time and with practice, it is possible to play accurately by obeying every rule of music—but the result may still be flat, insensitive and dead; it is without life or soul. That is like the legalism of a wrong use of Old Testament law. However, the concert pianist no longer focuses on those basic rules—she uses them and they are still essential if she is to play well—but now she concentrates on bringing life and soul into her music. Far from ignoring or destroying the rules she learnt in grade one, she now wants to give them greater value. She applies them in such a way as to express thought and feeling in order to make the music come alive and touch the soul—and she does so with hardly any conscious awareness of those basic laws. But if she makes a mistake, or is ever tempted to defy the rules of music, they are always there to bring her back into line. That is just how the New Testament Christian applies the law.

No more Law?

Writing to a young man on the subject of the law of God, John Newton may have slightly overstated his case when he remarked that, 'Ignorance of the nature and design of the law is at the bottom of most religious mistakes.' But perhaps he was not too far from the truth. It seems to be in fashion today for Christians with a theology that ranges widely from the 'Charismatic' to the 'Reformed' to dispense with the value of the Old Testament law of God. At the very time when the moral downgrade in western civilization is crying out for clear standards of right and wrong, many Christians have cut loose the Maker's instructions. Perhaps it is a reaction to the cold harshness of legalism; or more likely it may betray the influence of the existential philosophy of our age that refuses to accept absolute right and wrong and is comfortable to speak of 'contradictory truth'. But whatever the reason, so-called 'new covenant theology' that denies any value of the Old Testament law for the life of the Christian, is becoming increasingly popular.

There are few subjects where evangelicals present such a kaleidoscope of differing opinions than on the place of the law of God in the life of the Christian. They range from the Christian Reconstructionist who writes law books based on the Old Testament for the guidance of governments today and in preparation for their expected post-millennial age, to the dispensationalist and new covenant theologians who believe that the law should have no influence over Christians whatever. Michael Eaton in *A Theology of Encouragement*, assures us that the law has no claim whatsoever upon the Christian and although we can 'derive wisdom from it'—though what wisdom he does not define—we cannot apply it to the modern society or to the life of the Christian. In fact he goes further and suggests that only when we have wholly dispensed with the law of God can we possibly find full assurance of salvation.

Whatever arguments are levelled against the value of the law of God, we must take into account such biblical statements as:

'Do we, then, overthrow the law by this faith? By no means! On the contrary, we uphold the law' (Romans 3:31)

'The law is holy, and the commandment is holy and righteous and good' (Romans 7:12)

'Whatever was written in the former days was written for our instruction' (Romans 15:4)

'Keeping God's commands is what counts' (1 Corinthians 7:19 New International Version)

'But we know that the law is good, if one uses it lawfully' (1 Timothy 1:8)

'All Scripture ... is profitable for teaching, for reproof, for correcting, and for training in righteousness' (2 Timothy 3:16)

Verses like these hardly support the conclusion that Old Testament law has nothing whatsoever to do with the Christian. But what are the arguments against the Christian use of the law?

First, it is claimed that the Old Testament law is altogether too low a standard

We are told that the law is not sufficiently Christian in outlook. That is arguable, but what must be certain is that God did not reveal a low standard to his chosen people. We can hardly claim that the God who commanded Israel 'to be holy as I am holy' was prepared to settle for obedience to a low standard. Was his law adequate by which to measure that holiness? And if not, has the word 'holiness' radically changed its meaning from the old covenant to the new?

Some suggest that our Lord deliberately replaced the Old Testament law by his own teaching. In his book *Tablets of Stone,* John Reisinger claims that this is precisely what Jesus did in Matthew 5:27–28 by his instruction: 'You have heard that it was said, "You shall not commit adultery." But I say to you that everyone who looks at a woman with lustful intent has already committed adultery with her in his heart.' Reisinger believes that Jesus is saying that the seventh Commandment is not an adequate standard. But that is *not* what our Lord means at all. The introduction 'you have heard it said' is generally accepted as his way of referring, not to the Old Testament—which he normally introduces by 'it is written'—but to the teaching of the Pharisees. Thus our Lord is instructing his disciples that whilst the Pharisees limited the seventh Commandment to the act of physical adultery, there was much more intended by the Commandment than that. This is clear from the fact that the Tenth Commandment is all about the mind. In addition, Proverbs 6:25 'do not desire her beauty in your heart', 6:27 'Can a man carry fire next to his chest and his clothes not be burned?' and 7:25 'Let not your heart turn aside to her ways', explicitly refer to the inward lusting after a forbidden woman. In other words, Jesus was teaching his disciples, as he often did, how to correctly understand Old Testament law.

> *There was never anything wrong with the law of God. God himself gave it and it is his law*

There was never anything *wrong* with the law of God. God himself gave it and it is his law. This is why Paul reminds us that the law is 'holy, righteous, good and spiritual' (Romans 7:12, 14). It had to be, God gave it and it reflected his own character. If we say that the law is not sufficient for salvation, then Paul would agree, since it was never meant to be sufficient. If the law was final and adequate for salvation there would have been no need for Christ. Similarly, if we say that the law was weak, and powerless to enable us to keep it, then Paul would agree with that also: 'For God has done what the law, weakened by the flesh, could not do' (Romans 8:3). But far from being a low standard, it is 'the embodiment of knowledge and truth' (Romans 2:20). But it must be used spiritually, which is what Jesus taught, and not legalistically as the Pharisees taught.

Secondly, it is claimed that the law was for Israel alone

Reisinger believes that the Ten Commandments (Decalogue) are central to the covenant with Israel, and when that covenant was superseded by Christ, the Decalogue fell with it. In reply we may point out that whilst the law was a mark of God's special relationship with Israel, and was given to them as a great privilege and not revealed to the nations in general, yet Israel was intended to be an example to the nations. Their possession and practice of the law was meant to say to the surrounding tribes: this is how holy the only true God is and how holy his people live, and therefore this is how God expects all nations to live. By revealing the law to Israel alone, God was not suggesting that the nations could please themselves; and if he was, why then did he punish them for their immoral life-style? In fact, by what measure was it immoral if God's law was not their standard?

In Deuteronomy 4:5–8 God underlined the evangelistic value of the law by reminding his people that they were to be a witness to the nations who, learning of the laws of Israel may conclude: 'What great nation ... has a god so near to it as the LORD our God ... And that has statutes and rules so righteous as all this law?' This was one significant reason why God was so angry with David for his double sin of murder and adultery: 'You made the enemies of the LORD show contempt' (2 Samuel 12:14 *New International Version*). At that point of scandalous sin, David and Israel were no longer an example to the nations. We do not know what Jonah preached at

Nineveh when he finally arrived after his submarine adventure, but did he say nothing at all beyond the brief summary in Scripture: 'Yet forty days, and Nineveh shall be overthrown' (Jonah 3:4)? Surely, in order to convict the sin-branded conscience of the cruelly pagan Assyrians he must have preached the law of his God.

Significantly, in Deuteronomy 31:12–13, God included even the foreigners living in Israel among those who must listen to and obey the law: 'Assemble the people, men, women, and little ones, and the sojourner within your towns, that they may hear and learn to fear the LORD your God, and be careful to do all the words of this law, and that their children, who have not known it, may hear and learn to fear the LORD your God, as long as you live in the land that you are going over the Jordan to possess.' We cannot suggest that the phrase 'as long as you live in the land' means that God was perfectly content for them to abandon his law if they moved away from Israel. Does God have one acceptable standard for Israel and another for the rest of the world?

I took my driving test back in the 1960s in that old 4x4 Land Rover. Not only did I have to double declutch up and down the gears, but it had no automatic signals, and when manoeuvring I had to heave the wheel round! In those days there were brand new cars on the road that had smooth synchromesh gears, winking lights, and power steering. However, it did not occur to me to plead with my examiner that it was unfair that I should be judged by the same exacting standards as the guys in the brand new models—and apparently it did not occur to him either. The same rules were applied to both of us, and The Ministry of Transport made no concessions. Neither did the God of Israel make concession for the nations beyond the borders of the Promised Land; the same holy God and his holy laws stood in judgement upon all men. Israel was to be a light to the nations and her obedience to the laws of God would be an evangelistic witness.

To suggest that the law in general and the Ten Commandments in particular are part of the covenant with Israel and therefore have no binding authority of relevance once the new covenant was established in Christ, is to overlook one vital conclusion that must follow. If no one other than the Jews in the Old Testament were under an obligation to the law, in what sense did Christ die to redeem *us* from the curse of the law (Galatians

3:13)? How can Christ be said to have died to purchase our freedom from the consequences of breaking a law that we were not expected to keep in the first place?

Thirdly, Christ's claim that he had come to 'fulfil the law' is seen as an argument against its continuing value

The little word 'fulfil' in the Sermon on the Mount, is surrounded by three significant statements of our Lord. In Matthew 5:17 he claims, 'I have not come to abolish the Law or the Prophets', in the following verse he declares, 'until heaven and earth pass away, not an iota, not a dot, will pass from the Law until all is accomplished', and in verse 19 our Lord warns, 'Therefore whoever relaxes one of the least of these commandments and teaches others to do the same will be called least in the kingdom of heaven.' It is unwise to suggest that the phrase, 'these commandments' refers to the teaching of Christ that is to follow since the whole context is the enduring Old Testament Law, and verse 19 is an application of verse 18; in other words he is saying, 'the law lasts, and if you break it you will be least'. Besides, only in John 14:15, 21 and 15:10 do we have a record of our Lord referring to his own teaching as 'commandments'; that word is normally reserved for the Old Testament Law (for example Matthew 19:17 and 22:40).

How can Christ be said to have died to purchase our freedom from the consequences of breaking a law that we were not expected to keep in the first place?

Jesus had not come to get rid of the law, but to 'fulfil' it. But what did that mean? The same word 'fulfil' is found in the account of our Lord's baptism in Matthew 3:15 when he responded to John the Baptist: 'It is fitting for us to fulfil all righteousness.' By this he did not mean that he should do away with righteousness, but that he must do everything to discharge his obligation to it; he must do everything expected of him. Back in Matthew 5, the same word means to carry out and accomplish everything expected in the law. John Newton once wrote, 'It is an abuse both of law and gospel, to pretend that its accomplishment by Christ released believers from an obligation to it as a rule.'

But didn't Christ by his words and his actions abolish some of the law? No, all that he ever insisted upon was a proper understanding and application of the law of God. Here is one clear example: in his condemnation of the legalism of the Scribes and Pharisees he drew attention to their precise tithing of herbs. Whilst jibing at their pernickety insistence upon the minute counting of 'mint and dill and cumin', he complained that they had neglected, 'the weightier matters of the law: justice and mercy and faithfulness.' However what is particularly significant is the phrase: 'These you ought to have done, without neglecting the others'(Matthew 23:23); in other words their tithing was not wrong but they had placed insistence upon the letter of the law well above a life of love. Christ came to enrich the law, not destroy it; and he did this best of all by his life—his was the most beautiful expression of the law in action that this world will ever see. Newton claimed that Christ is the 'transcript of the law'.

His was the most beautiful expression of the law in action that this world will ever see

Fourthly, we are told that the fact that the laws of God are summed up by the simple command to love, implies that we no longer need the law

At the finale for the Queen's Golden Jubilee pop concert in her garden at Buckingham Palace on 3 June 2002, the catchy phrase: 'All we need is love, love is all we need' was sung with great enthusiasm by tens of thousands in the garden and outside in the Mall, and by millions around the world. This gospel according to the Beatles is taken up enthusiastically by many today—and Christians can fall into the same trap.

In Romans 13:8–10 Paul lists four commandments and concludes that all the others may be summed up in this way: 'You shall love your neighbour as yourself.' Similarly in Galatians 5:14 he claims that the entire law is summed up in a single command: 'Love your neighbour as yourself.' In the first of these two statements, Paul used one word that is translated by the words 'fulfilled' and 'fulfilling', and that word is the one used by our Lord at his baptism and in his Sermon on the Mount in Matthew 5:17. As we have seen, it simply implies fully carrying out rather than destroying. But the word translated 'summed up' in Romans 13:9 is interesting because it means what it says: to condense something into a summary. That is exactly what the law of love is—it is a summary of the whole law—not a replacement for it.

There can be no doubt about this conclusion because in Galatians 5:14 Paul is not making love a New Testament substitute for Old Testament law since his statement: 'You shall love your neighbour as yourself' is a quotation taken directly from Leviticus 19:18! Besides, by suggesting that the commandments can be summed up in this one rule that we should love our neighbour as ourselves, Paul cannot mean that *all* commandments without exception are summed up in this way. Whilst most of the Old Testament laws might be summed up in the delightfully simple phrase that we should love our neighbour, Paul knew his Old Testament sufficiently well to realise that at least the first three of the Ten Commandments related primarily to our love of God.

However, a summary does not dispense with the details; it encloses them by a simple statement. Let me illustrate: I may describe a collection of moulded steel, cast iron, electrical wiring, leather upholstery, reinforced glass, plastic, and an assortment of nuts, bolts and screws. But I summarise all this by telling you that I have just bought a motor car. That simple word 'car' does not destroy the detail, it merely summarises it. When our Lord was asked which one is the greatest commandment in the law, he replied by offering a short summary: 'You shall love the Lord your God with all your heart and with all your soul and with all your mind. This is the great and first commandment. And a second is like it: You shall love your neighbour as yourself. On these two commandments *depend* all the Law and the

Prophets' (Matthew 22:37–40). He made it quite clear that the summary did not dispense with the detail. This is apparent by the word that is translated 'depend'. It is used of leaves that hang from a tree or a door that is hung on its hinges. In this sense the emphasis is upon connection or dependence, hence the translation 'depend'; some translations actually use the word 'hang'. All the law and the prophets depend upon the law of love for their full and proper expression. But love no more means that we can do without law than the existence of trees means we can do without leaves or hinges means that we can do without a door.

You will sometimes be told that Christ left his disciples a new command that they should love one another. But he didn't! It is only a superficial reading of John 13:34 that arrives at this conclusion. There was nothing new in the command to love one another; our Lord was merely quoting—just as Paul did—from the law itself. So, what was new in the command that Christ gave? Look carefully at what our Lord says immediately following his quotation from Leviticus: 'Just as I have loved you, you also are to love one another.' That is radically new and uniquely Christian. There was nothing like this in the Old Testament law where the standard given was that we should love our neighbour *as we love ourselves*. Now, however, the standard is to love *as Christ loved us*. Here Christ expounds and applies the law. But you will notice that he uses the law as his foundation and then builds on it. This is what he meant by 'fulfilling' the law. The law told us *what* and even *how*, but our Lord pitches the *how* even higher.

Quite simply we need the law to guide and control our definition of love, because love alone is too subjective. Let me be very practical:

Two young people love each other, so they decide to sleep together. Is this right? How do we know? Love does not tell us, but the law does.

A man loves a woman and so he leaves his wife and family to go with her. Is this right? How do we know? Love does not decide, but the law does.

A man is cruel to his wife so her brother kills the brutal husband to protect his sister whom he loves. Is this right? Love does not tell us, but the law does.

Two men, or two women, enjoy intimate sexual relationships because they love each other. Is that right? Again, love does not tell us, but the law does.

A poor man steals to buy his children Christmas presents because he loves them. Is that right? Love may say it is, but it is the law that teaches us otherwise.

A woman lies to protect her friend whom she loves. Is that right? Only the law can tell us.

These moral issues are not answered by love alone. They are not even answered by love and a Christian indwelt by the Holy Spirit; if they were, all Christians would agree on all the examples I have given above, and as a pastor I would never have to remind disobedient Christians that their course of action is contrary to the perfect design of God. Here is the key: our moral decisions must be motivated by love monitored by law. The law restrains love from its excesses whilst love releases law from its harshness. It was the law of love that meant Christ could discharge the woman who was taken in adultery from the legal penalty of death. But love did not make her adultery right; the law condemned her and rightly so. This is a beautiful example of love and law in action: 'Neither do I condemn you; go, and from now on sin no more' (John 8:11). It is the grace of law when it keeps love in check.

The law restrains love from its excesses whilst love releases law from its harshness

Fifthly, we are reminded that the Christian is no longer under law but under grace

One of the most misquoted verses in the New Testament is Romans 6:14 where Paul states, 'You are not under law but under grace'. What exactly did he mean? He surely cannot be dismissing the value of law altogether since, as we saw earlier, Paul writes highly of the value of the law, and when he encourages Timothy that, 'All Scripture is … profitable for teaching, for reproof, for correction, and for training in righteousness' (2 Timothy 3:16), I doubt whether he meant all Scripture except the law. Michael Eaton concludes that as we walk by the Spirit we may fulfil the law 'accidentally', but that it has nothing to say to the Christian in his daily walk with God. Is this right?

It is clear from the context of Romans 6:14 that far from denying the value of the law, Paul is establishing a higher motivation in our life, 'For sin will not have dominion over you, since you are not under law but under grace'. The law is no longer our master and it no longer condemns us. Christ is our master and his death releases us from all the condemning judgement of the law. More than this, his Spirit enables us to understand the value of the law and delight in applying it to our lives. In a highly significant phrase in verse 17, Paul recognises that whilst we were once slaves of sin, in Christ we have now become obedient, 'from the heart to the standard of teaching to which you were committed'. We are now 'slaves of righteousness' (v 18). In his detailed and careful argument in Romans 7 and 8 about the law, Paul makes clear that the law standing on its own can only increase my sin and condemn me for it; it can neither give me life nor the power to overcome sin. However, once I am set free from the power and condemnation of the law by the Spirit of life in Christ, that which once was my enemy can become my friend. We are not saved *by* obedience to the law, but we are saved *for* obedience to the law.

We are not saved by obedience to the law, but we are saved for obedience to the law

Justifying grace assures us that to gain forgiveness and reconciliation with God we can have nothing to do with the law, and that to remain forgiven and reconciled, the law can have nothing to do with us. This is surely what Augustus Toplady meant in his hymn: 'The terrors of law and of God with me can have nothing to do; my Saviour's obedience and blood hide all my transgressions from view.' More importantly, it is what Paul meant here in Romans 6:14. Knowing that the power of the law to condemn me to the anger of a holy God has been for ever broken, gives me such joy in justifying grace. The law can never separate me from the love of God, for Christ is my Master and he alone has 'dominion'—lordship, rule, authority—over my life. That is the meaning of being under grace and not under law. Nothing more, but nothing less either.

Sixthly, the law is now written in our hearts so that we do not need the law written on stone

A frequently quoted promise from the Old Testament is Jeremiah 31:33. All are agreed that this refers to the new era of the Spirit after Pentecost: '"This is the covenant that I will make with the house of Israel after those days", declares the LORD: "I will put my law within them, and I will write it on their hearts. And I will be their God, and they shall be my people."'

The question is, precisely what does this refer to? Since Jeremiah refers to 'my law' six times and on every occasion it can only refer to the law of God (see 6:19; 9:13; 16:11; 26:4; 31:33; 44:10), it must be the Old Testament law that God writes on our hearts under the new covenant. But what does this mean? Are we to assume that none of the Old Testament saints ever kept the law of God joyfully, willingly, and wholeheartedly? Such a conclusion would be hard to square with the psalmist's expressions of love for God's word in Psalm 119 where on ten occasions he declares his 'delight' in the law, on seven he declares how he 'loves' God's law, and further comments how he has stored it in his heart (v 11), kept it with his 'whole heart' (vs 34, 69), and 'longs for it' (vs 20, 40). Surely the distinction is this: under the old covenant every member of Israel belonged to the people of the promise though not all lived by faith and therefore many obeyed the law grudgingly, but under the new covenant every member will be a true believer serving God and his law with a glad heart. David in Psalm 119 enjoyed the law in his heart under new covenant blessing, but he was exceptional.

Seventhly, the New Testament does not refer to the relevance of the law in the life of the Christian

This claim is far more imagined than real, and here are three texts, among others, to the contrary.

In 1 Corinthians 10:6–10 Paul provides us with four cameos of the disobedience of Israel in the wilderness which illustrate four of the Ten Commandments. Commandments 1, 2, 7, 10 are clearly in focus here and Paul concludes, 'these things happened to them as an example, but they were written down for our instruction' (v 11). More significantly is the fact that in Romans 13:9, Paul lists four of the Ten Commandments, embraces the rest by the statement: 'and any other commandment', and then summarises them by quoting, not from the teaching of Jesus, but directly from Leviticus 19:18. He offers not a word of hesitation or warning on the use of Old Testament law. As one writer comments, 'Paul appears to have no problem quoting from the Decalogue and leaving it at that.'

A third passage is 1 Timothy 1:5–11, which is an often overlooked but significant passage in this whole debate. Here Paul states that the law is good and is to be used—provided it is used 'lawfully'. Therefore there must be a right and a wrong way to use the law of God, and in vs 6–7 he refers to those who teach the law in the wrong way—though Paul does not define in what way they misused the law. However, he does indicate the correct use of the law: it is not needed for those who already obey its dictates (the just or righteous of v 9, and compare with Matthew 9:13 and Philippians 3:6) but it is for those who do not, whether Christian or non Christian. In other words, the law is a clear marker for righteous living; it has little to say to the righteous man—until he steps out of line. To underline this, Paul provides Timothy with a sin-list that follows the order of the Ten Commandments precisely (vs 9–10) and he concludes that these—and anything else that contradicts the law—is 'contrary to sound doctrine'. In other words, adherence to the law is part of what Paul calls 'sound doctrine'.

> *Keeping in step with the Spirit is never to be divorced from keeping in step with his law*

The grace of law

Both law and love are the grace of God. We are never to talk of 'grace *or* law', as if they are opposites—Paul tells us that the law is not 'contrary to the promises of God' (Galatians 3:21). Nor should we talk of 'grace *and* law', as if they are compatible differences. We will never find those two phrases in the New Testament. But we can speak of 'the grace *of* law'. Law was God's grace to define and confine sin, and it still is because it still does. Keeping in step with the Spirit is never to be divorced from keeping in step with his law.

Looking for a bridge between some of the Old Testament laws and the life of the Christian, Richard Lovelace in *Dynamics of Spiritual Life*, suggests that, 'The constant acts of choice they had to make between clean and unclean items was a kind of game preparation for the serious business of discriminating between the holy and unholy which is part of a walk in the Holy Spirit.' If that is so, then this is all part of the grace of law. It is the grace of God that instructed his ancient people Israel—and us through them—just how vital it is that our values of life should be very different from those of the world around us. And if we consider some of the rules are a little too fussy, perhaps God is saying to us: 'Think about it. The Christian conscience should be touch-sensitive to sin.'

When Christians 'talk down' the law of God, they do a serious disservice to the God of all grace who gave his rules to us in the first place; they equally do a great disservice to a world living in a moral maze with only the sin-branded conscience of society to guide it. For that matter, they do a great disservice also to a generation of young Christians struggling to learn just how they can claim that there are in existence standards stamped with God's authority. It is of little help for them to be told that the revelation of the law in the Old Testament is irrelevant for the twenty-first century, or even that though the world needs some of it, Christians need none of it. Wisdom will teach them that the one true God has given us his rules for perfect living, and that Christ by his life and teaching, and by his death and resurrection, has added a plus factor to those rules—not to replace them, but to renew them with life and love.

Law restrains love from its abuses whilst love releases law from its harshness. Love is the *how* that interprets and applies the *what* of law. This is why King Alfred the Great, who became the first king to unite much of England under his rule, placed the Ten Commandments at the beginning of the law book for his subjects and showed how they should be understood:

'by the love and compassion of the Lord Christ.' The puritan Thomas Watson once wrote, 'They who will not have the law to rule them shall have the law to judge them.' Or, as a wise old Methodist preacher once commented, 'We either keep the Ten Commandments or we illustrate them.' Better still, listen to David in the Old Testament: 'I find my delight in your commandments, which I love' (Psalm 119:47). It is remarkably sad that King David could declare: 'Open my eyes, that I may behold wondrous things out of your law' (Psalm 119:18), whilst many Christians three thousand years later can find nothing wonderful in them at all.

What is so wonderful about the law of God?

The law shows us how holy God is—though more clearly does the life of Christ.

The law shows us the horror of sin—though more clearly does the cross of Christ.

The law warns of judgement for disobedience—though more clearly does the agony of Christ at Calvary.

The law points to forgiveness and reconciliation with God—though more clearly does our Saviour's death and resurrection.

The law is holy, righteous and good—but a thousand times more holy, righteous and good is Christ. The grace of law always points away to Christ who died, not to bring an end to law but to the penalty of broken law and to the weakness of the law that cannot help us to keep it.

When Christians 'talk down' the law ... they do a serious disservice to the God of all grace

For the Christian, the law can never condemn. It has lost its power to cast any Christian into hell because Christ nailed all its demands to the cross (Colossians 2:14). I can now delight in the law because Christ has died to set me free to enjoy the grace of law.

HOW CAN THE WAY OF YOUTH BE PURE,
what guiding light can wisdom give?
Their path, O LORD, shall be secure
if by your holy word they live.

2 With all my heart I seek you, LORD;
O let me not from you depart!
To guard my steps from sin, your word
I safely cherish in my heart.

3 All praise, O gracious LORD be yours!
Teach me the truth of your decrees;
so with my lips I speak your laws,
your precepts and your promises.

4 As those who in their wealth rejoice
so is my joy to heed your ways;
my ears will listen to your voice,
my mind reflect, my mouth give praise.

5 As your decrees are my delight
so shall I not neglect your law;
here is my study, day and night,
here may I walk for evermore.

The Psalter 1912, Alt.
Praise! 119C Psalm 119:9–16 © in this version Praise Trust

ct.

Justifying grace

'By the grace of God I am what I am'
1 Corinthians 15:10

Wﾍen Paul wrote chapter fifteen of First Corinthians his purpose
was to convince the Corinthian Christians of the reality—the
essential reality—of the literal resurrection of Jesus Christ from
the dead. It was no 'conjuring trick with bones' as far as Paul was
concerned; no mere fable to describe the 'vivifying presence of Christ'.
Such myths may satisfy bishops and Bible critics, but they certainly would
not satisfy Paul. He had not hazarded his life riding stormy, pirate-infested
seas and trekking across harsh, bandit-ridden wastelands to tell the
Corinthians a make believe tale of fantasies—and he did not expect them
to risk their lives by believing such nonsense either. So, he taught them why
the literal, physical resurrection of Jesus Christ from the dead was so vital
to their faith and how they could be sure that the message was true; he even
provided them with a list of those to whom they could apply if they wanted
to take up references for the truth of his story—references from those who
had seen him for themselves. At the end of that list Paul declared, 'Last of
all ... he appeared to me also' (v 8). That was more significant than at first
appears, and perhaps this was what he was really driving at.

Paul had problems convincing the Corinthian Christians of his
authority, and as a result his relationship with them was stormy. The church
at Corinth had enough moral, spiritual, and doctrinal baggage to sink a
Roman galley, and more than once they rejected Paul and accused him of
pulling apostolic rank when he tried to correct the abuses within the
congregation. They did not appreciate his instructions or that he had any
right to order them what to do. Fortunately the end of the story is happier
than the beginning, but that doesn't immediately concern us. To convince
them of his authority as a true apostle, Paul insists that when the Lord had
finished appearing to all the others, he appeared also to me. It is as if he is
emphasising, 'Wasn't that magnificently odd of God to appear to me of all

people?' Then, immediately, Paul described himself as one who was 'untimely born'.

Paul used a vivid word here. 'Untimely born' (*ektroma*) referred to an abortion or a miscarriage and it was sometimes used as a word of abuse. Records show that it would be hurled contemptuously at someone who was despised. It was not unlike our word 'bastard' that started out in life simply as a descriptive word, but became in the course of time an insult. A modern colloquialism would be 'a waste of space', although that is far too gentle as an insult compared with the strength of this word. When used in the Old Testament (Numbers 12:12; Job 3:16; Ecclesiastes 6:3) it was always of something pitiable. Paul appears to be heading off the accusation of the self-styled 'apostles' in Corinth that he was an odd apostle. After all, he didn't come from Palestine like the others and he didn't follow around with Jesus like the mainstream apostles. In fact Jesus only appeared to Saul of Tarsus when he was no longer appearing to anyone else. Paul was painfully aware of his past as a violent, bad tempered, arrogant destroyer of Christians. So when the Corinthians contemptuously referred to him as an inferior apostle—a waste of apostolic space—Paul did not argue with that: 'You are absolutely right', he conceded, 'I am the least of all the apostles, and I want you to know that I mean it. I am no more worthy to be called an apostle than a stillborn child can properly be called a child, I am the least of the apostles.'

The word 'least' (*elachistos*) in verse 9 is a word that means the smallest in importance. Paul admits to being undeserving of the name apostle: 'I am literally not fit to be called an apostle.' Why did Paul feel like this about himself? This was a genuine expression of the word *tapeinos* that he urged upon the Ephesians when he told them to be, 'completely humble' (4:2 *New International Version*). But Paul had very good reason to think of himself like this because, again in verse 9, he tells us that he once persecuted the church. The word persecuted literally means 'to go after' somebody or to drive them out. The nearest we would have in modern idiom would be to 'go for' somebody. Seven times in his letters he admits that he once aggressively went after the Christian Church.

One example of this is found in Galatians 1:13 where Paul admits that in his former way of life he 'persecuted the church of God violently and tried to destroy it.' What an admission! This man was an enthusiast for persecution. In fact in Acts 26:11 he described his attitude towards the Christians as one of 'raging fury'! However, Saul of Tarsus was not content simply to persecute the Church intensely and passionately; he wanted to wipe out Christianity from the face of the earth. That became his one dedicated aim in life; it was Saul's great all-consuming ambition to go down in history as the man who stopped the Christian message from spreading. Saul of Tarsus would for ever be honoured by Judaism as the man who prevented this terrible scourge of the Nazarene from gaining a foothold in the Empire and therefore in the world. Paul never forgot that that was the man he was. And he could still hear in his mind, the words that echoed from the sky outside the walls of Damascus in that life-changing encounter with Christ, 'Saul, Saul, why are you persecuting me … I am Jesus whom you are persecuting.' In Galatians he adds that the first news of his conversion to Christ that arrived in Jerusalem was, 'He who used to persecute us is now preaching the faith he once tried to destroy' (Galatians 1:23).

It was Saul's great all-consuming ambition to go down in history as the man who stopped the Christian message from spreading

What is sin really?

Whatever sins Paul had committed—and there were many—this is where everything focussed. Saul of Tarsus was a Christ-rejecter. He fought against Christ. If anyone is to experience the grace of God, and if they are to understand what the word grace means, they must begin here. That is how we must see ourselves. We should never begin by focussing upon our particular sins, however terrible they may be. We may have wrecked our life and the lives of others by addictions, or cruelty or greed. But counting up sins is not the place to begin. Evangelistic sermons often make this mistake. Preachers can spend many pulpit hours listing sins, but at the end they will leave a sprinkling of hearers sitting comfortably and smugly thinking, 'Whew! He missed me!' Some will go away feeling confident that everybody else had been well and truly lambasted but they themselves are free from accusation; thankfully there are always others with more sins to their account than me. On the contrary, the great

Preachers can spend

many pulpit hours

listing sins, but at the

end they will leave a

sprinkling of hearers

sitting comfortably

and smugly thinking,

'Whew! He missed

me!'

issue that should confront everyone is that they are Christ-rejecters. And that is more important in our multi-faith society than at any time in the history of Christianity.

On one occasion, when Jesus had trounced the Sadducees on a point regarding the resurrection, the Pharisees weighed in. They were glad to see their opponents put down and they came up with a particular question that lay within their field of expertise. It was to do with the law of God, and that was decidedly their territory; no one knew more about the law than the Pharisees did. 'Teacher', they queried, 'Which is the great commandment?' (Matthew 22:34–46). The idea was to force our Lord to be selective with the Decalogue—the Ten Commandments; if he chose one above the others, they could accuse him of undermining the rest. But our Lord, always a step ahead of his opponents, bypassed Exodus 20 and went instead to Deuteronomy 6:5, 'You shall love the Lord your God with all your heart and with all your soul and with all your might.' This, concluded our Lord, is the first and great

commandment. In breaking that command—and all honest people must admit that they have—we have broken the greatest commandment and therefore we have committed the greatest sin. But more than this, at the same time, our Lord immediately went on to reveal himself as the Son of God. It was his insistent claim that to receive him was to receive God, and to reject him was to reject God. The record in Luke 10:16 makes this clear: 'The one who rejects me rejects him who sent me' (see also Matthew 10:40; John 12:44–45; 13:20; 15:21). As far as Christ was concerned, no one can love God and please him unless they accept the Son of God. To be a Christ-rejecter is to place ourselves outside the Kingdom of God, whether Jew or non Jew.

Precisely here is the great weakness of simply preaching against sins. Had Saul of Tarsus been among that group of Pharisees recorded in Matthew 22, he could well have been their spokesman because he was confident that his conscience was clear so far as the law of God was concerned. In fact years later when on trial before King Agrippa, Paul admitted that he had been brought up 'according to the strictest party of our religion' (Acts 26:5); and to the church at Philippi he goes so far as to claim that as for legalistic righteousness, he was 'blameless' (Philippians 3:6). His conscience was clear as he pounded down that dusty road to Damascus to throw Christians into prison and stamp out this new heresy. Saul had sin sussed. It was not his problem. That belonged to the Gentiles. No amount of preaching against sins would ever have convicted Saul of Tarsus; what finally convinced him were the words from heaven: 'I am Jesus, whom you are persecuting.' What Saul had to learn was that he was a Christ-rejecter, and that this was his most serious sin. If he did not love Christ, then he did not love God—however much he thought to the contrary. His heavy religion, his knowledge of the Old Testament law, his zeal as an enthusiastic supporter of Judaism: they all counted for nothing if he was a Christ-rejecter.

In our modern multi-faith society, it is politically correct to accept that there is truth in all religions. In fact there is. The truth revealed in world faiths is that the human race will always search after God. What is not true is that all roads lead to God and that the doors of heaven are wide open for all, irrespective of our philosophy of life; it is simply not true that religion or no religion makes no difference to a God of love. Pluralism demands a tolerant recognition that there are many roads to finding favour with God. Against such a background, there is little value preaching against sins.

After all, whatever a man's religion may be, he must have some answer to the problem of sin, whether it is listening to a holy guru, washing in a holy river, venerating a holy tooth, pilgrimaging to a holy shrine, engaging in a holy war or simply latching on to the right New Age 'channel'. To preach against sin may only drive him—with even greater zeal than before—to his chosen response to the problem. Every religion has its own answers to failure and sin. False answers they may be—but answers nevertheless.

What Saul of Tarsus needed to know was that for all his conceited self-righteousness and his religious zeal, he was rejecting God's *only* remedy to mankind's real problem. A sinner he most certainly was, but not because he committed this or that sin. Saul's greatest sin was that he rejected Jesus Christ and in doing so he rejected the very God whom he ignorantly thought he served. That is what Saul learnt on the highway outside Damascus.

In chapter one we introduced the life of John Newton. He was almost everything Saul was not. His formal education ended before he reached his teens and his future seemed destined for the short, inconspicuous average of a eighteenth century sailor—a bawdy, blasphemous and lecherous sot. Press-ganged onto a man-of-war at the age of nineteen, he refined his education with a philosophy to match his lusts and after fifteen months exchanged his Majesty's Navy for the slave trade in Sierra Leone. Within a short while he was a slave himself and his condition was little removed from that of an animal. By a remarkable turn of events Newton, shivering amidst the debris of a sinking ship and a tattered conscience, came to faith in Christ.

What was the difference between Saul of Tarsus and John of Wapping? One was a respectable, well educated and pious Jew convinced that he was serving God and keeping the law of God as best he could. The other was a blaspheming, drunken, debauched sailor determined to destroy belief in God. The two men could hardly be more different. But that is a completely false assessment of the two men. The only significant difference between Saul of Tarsus and John of Wapping was seventeen hundred years! Both of them were Christ-rejecters, ignorantly pitting themselves against the Lord himself. They were ignorant not because they did not know what they were doing, but because they did not understand the implications of what they were doing.

Before we can become a Christian, whoever we are and whatever our background, we must admit that we are Christ-rejecters. We may not have seen it like this, but unless we do see it in this way, we will never understand the meaning of the word grace. The road to becoming a Christian begins with an admission that our great sin is that we have rejected God by rejecting Jesus Christ. Never mind the catalogue of sins that fill up our life—however few or many, big or small we may consider them to be—the real issue is that we are rejecting God by rejecting Christ. Unless Christ is of first importance in our life, then we are rejecting him. If we do not accept this as our true condition then we cannot expect to share in his kingdom. 'I am Jesus', said the Lord to Saul of Tarsus, 'whom you are persecuting'. And Saul at last saw the reality of his situation. In a violent Atlantic storm in March 1748, so did John Newton.

What was it that changed Saul of Tarsus and John of Wapping? In 1 Corinthians 15:10 Paul writes, 'By the grace of God I am what I am, and his grace towards me was not in vain'; and in Galatians 1:15, when he had been underlining his once determined efforts to exterminate the Christian Church, he wrote, 'God set me apart before I was born and called me by his grace.' Even if the full horror of what Saul was doing had been slowly dawning upon him, there was no hope for him until he realised that he had made Christ his enemy. John of Wapping came to the same conclusion: 'I not only sinned with a high hand myself, but made it my study to tempt and seduce others upon every occasion.' Newton was an evangelist for unbelief, and years afterwards described himself as a common sailor whose 'Heart was hard, language profane, and conduct most profligate and licentious.' But above all, he realised that he had 'long laboured to destroy' the 'rich mercy of our Lord and Saviour Jesus Christ'. His greatest sin was to reject the very Saviour who had come to save him.

Many will rebel against this conclusion that we are all Christ-rejecters. It may not fit well with those who have been brought up in an evangelical Christian home or a strongly upright and religious environment. Perhaps we have always believed in Jesus and have always been sincere about God and Christian things. We may argue, 'I am not so bad. I am not like Saul of Tarsus or John of Wapping.' Perhaps not. We may not have sunk to the moral depths of John or risen to the religious heights of Saul, but we must never forget that the devil has his activists and his pacifists, his believers and his unbelievers, his successes and his failures. Grace is only experienced when we recognise that whatever else we thought we were, we have been Christ-rejecters—even when, as a child, we refused to allow Jesus to have first place in our life. Can we recall the time when we were not on side with Christ? Then whose side were we on?

Justifying grace

Paul uses the word grace around one hundred times in his fourteen letters. As we saw in an earlier chapter, grace was a common word in the first century, and we have on record a number of letters that include it. Here is one in which a pagan writes to a friend and says, 'If you are well it would be as I wish and much *gratitude* to the gods.' The word is *grace*, 'much grace (thanksgiving) to the gods'. In Romans 6:17 Paul turns the word into Christian use and writes, '*thanks* be to God'. But more especially, Paul invested it with a brand new meaning and made it one of the most important words in the New Testament. We read for example of 'the God of grace', and 'the grace of our Lord Jesus Christ', and 'the gospel of grace'. As we have seen, Paul uses it as a greeting in virtually all of his letters; it is here in 1 Corinthians 1:3, 'grace and peace'. When the word is used of God it refers to his kindness—his favour or goodwill—to those who are Christ-rejecters. However, grace is never simply a divine benevolence or goodwill; it is not condescending pity, kind thoughts or compassionate feeling. It is God's kindness or goodwill in action. Paul writes 'By the grace of God, I am what I am. And his grace toward me was not in vain.' Grace is always God in action.

So, precisely what is grace in action?

How many good deeds would be required to wipe away the guilt of Saul of Tarsus by his blasphemy against God, the murder of Stephen, the imprisonment of Christians and the destruction of churches? Or, how many good deeds, would be required to cancel the crude, bawdy and blasphemous songs that John of Wapping taught to sailors, his indoctrination of young men into his own unbelieving way of life and his cruel trade on the coast of Africa selling husbands and wives, parents and children continents apart? And how many good deeds are needed to blot out our sin of rejecting Christ? How much penitence is required for total absolution? How much do we have to pay to wipe the slate clean? How many great acts to cancel all the bad? The answer is—just one! But it is not ours, because we cannot pay. The one act of righteousness that can cancel our sin is that of Christ on the cross. Paul made this plain when he wrote: 'One act of righteousness leads to justification and life for all men' (Romans 5:18). But what is this 'justification'?

Whatever it is, justification has formed the bedrock of Protestant Christianity. The evangelist George Whitefield, wrote in his journal in 1736: 'It is the good old doctrine of the Church of England. It is what the holy martyrs in Queen Mary's time sealed with their blood, and which I pray God, if need be, that I and my brethren may seal with ours.' One hundred and fifty years later the evangelical Lord Shaftsbury wrote in a similar way when he described justification as: 'That grand doctrine, the very life of the Bible and the keystone of the Reformation.'

How many good deeds are needed to blot out our sin of rejecting Christ? ... The answer is—just one!

Each of the great doctrinal statements of the Reformation made a clear assertion on this subject of justification: the Augsburg Confession in Germany (1530), the Second Helvetic Confession in Switzerland (1566), the French Confession of Faith (1559), the Thirty Nine Articles of the Church of England (1571), The Westminster Confession of Faith of the Presbyterians (1649), the Savoy Declaration of the Independents (1658), and the Baptist Confession (1689). But these confessions were not inventing a new theology; it was clearly the teaching of the first century church led by the apostles, and it had never been lost among many of the great church leaders of later centuries.

However, the leaders of the Reformation in the sixteenth century across Europe, made clear their opposition to the medieval church that viewed salvation as a result of our good works of prayer, penance, charity, the purchase of indulgences, and the ceremonies and sacrifices of the church by which righteousness was infused into the penitent sinner; this righteousness might even be the surplus works of past saints into whose merit we can dip. In a similar way, it was taught that we could shorten the stay of our friends and relatives in purgatory by our own good works done on their behalf. All this had been stated plainly by church councils for centuries, and no amount of carefully crafted words, either then or now, could bring together the two opposites of justification by faith or justification by works.

But what did Paul mean when he wrote that Christ was 'delivered up for our trespasses and raised for our justification' (Romans 4:25)? Very few would deny that justification has to do with the death and resurrection of Christ and, since the time of the Reformation at least, there has been general agreement among evangelical Christians that justification refers to the declaration by God that, by the sin-bearing death and life-giving resurrection of Christ, the sinner is no longer guilty in God's sight. The great issue at the time of the Reformation in the sixteenth century was the claim by the Reformers that Christ took all our guilt, sin and punishment upon himself at the cross. The result was described in the language of the law court: the guilt of the sinner was passed to the account of Christ, and the Father counted his Son as the guilty one instead. In exchange, the righteousness of Christ was passed to the account of the sinner and thus the just anger of God against sin was satisfied. The word to describe this satisfying of the righteous judgement of God is 'propitiation'—which is found in 1 John 2:2.

The German Reformer in the sixteenth century, Martin Luther, called this, 'the wonderful exchange'. Justification was seen as a legal term in which the guilty sinner is declared 'not guilty' by God on the basis of Christ's death in place of the sinner—a substitute. This glorious offer of salvation, as the Reformers insisted, is to be received by faith alone and not by the services or ceremonies of the church. In the autumn of 1528 William Tyndale, who had given us the first printed New Testament in English two years earlier, described this great truth of justification in a powerfully poetic way. He was writing in *The Obedience of the Christian Man*—a book that was intended to persuade King Henry VIII that true Christians were loyal servants of the King, but which took the opportunity of telling the King what the gospel was really about. He described the death of Christ like this: 'God sent him into the world to bless us, and to offer himself for us a sacrifice of a sweet savour, to kill the stench of our sins, that God henceforth should smell them no more, nor think on them any more!' Jim Packer, a modern-day theologian, expressed it more plainly when he wrote, 'Jesus endured and exhausted the divine judgement for which we were otherwise inescapably destined.' In other words, justification has always been understood as having to do with the judgement of God against sin, the suffering and death of Christ and, by his resurrection, the complete acquittal of the sinner in the sight of God.

But that is all changing!

A new view today, represented by theologians Tom Wright and James Dunn, is that the Protestant Reformers got it wrong. As Wright understands it, in the first century the Jews had a narrow view that grace was confined to Israel. For the Jew, justification meant two things: membership of the covenant community of Israel—which was open only to Jews—and ultimate victory of Israel over her enemies. The key to understand justification, we are told, is chiefly about membership of the covenant community. In his letters, therefore, Paul's doctrine of justification was not primarily about a divine declaration of the 'not guilty' verdict through the sin bearing death of Christ, but about the fact that membership of the covenant community of God was now open to all.

Tom Wright and his fellow travellers believe that when Jesus died on the cross, he died as the representative of the whole Jewish nation, and the curse that he bore was the curse upon the Jewish nation for failing to be the light of the world. His resurrection therefore becomes the restoration after the curse of the exile. Wright claims that when Paul wrote in Galatians 3:13 that, 'Christ redeemed us from the curse of the law by becoming a curse for us', the 'us' is not non-Jews, but only the Jewish nation. Similarly the struggle against sin described by Paul in Romans 7:13–25 is not a personal experience but the struggle of Israel with the law. Thus Paul's letters to Rome and Galatia are not primarily about individual salvation, but about who are the people of God. Galatians was written to correct an over-zealous love of Judaism, and Romans was written to correct an over-zealous anti Judaism. Rather than the term 'justified by faith' Wright prefers to see our justification—membership of the community of God—as the result of our belief that by his death and resurrection Christ fulfilled all that Israel failed to be; we are therefore 'justified by belief'.

This reshapes the doctrine of justification by faith as evangelicals have always understood it. Sin as Christ-rejecting rebellion against God, is hardly the issue it seems; and such terms as Christ dying as our legal substitute, God crediting our sin to Christ's account, or sinners acquitted of their guilt, do not form a significant part of the vocabulary of people who hold this view. Paul's statement that, 'a person is not justified by works of the law but through faith in Jesus Christ' (Galatians 2:16) apparently now means no more than that by the works of the law no one will be reckoned among God's people. This may be a pleasant thought, but it is hardly robust—and it meant a great deal more than this for the converted university graduate from Tarsus. We must let Paul himself shape our thinking.

Justification by Faith according to Paul

The first three chapters of Paul's letter to the Christians at Rome is clearly a diagnosis of the personal guilt of everyone. To argue that this is only the guilt of Israel would be suspect to say the least in the light of his clear references to 'all ungodliness and unrighteousness of men' (1:18), to those who sin 'without the law' (2:12) and to the fact that 'none is righteous, no, not one ... for all have sinned and fall short of the glory of God' (3:10, 23). His diagnosis is severe and universal, and his conclusion is that 'by the works of the law no human being will be justified in his (God's) sight' (3:20). There is nothing that we can do to save ourselves. This opens the way for Paul to launch into his great exposition of justification by faith alone. We will make it simple.

In order to open up his teaching of sin put to Christ's account and righteousness put to our account, Paul introduces a familiar concept: 'To the one who works, his wages are not counted as a gift but as his due' (Romans 4:4). But Paul is about to dress up a very common word with a very special Christian meaning. The word for 'counted' is the Greek verb logizomai. It was a common word in finance and meant simply to reckon up or calculate. Whenever you do your own personal accounting that is what you are doing. You are reckoning up your money. In the first century the word was also used of passing money to someone's account—a direct debit—and the noun from this word was used for a finance office. But it was always a word that carried with it the idea of very careful reckoning. Unlike our phrase, 'I reckon' which has come to mean only 'I guess'.

Paul begins by employing the word in a normal, commonly used way. You count up the hours that a man works, you multiply it by the hourly rate and then you pay his wages. It is not a gift, he earned it; he deserved it and you pay it. It is all very simple. But, Paul continues, there is a divine reckoning as well; except that the divine reckoning is wholly different. Here are two men called Saul and John, and they have stacked up a great debt—whether ignorantly or knowingly makes no difference. What they need is someone to pass to their account sufficient funds to set them in the clear. The problem is that this debt is not money but wickedness—Christ-rejecting wickedness. Finance companies may be good at creating that, but they do not know how to deal with it. It is one debt that they can never cancel. Both Saul and John were Christ-rejecters and because of that there is a massive debit on their account and no amount of religious duty or change of direction could pay it off. At the very best, religious duty might be able to run up a little less debt in future. But the massive past debt, still stays—and that is true of us all. We can turn over a religious new leaf and become more socially acceptable, and by so doing we may think that we can reduce future debt. But if sin is ultimately defined as rejecting Christ, then we have done nothing to reduce that. It is something like this with Third World debt. If a government gets its political and economic house in order, it may slowly reduce the increase of its debt in the future. But what it cannot do is cancel the massive debt of the past. So what is the solution?

The solution is grace—justifying grace—and this is what God does for those who place their trust in Jesus Christ and do not even try to earn their salvation: God reckons righteousness to their account, or, as Paul expresses it: 'To the one who does not work but trusts him who justifies the ungodly, his faith is counted as righteousness' (Romans 4:5). However, there can be no such thing as faith until there is something for faith to rely upon. Faith has to be placed somewhere. In the same way there is no such thing as righteousness apart from a righteous life; righteousness is not some spiritual glue or heavenly star dust that is attached to us after religious rituals or sacred services. Righteousness can only be found in a righteous life. So, where can I find such a righteous life that can be credited to me in place of my unrighteous Christ-rejecting life? The answer is that it can only be the righteousness of Jesus Christ. It is his righteousness that is passed to my account.

When we talk of a man 'trying to justify himself' we mean that he is endeavouring to put himself in the clear, to show that he is not guilty, or at the very least to explain away his guilt. We can never do that in the sight of God because the simple fact is that we *are* guilty of rejecting his Son. But God can justify us by counting us as clean as Christ himself; he not only sets us free from the punishment our blame deserves, but counts us as no longer guilty of blame at all. On a number of occasions Paul wrote of the Christian as one who will be presented guiltless or blameless before God at the end of time (1 Corinthians 1:8 and Ephesians 1:4 for example).

God can justify us by counting us as clean as Christ himself; he ... counts us as no longer guilty of blame at all

But there is always a cost involved if one account is to be credited with the value of another, and the language of the Bible to describe this is vividly offensive: '(God) made him to be sin who knew no sin, so that in him we might become the righteousness of God' (2 Corinthians 5:21). What Paul wrote was quite literally: 'for us he was made sin'. Can it be possible that the eternal and sinless Son of God actually became our sin? The sheer offence of this leads some to conclude that it means only that he became a 'sin offering' for us. But that is not what Paul says. Certainly all the Old Testament sacrifices were sin offerings pointing forward to Christ. The bulls and goats, lambs and pigeons that died in the place of those who offered the sacrifice, could never in reality take away sin because a goat could never take the moral guilt of a human being (Hebrews 10:4). That terrible task was left to Christ alone. The very point Paul is making in the phrase 'for us he was made sin' is that his death was utterly different. He did what all the thousands of animal sacrifices together could not do. Christ became all that we are, so that we could become what he was. The one who was perfectly sinless was counted as a Christ-rejecting rebel so that we might be counted as sinless as he was! The sheer offence of this causes many to back off.

If Paul was emphasising the guilt of our sin put to Christ's account, Peter followed the same theology when he pointed to the punishment of our sin that Christ bore: 'Christ also suffered once for sins, the righteous for the unrighteous, that he might bring us to God' (1 Peter 3:18); here the little preposition *for* means literally: 'on behalf of', or 'for the sake of'. He took not only our guilt, but our punishment. Martin Luther, expressed this in a way as shocking as Paul, and it has caused no little debate among Bible teachers ever since. He was explaining the phrase in Galatians 3:13, 'Christ redeemed us from the curse of the law by becoming a curse for us— for it is written "Cursed is everyone who is hanged on a tree."' Luther explained that Christ was innocent as concerning his own person and therefore had no need to die under the curse of the law of God. But on the cross, in order that he might be a true sacrifice for the sins of the whole world: 'He is not now an innocent person and without sins, is not now the Son of God born of the Virgin Mary; but a sinner who has carried the sin of Paul, who was a blasphemer, an oppressor and a persecutor; of Peter, who denied Christ; of David, who was an adulterer, a murderer and caused the Gentiles to blaspheme the name of the Lord: and, briefly, who has and bears all the sins of all men in his body, that he might make satisfaction for them with his own blood.'

The one who was perfectly sinless was counted as a Christ-rejecting rebel so that we might be counted as sinless as he was!

This was strong stuff! And Luther knew it. He was not claiming that Christ ever ceased to be the Son of God but that he was counted in the sight of God the Father as a blasphemer, adulterer, murderer and all the other sins committed by men—as if they were his own! Luther asks whether it is absurd and slanderous to say that the Son of God became a cursed sinner and concludes, 'Then deny also that he suffered, was crucified and died.' For it is equally absurd and slanderous to claim that the sinless Son of God could become a curse for us and suffer the pains of sin and death; but that is exactly what Paul claims in Galatians 3:13.

Luther was right. This is justifying grace in action. It is a wholly inadequate view of the cross to see Christ only as a representative of rebellious Israel, fulfilling the role that Israel so miserably failed to discharge. But it is equally not sufficient to say only that Christ was punished as our substitute, in our place; he suffered far more than that. Christ did not merely bear our punishment and die under the anger of God against sin; he took our guilt as his own by taking our sin as his own. This is what is meant in those dreadful words of Paul: 'For our sake God made him *to be sin* who knew no sin, so that in him we might become the righteousness of God.' And when Peter writes 'He himself *bore our sins* in his body on the tree' (1 Peter 2:24), this is what he means. For Christ on Calvary, sin was not merely a burden to be born—it was a defilement to be felt.

> *For Christ on Calvary, sin was not merely a burden to be born—it was a defilement to be felt*

This is God giving himself for us, to do what we could never do—to pay the penalty of Christ-rejecting sin. But Paul made the death of Christ no lighter when he wrote, 'Christ has redeemed us from the curse of the law by becoming a curse for us' (Galatians 3:13). If Christ becoming sin is offensive, this claim by Paul that Christ was cursed on Calvary is more so! It is no casual remark of the apostle; it is the development of a carefully considered theme. In Galatians 3:10 he has claimed that all who fail to keep the law of God are under a justifiable curse of God and this means that all, without a single exception, stand under the judgement of God. The word 'curse' is far more than an expression of divine annoyance—it is a pronouncement of divine judgement. It is the just sentence by a holy God against all who reject his Son and disobey his law. The fearful penalty of *that* was paid by Christ on Calvary when he suffered the anger of his Father's judgement against sin. His agonized cry from the cross: 'My God, my God, why have you forsaken me?' expressed the terrifying depth to which the sinless Saviour felt the wrath of a holy God. To say that he went through hell on the cross has little reference to the physical suffering—many have suffered more lingering and excruciating physical pain than his—but it horribly describes what it meant for the Holy One to smart under the judgement of his Father for sin that belonged to us.

Justification is even more than the acquittal of the guilty: it is a declaration that those known to be guilty are perfectly righteous

We call justification 'justifying *grace*' because the direction of everything about the subject of justification is from God to us. Our only contribution to justifying grace is to be a Christ-rejecting sinner—beyond that, everything belongs to God. Justification is not a change in us—that is regeneration or new birth—rather, it is a change in how God sees us. This is why Paul can introduce the word 'glorified' after the word justified in Romans 8:30. Justified sinners are as fit for heaven as they ever will be.

Justification is more than a pardon

Although we say that justification adopts the language of the law courts, in a very real sense it is far from the language of any human law court. Legal language can cope with the judgement of the guilty and the acquittal of the innocent; but the acquittal of those known to be guilty violates all laws of justice. Yet justification is even more than the acquittal of the guilty: it is a declaration that those known to be guilty are perfectly righteous—and this by the supreme Judge who is always wise, fair and just. At this crucial point virtually all our law court comparisons fail us.

When we simply speak of Christ paying for our crime, we can understand that since it often happens that someone will pay the fine for another. Similarly, Christ as our substitute has some ring of familiarity about it: there have been heroic stories of a man owning up to the guilt of another and paying for it with his life. But Christ did more than any of this. He did not simply pay for our sins or even own up on our behalf—he became all that we are so that by a wonderful exchange we become all that he is.

Justification means not only that we are pardoned, but that in the sight of God it is as if the guilt was never ours!

Luther once expressed it like this: 'Lord Jesus, you are my righteousness, just as I am your sin. You have taken upon yourself what is mine and have given to me what is yours. You have taken upon yourself what you were not and have given to me what I was not.' This is precisely what Paul meant when he declared to the Christians at Corinth that God made Christ 'to be sin, who knew no sin, so that in him we might become the righteousness of God' in order that he could become, 'our wisdom and our righteousness and sanctification and redemption' (2 Corinthians 5:21 and 1 Corinthians 1:30). We have none of this apart from what we have in Christ. And this justification is final, for ever and complete. It can never be repeated any more than it can ever be undone. This is the reason for the strong note of total assurance that runs throughout the New Testament. Justification means not only that we are pardoned, but that in the sight of God it is as if the guilt was never ours!

If we ask, 'Why did our acquittal have to come this way? Why did it have to be so severe? Why was the punishment on Christ so ugly in every respect?' then we reveal how little we understand the absolute holiness of God and the utter sinfulness of sin. One day, when we stand before that God, we will understand how just the sentence was, how profound the sufferings of Christ were, and how full and complete is the salvation that is found in him.

In a beautiful conclusion to the benefits of justifying grace, Paul took up Psalm 32 and quoted from the first two verses: 'Blessed are those whose lawless deeds are forgiven, and whose sins are covered; blessed is the man against whom the Lord will not count his sin' (Romans 4:7–8). The theologians have a 'phrase for this, they call it: 'imputed righteousness' which is another way of saying, 'his righteousness is put to my account and counted as if it is mine'. If we prefer, instead of 'imputed righteousness' we can call it 'reckoned righteousness'. It is when the righteousness of Jesus Christ is credited or reckoned to our account. The debt is wiped out. To be certain of that is the first conscious experience of grace. It is on this ground that God can declare the repentant sinner 'Not guilty'. And that is a verdict that once given, will never be recalled. It will never be recalled simply because 'the righteousness of God' (2 Corinthians 5:21) now belongs to us.

Justification is as much the result of the resurrection of Christ as it is the result of his death

In God's accounting office and on the spreadsheets of the lives of Saul of Tarsus and John of Wapping, they were Christ-rejecters. That was the big issue. Neither of those two men ever forgot it. There may be a whole catalogue of things that they had done in the past, of which they were for ever afterwards ashamed, but the one thing that mattered most is that they lived as if God did not matter and as if Christ had not died for them. They lived without him and were content with this. But when Christ's righteousness was reckoned to their account, their debit column was covered and God promised never to reckon their sins against them again. An apostle Paul may be, a church planter and receiver of revelation from heaven, but Paul considered himself less than the least and not worthy to be called an apostle. That is grace—undeserved, justifying grace.

The resurrection and justifying grace

This chapter began with 1 Corinthians 15 deliberately because there is one other aspect of justifying grace that must never be forgotten. Justification is as much the result of the resurrection of Christ as it is the result of his death. To be true to Scripture, we should never speak of the justifying grace of God as if Calvary said it all. In a vital statement on this, Paul claimed, 'Jesus our Lord ... was delivered up for our trespasses and raised for our justification' (Romans 4:25). Now if Paul means what he says, our justification cannot be complete without the triumph of the resurrection; and for this reason Paul assures the Corinthians that, 'If Christ has not been raised, then our preaching is in vain and your faith is in vain ... you are still in your sins' (1 Corinthians 15:14, 17). Why does he say this? Because the resurrection is God's final 'Amen' to all that his Son accomplished and it is the guarantee of new life in Christ for all who are justified. He stands before the Father as a perpetual reminder that for those who are 'in Christ' there can never again be sin reckoned to their account—they are as innocent as if they had never committed one sin. That is a staggeringly daring claim and one that would be dangerously blasphemous—if it were not gloriously true.

In March 1748 John Newton was on his way back to England when he was conquered by Christ. The violent storm that smashed into the *Greyhound* and almost sent it to the bottom drove terror into the heart of this blasphemous sailor. Stumbling across the shattered deck Newton found himself praying his first prayer since childhood, 'If this will not do, the Lord have mercy on us'. But what had he to do with mercy? Or what right had he to expect a reply from God? For a day and a night he was tormented by his own profane songs and immoral life, but when he was at an end of himself and his own resources, and when the Bible verses stored in his mind as a child had utterly convinced him of his Christ-rejecting sin, he found peace with God through Christ. 10 March 1748 was the day when: 'The Lord sent from on high and delivered me out of deep waters.' Four weeks later the pathetic and starving crew eased their battered ship into the still waters of Lough Swilly. Later he wrote to his darling Mary, 'My first, half-formed prayers were answered. He whom the winds and seas obey, in a manner little less than miraculous, brought me in safety to Ireland.'

But God had done far more than that. He had led John of Wapping through the first lesson of undeserved grace, a lesson that Saul of Tarsus had learned seventeen hundred years earlier, and like Saul, John would live in the school of justifying grace throughout a valuable and fruitful life. Neither man would ever doubt that, 'By grace you have been saved through faith. And this is not your own doing; it is the gift of God, not a result of works, so that no one may boast' (Ephesians 2:8–9).

Justification by faith alone in Christ alone, was the front line of the Reformation battle, and we must not allow what the Reformers fought and died for to be diluted by a desire for ecumenical peace or theological innovation. A little after the time of Martin Luther, the Swiss reformer John Calvin wrote of this doctrine of justification by faith: 'Wherever the knowledge of it is taken away, the glory of Christ is extinguished, religion abolished, the church destroyed and the hope of salvation utterly overthrown.' Calvin was right.

JESUS, YOUR BLOOD AND RIGHTEOUSNESS
my beauty are, my glorious dress;
mid burning worlds, in these arrayed,
with joy I shall lift up my head.

2 Bold shall I stand on your great day
and none condemn me, try who may;
fully absolved by you I am
from sin and fear, from guilt and shame.

3 When from the dust of death I rise
to claim my home beyond the skies,
then this shall be my only plea:
Jesus has lived, has died for me.

4 O give to all your servants, Lord,
to speak with power your gracious word,
that all who now believe it true
may find eternal life in you.

5 O God of power, O God of love,
let the whole world your mercy prove;
now let your word in all prevail;
Lord, take the spoils of death and hell!

6 O let the dead now hear your voice;
let those once lost in sin rejoice!
Their beauty this, their glorious dress,
Jesus, your blood and righteousness.

NICOLAUS L VON ZINZENDORF 1700–60
Trans. JOHN WESLEY 1703–91
Praise! 778 © in this version Praise Trust

Incarnate grace

'You know the grace of our Lord Jesus Christ, that though he was rich, yet for your sake he became poor'
2 Corinthians 8:9

The apostle Paul was a brilliant communicator, and he found some smart ways of letting the churches know exactly what he expected of them. Sometimes he did this by posing a leading question. For example, the church at Galatia had been listening to those who were adding to the gospel; some were teaching that non-Jews could become Christians by faith in the sacrifice of Jesus Christ—plus. The plus factor was the essential observance of Jewish ceremonials; this changed the whole gospel into one of faith and merit instead of faith alone. In dealing with these 'Judaeisers', Paul asked them one leading question: 'Did you receive the Spirit by law or by faith?' (Galatians 3:2). Similarly, the church at Colossae was listening to those who tried to impose on them a detailed legalism of do's and don'ts. Once again Paul had a question for them: if they themselves had died in Christ to these elementary things: 'Why do you submit to regulations like: "Do not handle, Do not taste. Do not touch"?' (Colossians 2:20–21). Here at Corinth, the church was divided over its favourite leaders and best preachers; some preferred Paul, others Apollos, and others Peter. Paul had a simple question for them also: 'Was Paul crucified for you? Or were you baptised in the name of Paul?' (1 Corinthians 1:13).

However sometimes, instead of a question to silence the opposition, Paul used a comparison. He does precisely that here in 2 Corinthians 8. Paul was collecting famine relief for the suffering Christians in Judea, and he knew that the Corinthians could afford to give; in fact they had started well a year earlier but appear to have become a pretty tight-fisted lot more recently, and they had not fulfilled what they had promised. So Paul held up to them the example of the Macedonians who lived close by. In

2 Corinthians 8:2–5, he reminded the Corinthians how their neighbours had given out of their poverty as much as they could, and then a bit more. In fact they had pleaded for the privilege of giving and ended up by giving more than Paul had expected. What is more they gave themselves to the Lord also.

By now we can hear the Corinthians grumbling: 'It's Macedonians this and Macedonians that. Give us a break Paul.' So Paul switched attack and in v 8 he told them: 'I'm not commanding you, but I want to test the sincerity of your love by comparing it with the earnestness of others' (*New International Version*)—Oh no, here come the Macedonians again! But with the masterstroke of surprise Paul continued: 'For you know the grace of our Lord Jesus Christ, that though he was rich, yet for your sake he became poor.' What was he doing here? He was appealing to the Corinthians' grace for giving on the ground of the grace of the incarnation.

That word 'rich', can refer either to earthly wealth or spiritual wealth. Paul loved to link the word 'rich' with the word 'glory'—a word that refers to the full character of something or someone. Elsewhere he writes of 'the riches of his glory' (Romans 9:23), and 'the riches of his glorious inheritance' (Ephesians 1:18), and 'according to his riches in glory' (Philippians 4:19). The coming of Christ into this world at the incarnation—a word that means simply 'in the flesh'—is the greatest exhibition of God's grace. And this in turn is the most powerful incentive for Christian humility in the grace of giving.

Jesus before Bethlehem

To appreciate what Christ became we must understand what he was. Millions are born in dire poverty and millions more live their short lives owning nothing more than a few ragged clothes. Millions have died unjust and horrible deaths with their bodies thrown into common graves at best, without the dignity of being laid in the tomb of a rich man. So, how was the poverty of Christ remarkable? The answer to this is by an understanding of who and what he was. Paul describes the magnificence of Christ's power and authority before the incarnation by the simple claim: 'By him all things were created, in heaven and on earth, visible and invisible … all things were created through him and for him' (Colossians 1:16).

In 330 BC, at the age of 25, Alexander the Great of Macedonia crushed Darius the Great, King of Persia, and in doing so he made himself master of one million square miles and became many thousand times richer than anyone else on earth. Alexander was master of the Greeks, Pharaoh of Egypt and King of Asia. He set out to discover the limits of the world and to conquer it. Seven years later he was dead—Alexander had lost everything and he left little for history except a city bearing his name and the legends of his life.

By contrast, our King spoke a powerful word of command and the earth and heavens were created. Stars and planets spun in space, birds flew in the air, and animals walked on the earth; the wealth in every mine and the angelic hosts of heaven are all his. And yet he laid his glory by and he who was rich, for our sake became poor. That is the grace of incarnation. This is no little prince, president or prime minister tampering with justice and exploiting his subjects. Three B52 bombers can drop their payload and produce a crater one mile wide and fifty feet deep—I suppose that's power! At 08.15 on 6 August 1945 a single atomic bomb dropped over Hiroshima in Japan obliterated more than half of the city's seven square miles and annihilated over thirty thousand men, women and children in seconds—that is even more powerful! Throughout the history of the human race the largest capital expenditure of nations has been on the effort to produce the most powerful tools to obliterate their neighbours; as a result one hundred million people were killed in war throughout the twentieth century alone. Ultimate human power is always used for maximum human hurt. But our king of unlimited power used his supremacy for ultimate good. For our sake he made himself poor so that through his poverty we might become rich.

Ultimate human power is always used for maximum human hurt. But our king of unlimited power used his supremacy for ultimate good

When Daniel, 600 years before Christ, desperately needed to be reassured that there was a power more glorious and more powerful than the fierce armies of Nebuchadnezzar of Babylon, God gave him a glimpse of Christ in heaven: 'Behold … there came one like a son of man, and he came to the Ancient of Days and was presented before him. And to him was given dominion and glory and a kingdom, that all peoples, nations and languages should serve him; his dominion is an everlasting dominion, which shall not pass away, and his kingdom one that shall not be destroyed' (Daniel 7:13–14). Every empire known to man comes and goes: the ancient empires of Egypt, Assyria, Babylon, Persia, Macedonia, Rome, and the modern empires of Britain and Russia all rose to power by the might of their armies and then fell into virtual obscurity. The empire of Christ is everlasting, but he deliberately came into obscurity.

Instead of the sweet incense of heaven, he exchanged it for the sweat and stench of the place of execution

When John the apostle needed to be reminded of a power more powerful and a glory more glorious than the legions of Rome and the emperors Titus—who destroyed Jerusalem, and Domitian—who destroyed Christians, God showed him Christ in heaven: 'I looked and I heard around the throne … the voice of many angels numbering myriads of myriads and thousands of thousands, saying with a loud voice: "Worthy is the Lamb who was slain to receive power and wealth and wisdom and might and honour and glory and blessing!"' (Revelation 5:11–12). Few leaders willingly give up their power, they have it taken from them. Yet Christ gladly gave up the glory and splendour of heaven. He would always have been who he was even if he had not come to this earth, but he became what he was not—truly man, so that we might become what we are not—children and friends of God. Instead of heaven crying 'Holy, holy, holy', rough mobs shouted 'Crucify him!'. Instead of the honour and adoration of the angels, crude Roman soldiers beat him and spat on him. Instead of the sweet incense of heaven, he exchanged it for the sweat and stench of the place of execution. But why?

Was he really God—and man?

It is significant that some of the earliest heresies of the church centred not around the authority of the Scriptures, or the work of the Holy Spirit, but upon the person of Jesus Christ. Why was this? Not because the doctrine was not clear, but just because it was clear. The problem was not what to believe about Jesus being God—the Scripture could hardly be clearer on this—but how on earth could we believe it?

If he had been God alone then he could not have come here because we cannot see God and live. If he had been only man, there would have been no particular value in him coming here; many good men have set us an example before and since. But as both God and man he was unique. To avoid this incredible paradox, before the end of the first century the Ebionites claimed that he was only a spirit-filled man—the son of Joseph and Mary. The Docetists believed that Christ came disguised as a man—Jesus was the man who only 'seemed' to be divine. And the Gnostics lost sight of his humanity in a welter of secret knowledge and intellectual enlightenment. Within another one hundred years, Sabellius denied the three persons in one Godhead and taught that Christ was a mere man adopted by God for the occasion—and so Unitarianism was born: God acts in the three modes of Father, Son and Spirit.

No sooner had Constantine—the first Roman Emperor to adopt the Christian faith—painted the chi-rho symbol on the shields of his legionaries, than he found himself embroiled in a bitter debate among the Christians over whether or not Christ was truly God. With Arius heading up one side and Athanasius the other, this new convert from worshipping Isis and Mithras was well out of his depth. At Nicea in AD 325 Constantine called the leaders together, alternately threatened and lectured them on the need for unity, tried to force through a compromise, even offered a few definitions of his own, and at the end of it all invited them to supper in his palace. The apostle Paul would not have recognised it—times were certainly changing! But how to declare simply and plainly that Jesus of Nazareth, the uncreated Creator, was eternally God and, of the same nature and character, co-equal with his Father, seemed beyond the Emperor—and beyond most of the bishops as well!

The mysterious doctrine of the Trinity has always been a significant hallmark of Christian orthodoxy. To maintain the monotheistic faith of one God alone yet expressed in three distinct Persons each fully God, co-equal and in perfect and eternal harmony with one another, has always been too much for some to accept. But then, so has the wonder of the virgin birth, the miracles of Christ's ministry, the effectiveness of his death as our substitute in order to reconcile sinners to God, and the powerful event of the literal, historical resurrection. But the day we can clarify every part of our faith to the satisfaction of a cynical world, we will have nothing and no one left with which to stand in awe—God will have been reduced to the size of our imagination and explanation.

The true deity of Christ may be a mystery—but mystery is not inconsistency

The Scriptures rarely explain Christ's deity, but they frequently state it. In the Old Testament he is referred to as 'the Mighty God' in that undeniably Messianic verse in Isaiah 9:6, where the Hebrew *el el gibor* (literally: God, God the Mighty One) can never be made to refer to anyone other than the almighty, transcendent Creator. In the New Testament John plainly identified the one whom the seraphim worshipped with the cry 'Holy, holy, holy is the LORD of hosts; the whole earth is full of his glory!' as Christ himself—compare Isaiah 6:3, 10 and John 12:40–41. When Paul wrote to the Colossians that in Christ 'the whole fullness of deity dwells bodily' (2:9) he could hardly have expressed himself more plainly. The true deity of Christ may be a mystery—but mystery is not inconsistency. Of course we will find it hard to grasp the idea of two natures perfectly at ease in one person—especially when those two natures are as opposite as deity and humanity—but that makes it neither irreconcilable nor impossible.

But for our interest in incarnate grace the wonder was not so much that

Jesus of Nazareth was God, but that God became Jesus of Nazareth! We can see and hear that he must be God just by reading the account of his life and ministry; no one could do what he did and claim what he claimed unless he was God. But why did God become a man? That is explained only in the miracle of incarnate grace.

Why the incarnation?

When Anselm, the Archbishop of Canterbury in the eleventh century, tackled this question in his work: *Cur Deus Homo*? (Why did God become Man?) he came up—though at length as most theologians do—with two simple answers: first only God could make the way of salvation on behalf of sinners; no one else was either good enough or powerful enough. And second, since the human race was the offender and rebel, only mankind could put right the wrong. Thus, the one who made the way of forgiveness on behalf of sinners had to be both God and man.

The wonder was not so much that Jesus of Nazareth was God, but that God became Jesus of Nazareth!

No doubt this is true. But it could equally be argued that this is our reasoning; if God had chosen another way then that too would have been right. God *might* have come in the person of his Son without taking human nature; he *might* have come in the appearance of a man only—as Cerinthus the leader of Docetism believed in the first century; it *might* have all been a make-believe humanity. And if God had declared that that is what he was prepared to accept in place of the just punishment of rebel sinners, then that would have been enough. If God had decided that an angel was sufficient, then an angel would have been sufficient. But the fact is, God did not choose that way. God was not under an obligation to choose a particular way of salvation; he was not captive to some law beyond his control that demanded the life and death of the innocent on behalf of the guilty. If there is such a law—and there is—it is because God himself decreed it to be such.

A better way of understanding the grace and necessity of the incarnation is that Jesus of Nazareth had to be God to show us what God is like and to reassure us that the salvation he offers has the stamp of God's power and authority upon it. Equally he had to be perfect man to show us just how holy God's standard is—and therefore how far we fall from it—and to reassure us that as the God-Man he can perfectly sympathise and empathise with us in all things. This is a vital part of the phrase 'for your sake', and it is the glory of our God who is prepared to come to this sad world in order to show us, and in a way that perfectly fits our need, just what he is like. The grace of the incarnation is primarily for our sake, not for God's sake.

The grace of the incarnation is primarily for our sake, not for God's sake

All religions are groping after God—and well they might. Nothing is more human than to search for God; that is what makes humanity human. Paul recognised this in Athens when he reminded the great debaters that they were seeking God 'in the hope that they might feel their way towards him and find him' (Acts 17:27). Religion is human, but when religion arrives at its own conclusion it is a dead end. The only future in religion is by revelation, and the only full and final revelation is in Jesus Christ. We can never know God or understand God on our own. We cannot focus on God because his unapproachable holiness would blind us. Snow blindness is caused by the ultraviolet rays of the sun reflecting from the pure whiteness of the snow. In the vast expanse of a white snowscape, there is nothing for the eye to focus on, and nothing to protect the delicate eye from the searing rays of the sun. Just so, we cannot focus on God and his dazzling holiness—but Christ came to show us what the Father is like. There was no other way.

When the apostle described Christ here on earth, he did so like this: 'He is the radiance of the glory of God and the exact imprint of his nature' (Hebrews 1:3). Let me unpack that for a moment. 'The radiance of glory' is not a dazzling reflection, like the rays of the sun bouncing off a mirror or a wet road. *That* was the reflection of the glory of God that shone out from Moses' face when he came from the presence of the Lord (Exodus 34:29–35); his face shone with reflected glory, and therefore it was a fading glory. On the contrary, Christ's life does not *reflect* the glory of God, it *is* the glory of God. The writer goes further and underscores that Christ is: 'the exact imprint of his nature' (*New International Version* has 'exact representation of his being').

Instead of that word 'imprint' Paul could have chosen the word *eichon*, which is used in Matthew 22:20 'Whose *likeness* (portrait) is this?'; the same word is also found in the phrase '(Christ) is the *image* of God' (2 Corinthians 4:4). But he did not choose that word. Alternatively he might have used the word *morphe*, which is found in Philippians 2:6, 'He was in the *form* of God'. But he did not choose that word either. Instead he chose here in Hebrews 1:3 the Greek word *character* which surely needs no explanation. A literal translation of this verse would be: 'He is the radiance of the glory of God and the exact character of the actual reality of God himself.' How better could the apostle have expressed the truth that Christ is none other than in reality God, and that whatever we see, hear and learn about him during his life on earth, we see, hear and learn about God himself. Therefore in Christ, we are watching and hearing the very heart of God:

When we read of his love for little children
His tender dealing with the woman at the well in Samaria
His sympathy for the poor widow whose son had died
His healing of the lepers and the lame
His compassion for the hungry crowds
His tears over Jerusalem and at the grave of Lazarus
His pastoral comfort to Peter before and after his denial
His passionate warning to Judas before the betrayal
His prayer for the soldiers at Golgotha
His promise to the thief who died beside him
His loving care for his mother and disciple as he hung on the cross

This was the heart of the one who created the entire, unfathomable infinity of the universe, and who stood at the centre of the adoration of heaven. But he laid it aside because it was not appropriate that he should be seen like that here. What he had always been was masked by what he had become because that is what we needed to see and that is how we could understand God. He changed his appearance but not his nature.

I have a friend who is a hospital consultant and he motorcycles to work— much to the amusement of his staff. But when he stands at the bedside of his patients he lays aside his leather gear, his heavy boots and his crash helmet. They are not appropriate here. Nor does he wear his theatre mask, gloves and gown when he rides his motorcycle. Similarly his scalpel and forceps are not brought into church with him. He does not cease to be a motorcyclist or surgeon and he is never pretending to be something else. He is always what he is, which is everything that he is, but he wears the appearance of what is most appropriate. So Christ did not cease to be God, but now we see him as man, confined to space and time; a man who knew hunger and thirst, weariness and aloneness. His emotions were stirred, his heart was broken, his spirit was crushed, his body was racked with pain. He became poor so that we could understand what God is like.

Our Lord was equal with his Father, but here on earth he never used that reality for personal advantage

But, and this is most important, Christ never used his character as God to his own advantage. This is a point Paul seems to be making in a long debated claim: 'Though he was in the form of God, he did not count equality with God a thing to be grasped' (Philippians 2:6). That phrase 'a thing to be grasped' is interesting. It translates an uncommon word found nowhere else in the new Testament and not often outside the New Testament either. So Paul must have had a special reason for choosing it. Some commentators take it as a reference to something seized or grasped —like a prize or booty. Surely not! For Christ, equality with God was not a prize for doing well or a booty to be snatched; on the contrary it was his by eternal right. One writer has more recently shown that the reference is to something he had but did not use to his own personal advantage. That may be what Paul has in mind, and at least it fits well with the truth of the incarnation. Our Lord was equal with his Father, but here on earth he never used that reality for personal advantage.

When the crowd picked up stones to throw at him in Jerusalem, we are told simply: 'Jesus hid himself and went out of the temple' (John 8:59). There, surely, was evidence of his divine power. Similarly, just two chapters later, we find the Jews attempting the same thing: 'But he escaped from their hands' (John 10:39). At Nazareth, when they ran him out of town and up to the brow of a hill to throw him over so that his body would be crushed in the fall, Luke records almost absurdly: 'But passing through their midst, he went away' (Luke 4:30). In each case he refused to turn on those who abused him, and he used his silent sovereign power to still his enemies—but only because the appointed time, place and manner of his death had not yet arrived. That is the grace of the incarnation.

And when the time did arrive, he was still in full control. In Gethsemane 'a large crowd with swords and clubs' came to arrest him. What followed would be amusing if it had not been set against the sinister back-drop of the power of the prince of darkness. As Judas betrayed his Master with a treacherous kiss, Jesus stepped forward and quietly opened the interview: 'Who do you want?' A bold chorus came back: 'Jesus of Nazareth'. When he responded: 'I am he', the writer records: 'They drew back and fell to the ground'. That would have made a good front page story, and I can imagine that Peter now felt secure and strong in the thought that, at last, Jesus would assert his authority and end all this speculation about betrayal and death. But instead, he encouraged the soldiers to arrest him! Perhaps he stepped towards them, lifted some to their feet, and then held out his hands as if reminding them of what they must do. A still silence hung over the olive grove as the Son of God repeated his question: 'Who do you want?' This time I suspect the reply was little more than a whimper: 'Jesus of Nazareth'. Is there now a note of scorn in his voice: 'I told you that I am he. So, if you seek me, let these men go' ?

A few remembered their duty, gathered their courage and grabbed at Christ. All of a sudden Peter lost his cool, struck out with his sword, and in an ill-judged swipe lopped off the ear of an unfortunate servant—was it the official holding an arrest warrant from the chief priests? This desperate and defiant act was precisely what should have sparked a furious melee as the soldiers ripped into the small party of almost defenceless disciples. Instead, with apparently everyone rooted to the spot and Peter wondering what on earth he had just done, our Lord calmly walked across, healed the servant's ear and then, with a side glance to the rough gang, turned on his own well-meaning disciple: 'Do you think that I cannot appeal to my Father, and he will at once send me more than twelve legions of angels?'—more than seventy thousand regimental angels! Such a claim ringing out in the still and shadowy darkness of the olive grove, with the clear authority of the powerful voice of the Son of God whose veiled glory had sent the arresting party grovelling in the dust, must have been a scary experience for the quivering mob from Caiaphas. I can imagine them looking around nervously to see from which direction the first cohort of celestial soldiers might appear! For a moment a carpet of uneasy silence covered the scene. But no angels came. In the next moment the disciples lost their courage and fled, and the gang, having found theirs, closed in on Christ. The grace of the incarnation would never by-pass the cross.

He never used his power and glory for his own benefit; never as a final triumphant throw of his trump card over his enemies

Before Caiaphas they spat, punched and cursed Jesus of Nazareth — but he remained silent. And when the Roman governor warned him: 'I have authority to release you and authority to crucify you', the only response Pilate received was: 'You would have no authority over me at all unless it had been given you from above.' If on that point and at that moment he had been challenged to prove his claim, Christ would have remained silent—and all heaven with him. He only ever used his power for our sake.

It is significant that in some of the false gospels that appeared during the second and third centuries following the close of the New Testament, there are fanciful stories of Christ's childhood. This is the one area that the New Testament does not cover in detail and it was only to be expected that someone would try to fill in the gaps. However, the invented stories betray themselves immediately. In a false Gospel of Matthew we have two cruel stories of the childhood of Jesus in which he cursed a child who interfered with his game, and in each case the child died. Another story describes him throwing clay birds into the air so that they might fly away and amuse his friends. A *Gospel of Thomas* relates the story of Jesus killing a Pharisee who interfered with his game. All this is precisely what our Lord did not do. Throughout his life on earth, he never killed anyone, and he never encouraged his disciples to kill anyone. He never used his power and glory for his own benefit; never as a final triumphant throw of his trump card over his enemies, but only so that, 'The Son of Man must suffer many things and be rejected by the elders and chief priests and scribes, and be killed, and on the third day be raised' (Luke 9:22).

He suffered and celebrated, endured and enjoyed, just as we do—yet always without sin

All this Christ did so that we could understand the compassionate heart of the Son of God who, though he was unimaginably rich, became poor for our sake. Knowing that God is a holy and righteous being who will not wink at sin but will punish all who rebel against his authority, and seeing a world of suffering and pain, cruelty and disease, we may well be tempted to wonder if there is a God of compassion at all. But when we look at Christ, all doubts must be dispelled. In the record of his life 'we have seen his glory, glory as of the only Son from the Father, full of grace and truth' (John 1:14). This is the grace of the incarnation.

But there is another reason why Christ became poor, and that is so that we might find God and enjoy him for ever, secure in the knowledge that the one who came to die for us and who rose again to be a living and loving Friend and Saviour is perfectly able 'to sympathize with our weaknesses' (Hebrews 4:15). He suffered and celebrated, endured and enjoyed, just as we do—yet always without sin. The one who knew temptation and pain, and experienced all the human emotions that are common to us is the one best able to assist us in our need. To know that a friend cares and understands is a great comfort in times of need, but to know that that friend is God is a thousand times better. This is in part what Paul means when he adds: 'So that you by his poverty might become rich.'

At the time of his death, Alexander the Great was well advanced in his plans to conquer the Arabian world. Part of his greatness lay in his ability to plan. His forces were assembling, the baggage collected and the summer campaign almost ready. The advance army was on its way. And beyond that, Alexander planned to conquer and conquer until the world ran out! Plans. Great plans. Well-made plans. Then, a little mosquito achieved what all the armies of the world had failed to do—it drew the blood of Alexander the Great and killed him. All his plans ended with his death. He lived in splendour and was buried with honour, but his plans came to nothing.

Death was only inevitable for Christ because he chose it— not because he deserved it

But he who was a million times greater than all the world's great leaders laid plans and chose the time and fulfilled the detail. He who was immortal chose to die. Christ was the only man ever to walk this earth who chose to die. Many have volunteered for desperate and hopeless missions; others have willingly given their lives for a cause—good or bad; some choose suicide in the false hope of ending pain or gaining paradise. But no one chooses to die. They may choose the time and manner and place, but sooner or later death is the inevitable end of everyone who is born into this world. We have no choice. Death was only inevitable for Christ because he chose it—not because he deserved it.

He came to conquer the lives of men and women like us; and to carry this out he became poor—rejected, betrayed, despised and crucified in his body and his character. And the shedding of his blood was all part of the plan. It was the most important part of his plan. The death of world rulers always brings their finest moment to an end. Whether they die in battle or in old age loaded with riches and honour, all is at an end. For the year AD 1087, the Anglo Saxon Chronicle recorded the death of William of Normandy and concluded: 'Alas, how deceitful and untrustworthy is this world's prosperity. He who had been a powerful king, and lord of many a land, had then of all the land only a seven foot measure; and he who once was clad in gold and gems, lay then covered with earth.'

But this king was never more glorious than in his moment of death. There on the cross was revealed for us the true heart of God. That was his finest hour and the moment of his greatest power. For on that cross he carried our sin and guilt and punishment so that the anger of his Father against us would be deflected in his direction instead. His purpose was to reconcile us to God. To make us friends of God and to be with God for ever. And by his resurrection to guarantee all who trust in him a place in heaven: 'so that you, by his poverty, might become rich'—that is wealth beyond the treasures of this world.

How poor was poor?

When he who was the centre of adoration and worship in heaven came to this earth, he was born as a helpless baby and laid in a haybox. Just for a moment the hosts of angels announced his birth in a fanfare of heavenly glory to a handful of poor shepherds—then both angels and shepherds left him. Wise stargazers from a foreign land were led to the place where his parents lodged; they presented a few gifts to tide over the simple family— and then they left him too. Next on the scene were the merciless soldiers from Herod who massacred all the boys in Bethlehem—but their quarry had gone. And ever since, the name of that child and the cause of his followers have been the object of hate and bitter opposition across the world. He who was rich became poor.

They called him a glutton and a drunkard, a collaborator with quislings and a friend of the vilest scum in society (Matthew 11:18–19). They mocked that he was a sinner, demon possessed, a despised Samaritan (John 8:48; 9:24), even a traitor to the Emperor himself (John 19:12), and a blasphemer (Matthew 26:65). In spite of the ditty: 'Sticks and stones may break my bones but names will never hurt me', we all know that crucifying an innocent character can be a cruel form of persecution. And for the sinless Son of God—who had lived for always in perfect harmony with his Father—to be accused of treacherously siding with the dark enemy and of hurling insults at the Father, must have been a bitter hurt.

But he asked for it! Joseph and his mother fled to Egypt—a long-time enemy of Israel—and returned to live in Nazareth. Contrary to a Christian tradition, there is no firm evidence that Nazareth was particularly despised—though there are some grounds for thinking that it was looked upon with suspicion. Nathaniel's often-quoted comment: 'Can anything good come out of Nazareth?' may express no more than his surprise since Nazareth is never specifically mentioned in the Old Testament and therefore would seem to have no claim to the Messiah. Certainly the city—and it is referred to as a city and not a village in the Gospels—was remote in a high valley and perhaps aloof. What was significant, however, is the fact that when the crowd announced him as: 'Jesus, the prophet from Nazareth in Galilee' (Matthew 21:11), it was a comment of surprise—whoever heard of a prophet from Nazareth?

> *For the sinless Son of God … to be accused of treacherously siding with the dark enemy and of hurling insults at the Father, must have been a bitter hurt*

Why did he not return to Bethlehem? That was his birthplace and the town dignified with royal connections, being the birthplace of the great King David. Bethlehem was the expected birthplace of the Messiah for those with eyes to see (Micah 5:2) and surely it would have been more telling if he had been announced as 'Jesus from Bethlehem'. But he never was. Not once. Even Pilate knew him only as 'Jesus of Nazareth, the King of the Jews' (John 19:19). It was, of course, a common practice to designate a man by his hometown, so the frequent reference to him as 'Jesus of Nazareth' was not unusual. But why did God allow Joseph and

Mary to settle in Nazareth, knowing that would be the city of his upbringing? Why not Bethlehem—or better still Jerusalem? The simplest answer is that of Matthew 2:23, 'He went and lived in a city called Nazareth, that what was spoken by the prophets might be fulfilled "He shall be called a Nazarene."' But there is not one Old Testament prophecy precisely like this!

Of all the suggested solutions, the best would seem to be that which understands Nazareth as originally not a single town but the district of Galilee. Galilee was also known in the time of Christ as Gennesaret (Matthew 14:34; Mark 6:53; Luke 5:1) which was a not dissimilar word to Nazareth—compare the Greek *Gennasaret* with *Nazaret*. If this is the case, then the prophetic reference is to Isaiah 9:1, 'In the former time he brought into contempt the land of Zebulun and the land of Naphtali, but in the latter time he has made glorious the way of the sea, the land beyond the Jordan, Galilee of the nations.' Zebulun and Naphtali were the two tribes of Israel that occupied the area which marked the northern boundary of Palestine and that which was therefore most influenced by the foreign nations. Whenever fire came from the north—as it frequently did through the terrifying power of the Assyrians, Babylonians or Persians—it was these northernmost territories that were the first to feel the heat; and when captives were taken away by the conquering nations, these were the first to go and to be replaced by foreign nationals. At the time of Isaiah it was Assyria's turn to conquer, and all was darkness in Galilee, or Gennesaret, the land of the Nazarenes.

These northern territories became synonymous with fear and darkness, and by its remote contact with Palestine and its constant contact with foreigners, the city of Nazareth was doubtless viewed with a degree of suspicion. But the promise was that the people who walked in darkness would see a great light (Isaiah 9:2 and compare Matthew 4:12–16) and then followed the magnificent promise of the coming Messiah who would bring light even into this dark place: 'For to us a child is born, to us a son is given; and the government shall be upon his shoulder, and his name shall be called Wonderful Counsellor, Mighty God, Everlasting Father, Prince of Peace' (v 6). It was all the more tragic, therefore, that when the Light of the world began his ministry in his home town, he was soundly rejected (Luke 4:29).

But if the incarnate Christ chose to be known by the name of a remote and multinational city the reason may not be hard to grasp. That is precisely why he came—to reach people beyond Israel.

Even more to the point was the way he rode into Jerusalem, not on a fine horse or in a glittering chariot, but on the colt of an ass. The donkey was the most widely used beast of burden in the ancient East, and often still is, and it was no shame to ride on a donkey—unless you were claiming to be a king! In that case it would be ridiculous. The Roman persecutors later ridiculed their Christian victims by referring to them as *assinari*. When he submitted himself to the cruel indignity of crucifixion it only compounded the mockery of his claims. For the Romans, crucifixion was the death reserved, never for a Roman, but for the lowest common criminal; and it gave first century graffiti artists a field day to scrawl on walls pictures of a donkey-headed man spread out on a cross. For this reason Christians were not in a hurry to use the cross as a symbol of their faith, and they preferred the fish, or the letters alpha and omega (from Revelation 22:13—the first and last letters of the Greek alphabet) or the chi-rho monogram (the first two letters of the word *Christ*).

The incarnation was the hardest thing the Father and the Son ever did, and the one thing they did not have to do

The way the Triune God chose to make salvation possible was by the greatest act of grace possible. In a simple phrase the apostle summed up the before and after when he wrote, 'After making purification for sins (the *New King James Version* rightly adds the phrase 'by himself'), he sat down at the right hand of the Majesty on high' (Hebrews 1:3). In order to make purification for our sins, God chose the hardest way possible. He chose to send his Son to die. The incarnation was the hardest thing the Father and the Son ever did, and the one thing they did not have to do. It was not hard for the Son of God to create the world by a powerful word of command, and it is not hard for him to uphold the whole of the universe by that same powerful word. But it was desperately hard for him to become what he was not and suffer the scorn and ridicule of his creatures and submit to death in the jaws of Satan's final throw, and come here knowing that for a few terrible hours he would be rejected by his Father because he would become our sin in our place.

God chose a way of salvation that, beyond all doubt, demonstrated that the whole cost was born by himself; we could pay nothing. The incarnation was the only way. In the incarnation God stooped down to meet us at our point of need. How else could we know what God is like? How else could we be assured of his love and care? How else could we be certain that salvation was possible and secure? He did not do it for his sake, for he could have chosen any way he preferred; there must have been an easier way. But this way was the only way for us—though the most costly for him. That is the grace of the incarnation.

At the start we claimed that the coming of Christ into this world at the incarnation is the greatest exhibition of God's grace, and that this in turn is the most powerful incentive for Christian humility in the grace of giving. Now, Paul concludes in 2 Corinthians 8:12, in the light of an incarnate grace like that, if you are as ready to give as he was, you will hold nothing back in your service for one another –and that will be acceptable with God.

LET EARTH AND HEAVEN COMBINE,
angels and men agree
to praise in songs divine
the incarnate Deity;
our God contracted to a span,
incomprehensibly made man.

2 He laid his glory by,
took form in mortal clay;
unseen by human eye
the hidden Godhead lay;
infant of days he here became,
and bore the meek Immanuel's name.

3 See in that infant's face
the depths of Deity;
endeavour, while you gaze,
to probe the mystery;
let even angels gaze no more,
but bow and silently adore.

4 Unsearchable the love
that has our Saviour brought;
his grace is far above
the reach of human thought:
it is enough that God, we know,
our God, is manifest below.

5 He deigns in flesh to appear,
widest extremes to join;
to bring our vileness near,
and make us all divine:
and we the life of God shall know,
for God is manifest below.

6 Made perfect by his love
and sanctified by grace,
we shall from earth remove
and see his glorious face:
then shall his love be fully showed
and we shall be complete in God.

CHARLES WESLEY 1707–88
Praise! 364 © in this version Praise Trust

Invincible grace

'He who had set me apart before I was born and who called me by his grace' Galatians 1:15

Throughout his life Paul frequently looked back in sorrow and in amazement. Sorrow at what he once was—proud, self-confident, narrow-minded and arrogant; a bitter, Christ-rejecting, Christian-persecuting and Church-destroying extremist. And amazement at what he now is—the acknowledged leader of the Christian community, the privileged receiver of revelation from God, the model first century church planter, and above all a man with a passion to know Christ, a willingness to suffer for the faith he once laboured to destroy, and with a total conviction of the reality of heaven.

John Newton also provides us with a clear example of invincible grace, so we will use him often in this chapter. Like Paul, he was equally amazed at the change in his own life. When he first published his autobiography in 1764, shortly after he had settled as curate-in-charge at the parish church in Olney, he found himself the object of great interest. He wrote that from all over the nation: 'People come to stare. I am a mystery to them. Indeed, I am a mystery to myself.' What amazed Paul and John more than anything, was how they came to shift from their total unbelief and opposition, to their total commitment to Christ.

Over the centuries, Christians have debated the process of conversion. What makes a man or woman 'wake up' to the call of the gospel and turn to Christ in repentance? Most would agree that the answer lies somewhere in the word 'grace'. Paul leaves no room for doubt in Ephesians 2:8, 'By grace you have been saved through faith. And this is not your own doing; it is the gift of God.' Conversion is through the undeserved mercy of God who applies the righteousness of Jesus Christ to our account so that we can be justified—declared free from our guilt of Christ-rejecting sin. This is why grace is one of the most beautiful words in the Bible.

Whilst justification by faith has been called a hallmark of true Christianity, I would suggest that grace is the true hallmark, because grace comes before justification. Justification is God's verdict when all the merits of Christ's righteousness are put to our account, but grace is God's *willingness* to do so; in fact grace is God's eagerness and joy in doing so. Grace is not wrung from God reluctantly, it is given gladly, and what is more important, grace begins in eternity. Without grace in eternity there would be no justification in time.

But exactly when does grace 'kick in'? If grace describes God's eternal purposes to save me and justify me, when does it all take effect, and how? There have been a number of answers to that question in the history of the church. We will look at a few.

How can we respond to God?

Without grace in eternity there would be no justification in time

Some say that to respond to God, we have to exercise our will. God stands back and waits, and only when we call does he respond to us. It is all our initiative and God waits patiently. We are told that God would never command us to do what we cannot do, so the fact that he commands us to repent and turn to him must mean that we can do this without his immediate aid.

One obvious problem with this position is that there certainly *are* some things God calls us to do that he knows we cannot achieve. For example, he commands us to be holy because he is holy (Leviticus 11:45; 1 Peter 1:15) and Abraham was ordered, 'Walk before me and be blameless' (Genesis 17:1), but on this side of our transformation in heaven that is not fully possible; the standard is set before us as both an incentive to holy living and a reminder that God does not reduce his standards to suit our convenience. However, some writers have done just that, and they suggest that what God is really expecting is an 'all-round integrity and sincerity' and no more. But when our Lord defined the greatest commandment as: 'You shall love the Lord your God with all your heart and with all your soul and with all your mind', and the second as:

'You shall love your neighbour as yourself' (Matthew 22:37–39), he meant exactly what that appears to mean.

Others conclude that it is not quite like that. They say that it is true that the first faltering move towards God is ours, but as soon as we cry for help, God sends his Holy Spirit to sharpen our understanding and strengthen our faith. As the American evangelist Charles G Finney wrote in the middle of the nineteenth century: 'It is mine to be willing to believe and it is the part of God's grace to assist.' That looks as though we have to make the first call, and only then will God help us. The problem with this view is that it demands of us the hardest part—responding from our stubborn and rebellious mind and will—and it leaves for God the easiest part of assisting our progress. Our predicament is that we don't want God to start with—we are spiritually dead. It takes more power to start your car from stationary than it does to keep it moving. The initial turn of the ignition to wake up the vehicle draws massive energy from the battery; but once the engine is running, the battery can relax.

Others disagree with both these wait-and-see and cooperative agreement positions, and claim that as we are so very sinful we *must* have the Holy Spirit to take the initiative. To continue the automobile illustration, we need the Holy Spirit for a 'jump-start'. However, once we are alive to God, it is all up to us. We may resist even to the point of final rejection of the truth. In fact we may, and many do, surprise God by our stubbornness, and God is quite happy to have it this way because he loves this sort of 'open' relationship with us by which we choose the what, when and if of receiving grace. This is an increasingly popular approach today. It is known as 'open theology' or, with a slight variation, 'process theology'. God, we are assured, cannot ever be certain of our response to him but he enjoys relying upon our cooperation and will never compel us to do anything that we do not want to do. At the last moment Judas may not have betrayed our Lord, and that certainly would have surprised God since he had prophesied that very action of betrayal (Psalm 41:9).

In contrast to each of these views, the position taught by evangelical Christianity at the time of the Reformation in the sixteenth century and beyond, was that our response to God is all due to his grace from start to finish. We do not receive the Holy Spirit *when* we believe, but we receive the Holy Spirit *so that* we can believe.

This conviction is based upon evidence found throughout Scripture, and it is especially seen in Galatians 1:15–16 where Paul expresses his gratitude and amazement that it was grace alone that set him apart 'before I was born', 'called' him and revealed Christ to him. Such a view is also based upon our helpless condition before conversion. Paul describes it in this way: 'You were dead in the trespasses and sins in which you once walked' (Ephesians 2:1). Before our conversion we were living a spiritual death even in an active life. Therefore in a real sense our freedom was lost. We could make many moral and ordinary choices, and at times good ones; not all religious or non-religious morality is bad morality. But in responding to God we are helpless.

We do not receive the Holy Spirit when we believe, but we receive the Holy Spirit so that we can believe

In 1517 Martin Luther, the German Reformer, wrote a book entitled *The Bondage of the Will*; it was an argument against the Dutch theologian, Desiderius Erasmus, who believed that we could respond to God by our own power. Commenting upon our Lord's words: 'No one can come to me unless the Father who sent me draws him' (John 6:44), Luther wrote, 'Christ declares not only that the works and efforts of "freewill" are unavailing, but that even the very word of the gospel is heard in vain.' He went on to assert that we have no power of our own to respond to God. It is not just that we *will not* respond, the reality is that we *cannot* respond. In fact, Luther was simply following Augustine in the fourth century who claimed that before the Fall mankind was free not to sin, but after the Fall mankind was not free not to sin. Or, in the words of the apostle Paul: 'The natural person (the word refers to someone who is without the Spirit of God) does not accept the things of the Spirit of God, for they are folly to him, and he is not able to understand them because they are spiritually discerned' (1 Corinthians 2:14).

In Romans 8:5–8 Paul expressed the hopeless helplessness of what he called the 'flesh'; in this context the word refers to our sinful nature: 'Those who live according to the flesh have their minds on the things of the flesh, but those who live according to the Spirit set their minds on the things of the Spirit. To set the mind on the flesh is death, but to set the mind on the Spirit is life and peace. For the mind that is set on the flesh is hostile to God, for it does not submit to God's law; indeed, it cannot. Those who are in the flesh cannot please God.' This is all very plain even though not very pleasant. In his first chapter in Romans, Paul presented a bleak picture of humanity. He wrote of a will in rebellion against the truth (v 18), and without a love for God (v 21), a futile mind and a foolish heart (v 21), emotions out of control (vs 24–27), a life filled with all kinds of wickedness and a conscience corrupted so that it is no longer reliable (v 32). When we package all this with the fact that we are dead towards God (Ephesians 2:1), hostile to God (Romans 8:7), blind to the truth (2 Corinthians 4:4) slaves to sin and Satan (Romans 7:14; 2 Peter 2:19), and incapable of responding to God (John 6:44). It is not a pretty picture. In fact, it is all very depressing and hardly surprising that modern religions and sociologists are not comfortable with such a diagnosis.

So, if our nature is helpless, is it all hopeless? That is exactly the point at which Paul's claim in Galatians 1:15–16 comes in: 'He who had set me apart before I was born ... called me by his grace (and) was pleased to reveal his Son to me'. That is invincible grace.

First, the invincible grace of God's choice

This grace that determined our salvation was according to God's own purpose—not ours—before time began. Elsewhere Paul expressed it another way when he told the Ephesian Christians that they were 'chosen in Christ before the foundation of the world' (Ephesians 1:4); and he made the same claim in 2 Timothy 1:9, 'Called ... not because of our works, but because of his own purpose and grace which he gave to us in Christ Jesus before the ages began.' Twice in the Revelation of John we learn that our names were written in the book of life before 'the foundation of the world' (13:8; 17:8).

This is the meaning of that striking word 'predestined' that Paul uses in Romans 8:29–30 and Ephesians 1:5, 11. The Greek word is made up from a little preposition that means 'beforehand', and another word from which we gain the English word 'horizon'. The verb *horizo* originally referred to the act of dividing or separating one thing from another. For us the horizon refers to the dividing line between earth and sky; in the New Testament it is used of a boundary or limit (Acts 17:26). Up in the sky we have a group of brilliant stars that are called Orion, named after the god of Greek mythology, the great hunter—it is the same word.

So we may say that the word predestined means that we have been brought within God's horizon from before the beginning of time. God plans what he will see and sees all that he has planned—and every Christian is part of that.

God plans what he will see and sees all that he has planned—and every Christian is part of that

The God who created the universe of stars and planets, who planned the laws of science and the exact regulation of this complex world, the God of the infinity of space and the eternity of time, of majestic holiness, fearful justice and sovereign power, is the God who, before time began, chose those who would be saved, and he credited grace to their account. He determined even then, to deal with them favourably and not as their sins deserved. He keyed in their names to the database of citizenship in heaven—or in old speak, he wrote them in his book! It is for this reason that Paul can confidently claim that the solid foundation of God's kingdom has a seal that reads, 'The Lord knows those who are his' (2 Timothy 2:19). It was not that God woke up when he heard us call but we woke up when he gave us grace to call. There is a world of difference between the two.

No one knew this better than John Newton, and writing to a friend on this subject he drew his attention to John 3:27, 'A person cannot receive even one thing unless it is given him from heaven.' The converted blasphemer and drunkard went on to challenge his correspondent by reminding him of the broad road to destruction that once we were all walking: 'Were not you and I in this road? Were we better than those who continue in it still? What has made us differ from our former selves? *Grace*.

What has made us differ from those who are now as we once were? *Grace.* Then this grace ... must be differencing or distinguishing grace; that is, in other words, electing grace.' Newton was well aware of his own state at the time of his remarkable conversion to Christ and so he continued, 'We know that the Lord foresaw us in a state utterly incapable either of believing or obeying, unless he was pleased to work in us to will and to do according to his own good pleasure.'

Newton had in his congregation a wise old lady who, when challenged on the subject of predestination, responded, 'Oh, I settled that long ago. If he had not chosen me before I was born, he certainly would have seen nothing in me worth choosing me for afterwards.' And Saul of Tarsus was not ashamed of grace like that. In just the same way God told the young prophet Jeremiah: 'Before I formed you in the womb I knew you; before you were born I consecrated you; I appointed you a prophet to the nations' (Jeremiah 1:5). That purposeful grace of God was not peculiar to Jeremiah, it is true for all who find Christ as Lord and Saviour.

Too many Christians spend too much of their time either arguing or worrying over this great truth of predestination, when all that God intends for us is that we should bask in the light of it. To change the picture—it is a comfortable armchair to relax in. The only people who need to worry about it are those who do not know it to be true for themselves. For all who have sincerely turned from their sin to Christ, this is one of the most reassuring doctrines found in the Bible. Luther expressed his enjoyment of this grace of God like this: 'I have the comfortable certainty that I please God, not by reason of the merit of my works, but by reason of his merciful favour promised to me; so that, if I work too little, or badly, he does not reckon it to me, but with fatherly compassion pardons me and makes me better. This is the glorying of the saints of God.'

When the sun finally breaks out after a long, miserably cold and wet winter, I suppose there may be some people who are so terrified by the thought of skin cancer from the harmful ultraviolet rays of the sun that, before they venture out, they dress themselves in their winter coat, scarf, hat and gloves for protection. For most of us, however, we are so delighted at the rediscovery of all the benefits of God's sunshine that we throw off our winter clothes and enjoy the warmth and light of God's gracious gift.

With this great truth of God's electing grace, we are not to argue and squabble over it, still less try to protect it from the accusations of an unsubmissive mind; we are to go out and take pleasure in its warmth, strength and security. All that God wants us to do with this great truth of election is to enjoy it.

Secondly, the invincible grace of God's care

The grace that knew us from eternity, determined our salvation, and settled our names in the database of heaven was also the grace that maintained a watchful care over us long before our conversion; in fact, from the moment of our birth. The Puritans had a word for this; they called it 'prevenient' grace. That word is from the Latin *praevinire* which means to come beforehand or precede. Our English word 'prevent' came from this Latin word, and originally it referred to someone who precedes or goes before us; unfortunately, over the course of time the word 'prevent' has come to refer to something that gets in our way or hinders us. But 'prevenient grace' refers to God's preparation in our lives when he prepared the way before our conversion. We may call it 'preparing grace' if we wish. Certainly at times he 'got in our way' to ensure that we kept to the path that he had chosen for us, even though we did not know this. Our birth, family, education, friends—even our decisions—were all in the hands of the One who had chosen us for salvation.

All that God wants us to do with this great truth of election is to enjoy it

Saul of Tarsus was a well-educated Jew, highly regarded and with good connections; he was a Roman citizen and possessed a sharp mind, a strong will and a firmly disciplined life. This was all true long before he became a Christian, but it meant that once converted, Paul the Apostle had easy access into the synagogues throughout the Roman Empire and this formed the basis of his strategy when he became a Christian evangelist. As a violent persecutor of the Christians, he knew also how their opponents thought and schemed. Though Paul did not appreciate it beforehand, this was all part of God's prevenient grace in the life of one who would be 'a chosen instrument of mine to carry my name before the Gentiles and kings and the children of Israel' (Acts 9:15).

As a young boy, John Newton had his mind stored by his godly mother with Bible verses and hymns from the collection of Isaac Watts. This was later used by God in his experience of conversion when those verses came flooding back to his memory. John possessed a very retentive mind—he learnt to read at the age of four and began Latin at six—enjoyed a gift of putting thoughts into verse, and he was a natural leader. All this prepared him for his later service for God.

If we look back at our own lives, it is not difficult to see the plan of God in our family connections and upbringing, our natural ability and interests, perhaps also our enjoyment of reading, studying or just arguing! We may have been 'open to religion', or impressionable, or naturally sceptical, even cynical. So many roads closed, or opened, that at the time were frustrating or forwarding our plans; then we could see no purpose, but much later on we could see how everything worked towards our conversion and subsequent Christian service. Whatever our background, personality or interests, we can now see how it was all being used by God to prepare the way for our future.

However, prevenient grace is not only God's preparation, but also his providence. Those 'unseen footprints' of God (Psalm 77:19) by which he protects and guards us until the time of our conversion—and beyond—is all part of invincible grace. Our lives are full of occasions of remarkable protection and the strange coincidences that brought us first into touch with the message of the gospel. We know very little about the early life of Saul of Tarsus, though we do know of his presence at the death of Stephen which clearly made an impact on his conscience. Of John Newton we know much more. As a boy he was once thrown from his horse and narrowly avoided being impaled on a wooden stake. On another occasion he missed by a few minutes a boat that was to take him and a young friend to visit a man-of-war lying at anchor—the boat capsized and his friend was drowned. Years later, as a godless sailor, Newton had organised a drinking bout during which his hat blew over the side of the ship; in his stupor he was about to clamber after it, thinking it was just a few feet away, when his shipmates pulled him back from certain death since Newton could never swim. In fact, John's life was full of examples of prevenient grace; though at the time he never recognised the hand of God and these 'lucky' escapes from death were simply good stories to tell over a jug of beer.

Perhaps the greatest evidence of prevenient grace in Newton's life was the incredible series of coincidences that finally brought him back from the coast of Africa. John was by now trading for slaves on the coast of New Guinea and was preparing for a mission inland. Before he set out he was planning to fight a duel with another trader who had crossed him; his pistols were chosen and ready for what he intended to be a contest to the death. The day before the arranged duel, a ship passed the point where Newton and a colleague were working and, being in need of some items to take inland with them, they sent up a signal for trade. It was very unusual for ships to pass this part of the coast at this time of the year, and the captain at first decided that since his ship was already past the convenient point for returning he would simply ignore the signal; however, he suddenly changed his mind, hove-to and received Newton's trading partner on board. Almost the captain's first question was to enquire whether the young man knew of a John Newton anywhere on this coast! He had received orders from Newton's father via the owner of the ship that if he ever located Newton, he was to bring him back to England at whatever cost. John had not been heard of in England for more than eighteen months. His life was packed with such examples of God's prevenient grace. But the same happens to all who are chosen for faith in Christ—though we are mostly unaware of these unseen footprints and they are not always dramatic.

Some years ago our church embarked on a large rebuilding programme and moved off our premises for nine months. For Sunday services we met in a local parish church hall and unknown to us a retired Scotsman, who lived opposite the hall, was watching our congregation coming and going each week. Intrigued, he wrote to a friend in Glasgow and commented on these people who had suddenly appeared at the parish hall. As it happened his correspondent was a Christian and she knew exactly who these people were. She told him to get on his bike as soon as they moved back to their new building and worship with them. John did as he was told, was converted to Christ, and later married his adviser from Glasgow! However, that episode was not the only example of prevenient grace in his life. John had fought all through World War Two and was nicknamed 'bomb-proof Jock'—so many of his comrades were killed around him but nothing ever hit Jock. Until he became a Christian he had always thought he was just lucky, but now he understood why his life had been so often and so remarkably preserved.

Prevenient grace is rarely requested and mostly unrecognised. Through Isaiah God told Israel, 'I revealed myself to those who did not ask for me; I was found by those who did not seek me.' That is invincible prevenient grace. It is equally God's invincible grace when he holds back his anger upon our sin: 'He restrained his anger often and did not stir up all his wrath' (Psalm 78:38).

But this invincible grace of God does not cease at the point of our conversion. John Bunyan, the seventeenth century mender of pots and pans who was converted to Christ, expressed it like this: 'All the providences and dispensations that come upon his elect people are not intended to destroy them, but to humble them so that they might trust him even more. Sometimes God even allows his chosen people to fall into temptation and sin, but only with a better purpose in view.' This is what Paul meant when he reminded the Philippians that 'he who began a good work in you will complete it at the day of Jesus Christ' (Philippians 1:6). John Newton discovered this when, shortly after his conversion, he sailed as first mate on the *Brownlow*. Confident that he could live consistently as a Christian in the cruel and godless environment of a slave-trading ship, he soon found himself to be 'almost as bad as before'. Only a fever that brought him close to death, and another remarkable incident in which he ought to have been drowned, arrested his backsliding and restored him to a humble trust in Christ alone for both salvation and the strength to continue as a Christian.

John Bunyan spent twelve years in prison for preaching the gospel of

Prevenient grace is

rarely requested and

mostly unrecognised

Christ, but it was here that he wrote his classic: *The Pilgrim's Progress*; however, he told his own story in the less well-known *Grace Abounding to the Chief of Sinners*. From his own experience Bunyan wrote of this invincible grace: 'Oh, what love, what care, what kindness and mercy I now saw blending with the most severe and dreadful of all God's dealings with his people! He would let David, Hezekiah, Solomon, Peter and others fall, but he would not let them fall so low as to commit the unpardonable sin to descend into hell for sin.'

Thirdly, the invincible grace of God's call

For those predestined to eternal life, there is always a time when God's grace 'gets through'. For Saul of Tarsus that moment was outside the walls of the city of Damascus in the year AD 30, for John of Wapping it was on a broken ship in mid Atlantic in March 1748. Whenever we hear the call of God with ears that are listening and a mind that can understand, it is at a moment God has planned from eternity. This is what is meant by the phrase 'called according to his purpose' in Romans 8:28. It is that moment when God speaks personally and we must respond. By 'must', I do not mean that we ought to, but that we cannot do other than respond; there is a divine compulsion about this call. God is speaking to us personally—and we know it! For Saul it came in a vision and an audible voice, for John it came through a terrified conscience and the recollection of many verses from the Bible. For each it is personal and particular; there is no set pattern.

Some refer to this as the 'irresistible' call of God. John Newton preferred the word 'invincible' because he knew that we can resist the call of God—and he often did—but finally we cannot win; God always has his way. Saul had obviously been resisting the nagging of his mind and conscience and that is why the Lord told him, 'It is hard for you to kick against the goads' (Acts 26:14).

In *Grace Abounding*, Bunyan traces the invincible grace of God's call in his own life. He tells of the occasion when he was in the town of Bedford and overheard a group of women sitting at their doorway and talking about religion. His conscience was already troubling him and he deliberately listened-in to their conversation. Their talk both intrigued him and troubled him because they seemed to have found a new world that he was a complete stranger to, and their experience of God and salvation was well beyond anything he himself could understand. He slipped away and went on with his business but he commented, 'Their talk and conversation followed me.' He could not get out of his mind the things they had been saying, and the assurance and joy that they had. Bunyan's conscience was troubling him. Invincible grace was at work in his life. In his case the path to salvation was a long and hard one; he went through an agony and torment of conscience before finally he found peace with God. In fact he discovered that Martin Luther's commentary on Paul's letter to the Galatians was, 'The best of all the books that I have ever seen for a wounded conscience.'

In his poem *The Hound of Heaven*, Francis Thompson, a Roman Catholic in religion, described the work of this invincible God as a great beast (he did not mean that in a bad sense) following relentlessly the one he loves even though that person is struggling to get away from him. Thompson, who died in ill health and poverty in 1907 at the age of forty-eight, began his powerful poem in this way,

> 'I fled Him, down the nights and down the days;
> I fled Him, down the arches of the years;
> I fled Him, down the labyrinthine ways
> Of my own mind; and in the mist of tears
> I hid from Him, and under running laughter.
>   Up vistaed hopes I sped;
>   And shot, precipitated,
> Adown Titanic glooms of chasmed fears,
> From those strong Feet that followed, followed after.
>   But with unhurrying chase,
>   And unperturbèd pace,
> Deliberate speed, majestic instancy,
>   They beat—and a Voice beat
>   More instant than the Feet—
> "All things betray thee, who betrayest Me."'

God would not let him go but followed him in all his attempts to break free. Francis Thompson continued by describing the man who runs from God, turning to the world for its pleasure, longing to find love, and then, hungry, thirsty and discontented, he is stripped of all he hoped would satisfy him; his life crumbling around him:

> 'In the rash lustihead of my young powers,
>   I shook the pillaring hours
> And pulled my life upon me; grimed with smears,
> I stand amid the dust o' the mounded years—
> My mangled youth lies dead beneath the heap.
> My days have crackled and gone up in smoke,
> Have puffed and burst as sun-starts on a stream.'

Finally, with the hound of heaven never giving up the chase, he discovers that the heavy hand of suffering and pain that he thought was for his harm, was in reality the only love that he, unworthy as he is, could ever expect. He hears the voice of the one who reminds him that human love has to be merited, but that he has merited nothing:

> "How little worthy of any love thou art!
> Whom wilt thou find to love ignoble thee,
>   Save Me, save only Me?
> All which I took from thee I did but take,
>   Not for thy harms,
> But just that thou might'st seek it in My arms.
>   All which thy child's mistake
> Fancies as lost, I have stored for thee at home:
>   Rise, clasp My hand, and come!"'

How much Francis Thompson understood of the theology behind his poem we can only guess, but Paul of Tarsus and John of Wapping would not only have appreciated the theology, they would have recognised how very closely it expressed their own experience. Paul referred to himself as the 'foremost of sinners', and John certainly knew a 'mangled youth grimed with smears' the details of which he once longed could be 'buried in eternal silence'.

But this work of the Spirit is not simply external impressions. Peter wrote of Christians being 'partakers of the divine nature' (2 Peter 1:4), and that is one of the most significant phrases in the New Testament. If all that we have said about the tragic state of human nature after the Fall is true, then God must not only take the initiative but he must also provide all that is necessary for us to be able to respond to him. In biblical terms this is the new birth, or regeneration, without which, according to our Lord himself, no one can see the kingdom of God (John 3:3); and, again by our Lord's own claim, this is a sovereign work of the Spirit (v 8). It is not for us to be fussy over the time-sequence of regeneration and conversion, or to know precisely the moment of the Holy Spirit's first work in our life or the exact time of our new birth; but we must surely agree with Luther that, 'Through the drawing of the Holy Spirit, God makes willing men out of the obstinate and unwilling.'

Grace to be willing

It is natural to object to the idea of God forcing us against our will to bow to Christ in repentance. I could not agree more. Whoever believes that God forces men and women unwillingly into the Kingdom of God? He will not frog-march or press-gang people into his kingdom; he is not argumentative and belligerent. On the contrary, he seeks willing volunteers for his service. Matthew illustrated this by borrowing a lengthy quotation from Isaiah to reveal that Christ will not break a bruised reed or quench a smouldering wick (Matthew 12:18–21). In his determination God is gently firm and kindly resolute.

The fact is that he works upon our will by his Spirit, sometimes by gentle wooing and at times by the harsh treatment of our circumstances; sometimes he leaves us to run and we try the world and all its pleasures— like the man in Thompson's *The Hound of Heaven;* sometimes we suffer pain and disappointment. At times we cry out *against* him; but always that Hound of Heaven pursues us, until at last we long *for* him and cry out *to* him. From all who have been 'appointed to eternal life' (Acts 13:48) he will ultimately and inevitably win willing repentance, devoted love and believing trust. This is no new teaching, because as far back as the time of Moses the nation of Israel was encouraged to believe that God would work in their lives: 'So that you will love the LORD your God with all your heart and with all your soul' (Deuteronomy 30:6). That is invincible grace. God is a great huntsman—he always hits his mark.

God's agency in this prevenient grace is twofold—and no more. He uses the Holy Spirit and the word of God—by which we mean the Scriptures. The human will is not a third agent in cooperation, as if God cannot succeed by his Spirit and his word unless we agree to allow him. Lazarus had been four days dead and, in a warm climate, Martha wisely pointed out that there would be an offensive smell if the tomb were to be opened. Nevertheless the stone was rolled from the mouth of the cave and Lazarus 'came out, his hands and feet bound with linen strips' (John 11:44). But Lazarus did not come out of the grave because the stone was removed, still less because he considered it an attractive option, or because he decided not to be dead any longer. There were just two forces that combined to bring Lazarus out of the tomb: The commanding voice of the Son of God and the reviving power of the Spirit of God. Nothing less and nothing more is required for our new birth.

God is a great huntsman—he always hits his mark

The way that God applies grace is not by the Spirit alone as some would suggest, or by the word alone, as others propose, but by the Spirit *and* the word. It is not that God sometimes uses the Spirit instead of the Scriptures; so-called spiritual illumination that comes apart from God's revealed word is often very dangerous. Equally it is not that at other times he will use the word instead of the Spirit, as if we can rely upon the moral force of the truth of the Bible to awaken sinners. On the contrary, it is God's normal way to use the word by his Spirit to convince of sin, of righteousness and of judgement. No spiritual experience or persuasive argument is sufficiently powerful to awaken a Christ-rejecting sinner to new life.

I said the word and the Spirit are God's 'normal way' of applying his grace to a sinner, because I recognise that where there are no Scriptures, and no evangelist either, then God may send his Spirit to employ other ways to bring the knowledge of his Son. I do not doubt the stories of those across the world of Islam where the Bible is unknown, who are introduced to

Christ through a dream or vision; God is free to reach into the lives of his elect in any way he chooses, but it will always be through his Holy Spirit. And his way of saving sinners and of growing Christians, in normal circumstances is always by his Spirit through the word.

This is why the Scriptures are called 'the sword of the Spirit' (Ephesians 6:17); and for this reason, 'walking in the Spirit' and 'keeping in step with the Spirit' (Galatians 5:16, 25) are to be defined as obedience to the Bible. When Peter encouraged the young churches that, 'His divine power has granted to us all things that pertain to (are relevant for) life and godliness' (2 Peter 1:3), the 'all things' are described in the next verse when he writes of the promises of God and the Christian being a 'partaker of the divine nature'. That is the word and the Spirit. With those two we have all that we need to become a Christian, and all that we need to continue as a Christian.

There was a time when Christians often seized the opportunity to review the invincible grace of God in their lives both before and after their conversion. We sadly neglect this today, and this is partly because we have been given the impression that we are somehow smart to respond to the call of God and that the first inclination of our heart and mind towards the Creator was more our work than his. We have wandered a long way from the theology of the old hymn by W Spencer Walton:

There were just two forces that combined to bring Lazarus out of the tomb: The commanding voice of the Son of God and the reviving power of the Spirit of God

> O the love that sought me!
> O the blood that bought me!
> O the grace that brought me to the fold,
> wondrous grace that brought me to the fold!

Chapter 7

Or, as Josiah Conder expressed it more fully over one hundred and fifty years ago:

MY LORD, I DID NOT CHOOSE YOU
for that could never be;
this heart would still refuse you
had you not chosen me:
you took the sin that stained me,
you cleansed and made me new;
for you of old ordained me
that I should live to you.

2 Unless your grace had called me
and taught my opening mind,
the world would have enthralled me,
to heavenly glories blind:
my heart knows none above you;
for you I long, I thirst,
and know that if I love you,
Lord, you have loved me first.

JOSIAH CONDER 1789–1855
Praise! 691

Forgiving grace

'The grace of our Lord overflowed for me with the faith and love that are in Christ Jesus' 1 Timothy 1:14

The outcome of his approaching trial before Nero was all too predictable, and in preparation Paul had been moved from house arrest to a prison somewhere in the city of Rome. By now he had been a Christian for more than thirty years—at a reasonable estimate that placed him somewhere in his mid 50s—and he reviewed his life in a letter to one of his early converts who was by now the young pastor at Ephesus. Perhaps Paul sat thoughtfully in his prison and reflected sadly on his past. He knew that he did not deserve the invincible grace that chose him from before the world began, or the justifying grace that reckoned Christ's righteousness to his account. There was so much in his past life of which he was miserably ashamed and which he could never forget.

We can never entirely forget our life before Christ conquered us—nor should we. That which Paul wanted to put behind him in his race for the prize (Philippians 3:13–14) was not his past life, but his recent achievements. For many, there are things we have done for which we are both embarrassed and mortified and they frequently return to haunt us. It is no use anyone telling us to 'forget them' because we cannot. Some things are so indelibly written on our mind that only the transformation of heaven will finally erase them. When he wrote his autobiography, John Newton longed for some of his past life to be 'buried in eternal silence' and for this reason, unlike modern writers with a good story, he did not detail it for us; but he admits that so much of it he could never erase from his mind.

When Paul reminded Timothy that the law is made not for the righteous 'But for the lawless and disobedient, for the ungodly and sinners, for the unholy and profane, for those who strike their fathers and mothers, for murderers, the sexually immoral, men who practise homosexuality, enslavers, liars, perjurers and whatever else is contrary to sound doctrine' (1 Timothy 1:9–10), he must have been overwhelmed at the thought that purposeful grace brought him into the ministry of a gospel capable of dealing with people like this. To Timothy's response that Paul, with all his religious zeal before his conversion and his spiritual successes since, could hardly be compared to such dreadful people, Paul was insistent, 'I was a blasphemer, persecutor, and insolent opponent' (v 13); and in case this did not persuade the young pastor, Paul described himself as the foremost of sinners (v 15)—and he meant it. Paul was aware not only of undeserved and purposeful grace, but of an abundant, unlimited and forgiving grace that was always available whenever he needed it. There is no adequate human illustration for God's abundant grace, because sooner or later ours runs out—but God's grace once committed, never fails.

> There is no adequate human illustration for God's abundant grace, because sooner or later ours runs out—but God's grace once committed, never fails

Have you ever wondered just where the 'faithful saying', that Paul refers to in verse 15, comes to an end? Does it stop after the word 'sinners', or after the word 'foremost'? Paul is saying to Timothy: 'I want you to tell those people in Ephesus that this is a trustworthy saying; it deserves that everyone should accept it; it is the good news in brief and here it is: "Christ Jesus came into the world to save sinners". And Timothy, let them know that I am the worst. Whenever you talk about Christ dying for sinners, tell them about me; tell them about the undeserved grace that saved me and the abundant grace that goes on and on forgiving me; and you can tell them that of all sinners Saul of Tarsus was the worst.' The word 'foremost' that Paul used here may refer to the first in time, place, influence or honour. Of all the concerted and organised persecution that would come upon the Christian church over the next two thousand years, Paul wanted it to be known that he was responsible for the first and the worst. To murder anyone is bad, but to strangle a child in infancy is especially evil; that is what Saul of Tarsus had set out to do to the infant church.

How bad is worst?

In Galatians 1:13 Paul tells, 'how I persecuted the church of God violently and tried to destroy it.' The word for 'violently' is *huperbole* from which we get our English word, 'hyperbole'—something that is greatly exaggerated. Paul admits that his persecution of the church was totally and unreasonably exaggerated; it was utterly excessive and completely irrational. Is that claiming too much? Not at all: this man had been motivated by nothing other than a desire to destroy the Christian church before it could take root. It is recorded in Acts 8:1–3 that he was 'ravaging the church' and went from house to house to drag off men and women who believed in the gospel to throw them into prison—even the women were not safe from his bitter hatred. That was Paul's first house-to-house visitation. And in Acts 26:11, when he was on trial and yet again giving his testimony, Paul looked back and admitted, 'I punished them often in all the synagogues and tried to make them blaspheme, and in raging fury against them I persecuted them even to foreign cities.' This man was a vicious and evil force to be reckoned with. He was hell-bent on a search and destroy mission to exterminate all who counted themselves disciples of Christ. Tragically, as he looked back three decades later, his own conversion had precluded him from securing their release; how many men and women died in those foul prisons because Saul of Tarsus had put them there?

But it was much worse even than that. The simple statement at the death of Stephen in Acts 7:58 records, 'The witnesses laid down their garments at the feet of a young man named Saul', and the first verse of the next chapter adds, 'and Saul approved of his execution.' The death of Stephen was a highly illegal action. No one had the right of capital punishment in the Roman Empire—the 'right of the sword' as it was known—apart from the Roman authorities themselves. This is exactly why the Jews had to gain Pilate's consent to the death of Jesus. And it is also why, years later when Paul himself was witnessing in the Temple area in Jerusalem and the mob were about to kill him, the commanding officer of the Roman garrison

Chapter 8

turned out his troops to rescue the intended victim. It was of no immediate concern to the tribune what the issue was; all he knew was that an illegal assassination looked likely and so he ordered his men to bring Paul into protective custody whilst he sorted out the matter (Acts 21:27–36).

Thirty years earlier, at the death of Stephen, Saul was a well known young lawyer—a rising star in the legal profession; as soon as the mob saw him they threw down their cloaks at his feet; that was a deliberate act with a definite intention. The unspoken support of Saul of Tarsus implicated him in the assassination and gave the whole murderous episode an appearance of legality; and Saul of Tarsus silently accepted the responsibility. Looking back as he wrote to Timothy, Paul was astounded at himself. He had stood there and let Stephen die. For ever after, Paul carried with him the doubtful privilege of being on record as the man guilty of the death of the first Christian martyr. We are all responsible for our sins, but none of us can predict their influence and outcome.

Paul was not simply an illustration of forgiving grace, he was an example of it

This was all so clear as Paul sat in his Roman prison. In his mind he could see the face of Stephen which appeared like the face of an angel, and he could still hear the rocks as they thudded into the skull of the young evangelist. He saw again the bloody face of that fine and fearless Christian soldier. And Saul of Tarsus was the one man present who had the authority to intervene. I imagine that when he wrote the words to Timothy: 'Christ Jesus came into the world to save sinners, of whom I am the foremost', Paul put down his quill, hung his head in shame and tears blotted his scroll. But here is the glory of the gospel: 'I received mercy for this reason, that in me, as the foremost, Jesus Christ might display his perfect patience as an example to those who were to believe on him for eternal life.' Paul was not simply an illustration of forgiving grace, he was an example of it.

In September 1775 John Newton was visiting London. It was nearly thirty years since his own conversion and he was now a minister of the gospel. As he so often did on these occasions, the converted slave trader preached to the inmates of the notorious Bridewell Prison. A few years earlier crowds had satisfied their sadistic pleasure by watching the women being flogged at Bridewell. Newton wrote home to Sally—one of the maids in their home in Olney—and described the one hundred or so in his congregation as 'housebreakers, highwaymen, pickpockets and poor unhappy women such as infest the streets of the city, sunk in sin and lost to shame.' He described how he had given his testimony and then preached from the words of Paul: 'Christ Jesus came into the world to save sinners, of whom I am chief.' By the time he had concluded, Newton confessed, 'there were many tears in that place, including my own.'

Like Saul of Tarsus, John of Wapping also knew that so much of the damage he had done in his unconverted years could never be undone; and, like Paul, John may not have killed with his own hands, but his involvement in the slave trade meant that he had sold husbands and wives, children and parents a continent apart. Hundreds of black Africans that he had bought had died cruelly on the plantations, or else he had rolled their bodies into the shark infested waters when they succumbed to the choking filth below decks. But more than this, his ready tongue and sharp wit had influenced many young men into his bawdy and blasphemous brand of unbelief. One way or another, John Newton had destroyed more lives than he cared to remember. When we can no longer weep for our sins, we have lost our understanding of grace.

When we can no longer weep for our sins, we have lost our understanding of grace

Saul of Tarsus never ceased to be ashamed of his past. But he never ceased to bask in the joy of the abundant grace that freely forgave him and covered all his sins in that magnificent act of undeserved grace that reckoned Christ's righteousness to his account. God's forgiving grace was received by Paul when he came trembling and repentant to the Lord of all forgiveness.

The grace of forgiveness

Well into the Middle Ages the study of mathematics was regarded with either suspicion or derision. Abelard, the French philosopher of the twelfth century wrote of it as 'a nefarious [evil] study'. Long before that, in the time of the Roman Empire, the Theodosian Code of AD 394 passed the sentence of death upon all 'mathematicians'—mainly because of their alliance with astrology, fortune telling and divination. As a schoolboy I had different reasons for agreeing with the Emperor Theodosius!

When King David took up the study of maths it was one of the greatest mistakes of his life. 2 Samuel 24 records that he ordered a census of his fighting men, and for that act of arrogance both he and the nation suffered. Almost immediately David owned up to his sin: it seemed to lie like a terrible weight upon him. He vividly expressed the experience of a man under conviction in Psalm 32 when he complained of the heavy hand of God: 'my bones wasted away through my groaning all day long' and 'my strength was dried up as by the heat of summer' (vs 3–4). One thing David was acutely aware of was that the mathematics of God is perfect. He must have felt that if God counted up his sins they would amount to far more than the million and a quarter men he had counted under arms. But David also knew that the happiest man on earth was the one 'whose transgression is forgiven, whose sin is covered … against whom the LORD counts no iniquity' (vs 1–2). Forgiveness is when God stops counting up our sin.

Forgiveness is when

God stops counting

up our sin

Whilst the prophet Hosea warned the nation that God stored up their sins (Hosea 13:12), Job in his painful misery looked forward to death—and beyond it to what he calls his 'renewal'—when he would discover that God was no longer watching over his sin, that his transgressions were 'sealed up in a bag' and covered over for ever (Job 14:14–17). God offered the people exactly this hope when, through Isaiah, he introduced himself: 'I, I am he who blots out your transgressions for my own sake and I will not remember your sins' (Isaiah 43:25). This divine amnesia is underscored through

Jeremiah: 'I will forgive their iniquity, and I will remember their sin no more' (31:34). When sin is forgiven by God it will never be recalled, neither in time nor in eternity.

God adorned his promise of forgiveness with picture after picture to convince his people that it is not a mere passing mood or transient warm feeling, but that forgiveness is final and for ever: He will replace their scarlet sins with the whiteness of snow (Isaiah 1:18), cast their sins behind his back (Isaiah 38:17), sweep them away like a dissolving cloud or mist (Isaiah 44:22), tread them into the ground without trace and cast them into the depths of the sea (Micah 7:19). But of all his pictures, one of the most telling is understood more today than when David first passed it on:

The Lord is merciful and gracious,
slow to anger and abounding in steadfast love.
He will not always chide,
nor will he keep his anger forever.
He does not deal with us according to our sins,
nor repay us according to our iniquities.
For as high as the heavens are above the earth,
so great is his steadfast love towards those who fear
      him;
as far as the east is from the west,
so far does he remove our transgressions from us.
Psalm 103:8–12

When sin is forgiven

by God it will never

be recalled, neither in

time nor in eternity

The earth is not quite round. The equatorial diameter is greater than the polar diameter—in other words, it's a bit fatter than it is tall, by around twenty-seven miles. Whereas we talk about the North Pole and the South Pole—and great explorers like Robert Falcon Scott, Ernest Shackleton and Roald Amundsen have left us their records of these poles—there is no West Pole or East Pole. Our psalmist, knowingly or unknowingly, measured the greatest distance, which is from east to west. Here there are no fixed points; to travel from east to west is endless. That is how far God removes forgiven sin.

Similarly, when David looked up into the sky, if he troubled to count he could see around 4,500 stars on a clear night. What he did not know was that in the great splash of light across the heavens that we call the Milky Way, there could be in excess of thirty thousand million stars. And beyond that? The only certain knowledge that we have added since the time of David almost three thousand years ago is that there is far more universe beyond our furthest probes. For all our science we are no nearer to understanding how high the heavens are above the earth. That also, is how far God removes forgiven sin from us.

In the New Testament the pictures are no less powerful. Paul tells us that God has, 'forgiven us all our trespasses, by cancelling the record of debt that stood against us with its legal demands. This he set aside, nailing it to the cross' (Colossians 2:13–14). That is typical of Paul tumbling over himself with imagery. The phrase 'the record of debt' translates just one word in the Greek (*cheirographon*), and although this is the only use of the word in the New Testament, it was commonplace in the time of Paul. It referred to a certificate of debt written with one's own hand—a promise that in due time the debt would be repaid. Once paid, the bill would be literally crossed out and cancelled. Twenty years after the death of Paul, the governor of Egypt acquitted a prisoner on trial and 'gave orders that the bond be crossed out.' When that was done, the captive was released. Paul could not have chosen a more appropriate picture.

The 'record of debt' that Paul refers to here is not simply the broken law of God, but more particularly the record of our life that we have ourselves written. By our Christ-rejecting sin we had signed our own death warrant. Our own life 'stands against us'—the word refers to an adversary—and we become our own worst enemy; acknowledging a debt that we could not possibly repay, even if we had all eternity to try. This is exactly how Paul felt. In Romans 7:15–19 he records, 'I do not understand my own actions. For I do not do what I want, but I do the very thing I hate … I know that nothing good dwells in me, that is, in my flesh. For I have the desire to do what is right, but not the ability to carry it out. For I do not do the good I want, but the evil I do not want is what I keep on doing.' Yet—amazing grace—God crossed all this out. He cancelled and obliterated the charge sheet.

That language is not too strong, because the simple word 'cancelled' was used of the practice of washing out the writing on a papyrus scroll so that it could be used again. Our grubby and smeared life is washed clean so that God can write with us a new life. The Christian has a brand new recycled life. But how did God do this? He took it out of our way by nailing it to his cross. Only once do we read of the nails of the cross, and that was when Thomas demanded to see the nail prints in his hands as proof of the risen Christ (John 20:25). Paul pictures the nails fixing not his Lord to the cross but Paul's own sin in his Lord to the cross. This death of Christ taking our sin, as we saw in a previous chapter, led to justification. Forgiveness is the experience of justification.

The word 'forgiven' in Colossians 2:13—the verb is *charizomai*—is derived directly from our beautiful noun 'grace' (*charis*), and it means 'to show oneself gracious'. However, in Ephesians 1:7–8 Paul uses an altogether different word: 'In him we have redemption through his blood, the *forgiveness* of our trespasses, according to the riches of his grace, which he lavished upon us, in all wisdom and insight ...' Here 'forgiveness' translates a word meaning to release or set free and it was a common word for the release of prisoners. The vivid picture of the prison doors opened and the captive walking free may be what was in the mind of the apostle—who at the time of writing was *The Christian has a brand new recycled life* under house arrest in Rome! But, once more, the freedom is not due to anything we have done, it is a freedom gained by the blood of Christ— much as Barabbas was released in exchange for the death of the Man whose blood the mob screamed for (Matthew 27:16–26).

But linking 'forgiveness' with 'redemption' is no coincidence for Paul. The word 'redemption' that he uses here is unusual. Redemption was common enough in the first century, but Paul chose a form of the word that occurs ten times in the New Testament and fewer than that in all other known literature of the day. Perhaps he deliberately chose an irregular word to press home a Christian distinctiveness. There is an ongoing debate about whether Paul's use of the word 'redemption' applies chiefly to the slave market, prisoners of war, or to the Jewish practice of redeeming the first-born. The picture of the slave market is that of someone paying the price for a slave and then setting him free—it was known as 'manumission'; if he could save sufficient money, a slave could even buy his own freedom. Prisoners of war were frequently held as a ransom; it was part of the bounty of warfare, and the more prosperous the prisoner, the higher the price. On the other hand the Jews were familiar with their own history of redemption which was very different. The first born, whether human or animal, belonged to the LORD, and it could only be redeemed by the payment of a redemption price (Numbers 18:15–17); a man guilty of manslaughter could similarly redeem his life by a payment (Exodus 21:28–30). But whichever picture is intended, and perhaps the slave market would be chiefly in the mind of the congregation at Ephesus, the picture was certainly one of release from captivity or death as a result of a payment made. In this case Paul is insistent that the payment is nothing less than the blood of Christ.

However deep the dye, however ingrained the stain, however hurt our conscience may be and whatever guilt may plague our mind and soak into our soul, forgiveness by the blood of Christ is full, free and for ever.

However deep the dye, however ingrained the stain, however hurt our conscience may be and whatever guilt may plague our mind and soak into our soul, forgiveness by the blood of Christ is full, free and for ever.

When we know our sins are forgiven, we can be sure that they are blotted out, no longer reckoned against us, sealed up and cast away from God's sight; they are forgotten by God, trodden into the ground, cast into the deepest ocean, removed as endlessly as the equator and as distantly as the infinity of space; the record is removed, the slate wiped clean and all is replaced by the pure whiteness of snow. We are set free from the penalty and imprisonment of sin. And all through the blood of Christ on Calvary.

But there is a condition attached to forgiveness!

The grace of repentance

I am always uneasy when I hear people talk about 'free grace'. I know what they mean, but it can be a very misleading phrase. In two important respects grace for forgiveness is not free at all. First of all, we must never forget that grace is offered to us at a massive cost. The most valuable gift that the human race could ever receive is grace. But grace for us meant hell for Christ. He who was pure in thought, word and action became vile with our sin; he who was the subject of angelic adoration became the object of the Father's anger; he who had enjoyed eternal harmony with his Father endured estrangement on Calvary; he who cast out Satan from heaven became the victim of satanic fury—Calvary was in one terrible sense the hour of the power of *But grace for us meant* darkness (Luke 22:53). He, the sinless Son of God, fell under the onslaught of evil and the *hell for Christ* fearful frown of his Father. That is the cost of free grace. When Paul wrote, 'Christ loved us and gave himself up *for* us a fragrant offering and sacrifice to God' (Ephesians 5:2), that little preposition means 'on behalf of' or 'for the sake of'. It seems hardly possible that such a blighted and cruel death should be a 'fragrant offering'. But that is what 'free grace' means.

However, grace for forgiveness is not free for another reason. Forgiveness never comes alone. There is always a condition attached—conditional forgiveness. But can there be conditional forgiveness without compromising the great theme of free grace? Yes, because the only proper use of the phrase 'free grace' is the grace that chose us in eternity without any reference to our merit—that is the invincible grace we have already considered in chapter seven. From there on grace is both costly and conditional.

The condition attached to the experience of receiving grace is called *repentance*. In the New Testament the word 'repentance' is made up from two words: a preposition plus the noun for 'mind'. Repentance means to change our mind—to turn and return to God. To do this, we own up to our sin of rejecting Christ, hate the sin that sent him to the cross, and return to the God who made us—and all with a loving obedience that is determined to live to please him in the future. Repentance begins in Paul's phrase: 'Christ Jesus came into the world to save sinners, of whom I am the foremost.' That was his unqualified admission of guilt.

Forgiveness and salvation are never offered by God—either to his backsliding people or to a pagan world—without repentance. Repentance is an invariable condition for forgiveness. The Hebrew word translated 'forgive' in the Old Testament comes from a root meaning 'to bear' or 'carry away'. Although it only occurs something over thirty times its meaning is found in many other words, like 'atonement', for example. In a vivid illustration of the word, Joshua warned the people that God would not forgive them unless they turned from their idols and returned to the Lord; only then would he be fully reconciled to them and they to him (Joshua 24:19–27). There could be no forgiveness without a radical change, and when that condition was satisfied, a full and open relationship would be restored.

Repentance is an invariable condition for forgiveness

Again speaking to Israel God promised, 'If my people who are called by my name humble themselves, and pray and seek my face and turn from their wicked ways, then I will hear from heaven and will forgive their sin and heal their land' (2 Chronicles 7:14). The 'if' is a condition attached to restoration. At the time of the exile God commanded, 'Repent, and turn from all your transgressions, lest iniquity be your ruin' (Ezekiel 18:30, see also 14:6). And again just two verses later: '"I have no pleasure in the death of anyone", declares the LORD God; "so turn and live."' Through Jeremiah God urged his people in exile: 'If you return, I will restore you, and you shall stand before me' (Jeremiah 15:19). This is typical of God's approach throughout the Old Testament; the abundant grace of God is obtained only after true repentance.

Perhaps nowhere is this more clearly seen than in the response of Nineveh to the preaching of Jonah; the salvation of that pagan city was conditional upon their true repentance (Jonah 3:1–10). Not only did their actions demonstrate a true sorrow for sin, but the King's command that the people must, 'turn everyone from his evil way' included precisely the word used by God to Israel. The word 'turn' is frequently translated 'repent' in our Bibles, though the Hebrew word *shoob* literally means 'return'. Among all his false teaching, Elihu mixed in some true theology in his poor comfort to Job: 'God opens their ears to instruction and commands that they return from iniquity' (Job 36:10). The last recorded words of Job to his creator are these: 'Therefore I despise myself, and repent in dust and ashes' (42:6). Here Job uses a stronger word (*nawkham*) that means to be sorry or grieved. Only then was everything restored to him.

Not once in the Old Testament did God ever forgive without first demanding repentance. There is a phrase used in the time of Jehoiakim that makes this frighteningly clear. A run of bad kings in Judah had left God with no choice but to bring severe judgement upon the nation. The Babylonians swept across the land in their slaughtering tradition and they were followed by bands of Syrians, Moabites and Ammonites who mopped up all that was left. There was just no let up. But clearly God was waiting for the people to turn, and they did not. There was no sorrow, no repentance, and no change of mind or heart. And then comes the awful phrase: 'The LORD would not pardon' (2 Kings 24:4) or, as another translation has it: 'The LORD was not willing to forgive.' God will never pardon if we do not repent. That is his condition attached.

The same theme is even more evident in the New Testament where the Greek word *metanoeo* means a complete change of mind for the better. John the Baptist came with a straightforward message: 'Repent, for the Kingdom of heaven is at hand' (Matthew 3:2); and he demanded change. In case anyone should suggest that Jesus had a softer message, almost his first words at the commencement of his own ministry were, 'Repent, for the kingdom of heaven is at hand' (Matthew 4:17). And nothing had altered when he sent his disciples to preach: 'So they went out and proclaimed that people should repent' (Mark 6:12).

At Pentecost Peter followed his Master's example, and when the crowd begged to be told what they must do in response to his message he commanded, 'Repent and be baptized every one of you in the name of Jesus Christ for the forgiveness of your sins' (Acts 2:38). It was the same in Peter's next sermon: 'Repent therefore, and turn again, that your sins may be blotted out' (3:19). Here Peter used the word for 'repent' but then added that they must 'turn again'. It is the word *epistrepho* which is the same as the Hebrew *shoob*, but it is in the active form and not the passive, which means not that they must 'be converted' but that they must turn themselves; it is also an imperative—an order!

If we ask where this ability to turn comes from, Peter has his answer ready for that also. On trial in Jerusalem, he insisted that through Christ alone God would 'give repentance to Israel and forgiveness of sins' (Acts 5:31). It was never doubted in the infant church, that repentance itself was a gracious gift from God. The conversion of the household of Cornelius convinced them that to the Gentiles also: 'God has granted repentance that leads to life' (Acts 11:18). Like John the Baptist and Christ himself, the apostolic church believed in a baptism of repentance as a precondition for receiving forgiveness (Acts 19:4; 13:24).

Paul carried forward the same message. When preaching at Athens he uncompromisingly declared, 'God commands all people everywhere to repent, because he has fixed a day on which he will judge the world in righteousness' (Acts 17:30–31). He later reminded the Ephesian elders that his invariable message to both Jews and Greeks was that they must turn to God in repentance and have faith in Jesus Christ (Acts 20:21). Similarly, when on trial in Jerusalem, Paul declared to King Agrippa exactly what his message had always been; everywhere he went it was simply this: '(I declared that) they should repent and turn to God, performing deeds in keeping with their repentance' (Acts 26:20). Notice here that Paul used precisely the same two words that Peter had used in Acts 3:19. Paul was just as consistently insistent in his letters. He reminded the Christians at Rome that the goodness, forbearance and longsuffering of God was 'meant to lead you to repentance' (Romans 2:4). Likewise the believers at Corinth were encouraged not to forget that it is only repentance that can lead to salvation (2 Corinthians 7:9); and Timothy was told that repentance alone leads to the knowledge of the truth (2 Timothy 2:25).

Repentance, like faith itself, is a gift of God. But like faith also, without repentance it is impossible to find forgiveness and reconciliation with God. And without these two, it is impossible to please God, know God, or enjoy God. In other words, repentance is an essential condition for salvation—which is a full restoration of our shattered relationship with God. If repentance itself is a gift of God—which it certainly is—it is no less a condition for the experience of forgiveness and reconciliation. No proper understanding of the Bible can avoid this conclusion.

Three words can never be divorced: repentance, forgiveness and reconciliation. These three can never be separated; you cannot have one without the others, you cannot even have two without the third. All three must be present and they must be present in this order: repentance, forgiveness and reconciliation. This is a vital conclusion, and therefore it is better that we are absolutely sure of it now because the implications we are about to discover may not be agreeable to some—and it is too late to backtrack when we find out that we do not like what we have let ourselves in for! Unfortunately few evangelicals have a proper understanding of forgiveness.

Three words can never be divorced: repentance, forgiveness and reconciliation

Unconditional forgiveness is a low view of forgiveness

One of the most misunderstood words in our society today is the word 'forgive'. And sadly, Christians have allowed the word to be defined by the world rather than by the Bible. You may be surprised to learn that on this subject of forgiveness society, generally speaking, believes in unconditional grace. They probably have never heard the phrase and they have no idea what it means, but they believe it. A few years ago a head teacher, Phillip Lawrence, was knifed by a thug when he went to aid one of his pupils. Some time later his widow was being interviewed on the media and she is reported to have said, 'When Phillip died everyone assumed I had forgiven. I cannot tell you anything about forgiveness.' I was so glad to hear Frances Lawrence say that because she bucked the trend: let me explain what I mean.

In the cruel and violent world in which we live there seems to be plenty of opportunity for Christians to show forgiveness, but not just Christians. After the latest terrorist outrage or senseless drink-drive murder, the public waits for the early response of the bereaved: 'I forgive the people who did this terrible thing.' That is trumpeted as a great example to us all, a great victory. But if they cannot muster the emotional courage to utter those saintly words, society reckons they have failed. Society doesn't say as much, but it has implied it by extolling those who do manage to 'forgive'. Consequently Christians, not wanting to be morally wrong-footed by an unbelieving world on the subject of forgiveness of all subjects, have convinced themselves that a public announcement of forgiveness is the right thing to do.

In January 1999, Stewart Staines and his two sons aged 8 and 10, were burnt to death as they slept in their jeep in Manaharpur, India. He and his wife Gladys had been working among leprosy sufferers. Gladys immediately decided to stay on with her thirteen year-old daughter. But the other thing she did immediately was to forgive her husband's killers, and she claimed that it was, 'A spontaneous act'. She went on to say that it took away the bitterness from her heart. That was very commendable, and I do not doubt at all that it took away the bitterness from her heart. I have no criticism of Gladys Staines. But not all can rise to that, and my question is, did she have to forgive? Was she under an obligation to forgive? Was she even right to forgive? Was it essentially Christian for her to forgive? I will set out this subject in five statements.

First. God in Christ is our pattern for all responses in life

This should hardly require proof for the Christian. One great purpose of the incarnation was that we could more easily focus upon what God is like and what he expects of us. Christ 'suffered for you, leaving you an example so that you should follow in his steps' (1 Peter 2:21). Christ is always our example. He is our model in holiness, service and priorities and he must therefore be our model in this whole question of forgiveness as well. When the apostle wrote about the relationship between husbands and wives he instructed husbands to love their wives: 'as Christ loved the church' (Ephesians 5:25). In the pattern of our forgiving others it can be no different, we are to forgive: 'as God in Christ forgave you' (Ephesians 4:32 and Colossians 3:13). This can only mean that in every respect, the way we are to forgive is to be modelled on the forgiveness we receive from God in Christ.

Secondly. In Scripture God never forgives unconditionally

As we have already seen, God's forgiveness is dependent upon repentance. Certainly this is a repentance that is won from us by the invincible grace of God, but it is nevertheless a repentance that is a condition if we are to receive God's grace in forgiveness. The forgiveness that follows repentance is full, unreserved and eternal. Throughout the Old Testament and into the New Testament, the message of God through the prophets, John the Baptist, our Lord himself, and the apostles was consistently to call for repentance as a condition of receiving forgiveness. This fact is crucial to the whole debate. If God is our pattern, and that pattern is seen most clearly in Christ, then we must ask why we are expecting mere men and women to forgive those who sin against them regardless of the offender's response. God himself never forgives in this way.

This is a significant pastoral issue. When a man's child is killed by a drunk driver or by the deliberate act of a terrorist we are asking him to do what we expect of no one else. Society does not forgive, they say to the police: 'Go and find the murderers'—that is not forgiveness. The police set out to hunt down the killers—that is not forgiveness either. And, as we saw earlier, God does not forgive; he demands repentance first. So, with society, the law enforcers and God himself standing aside, we ask the emotionally bruised to muster with superhuman courage the devout words: 'I forgive'.

Thirdly. In Scripture forgiveness always involves reconciliation

In his popular book *Total Forgiveness*, R T Kendall claims that on our part there must be, 'Total forgiveness even when there is not a restoration of relationship. One must totally forgive those who will not be reconciled.' The problem with this statement is that we must ask, where in the Bible did

God ever forgive like this? Never did God forgive and still allow those forgiven to remain his enemy.

Those who refuse to repent do not receive forgiveness or reconciliation with God. God may not deal with them as their sins deserve but that is not forgiveness—it is the grace of mercy or compassion. Forgiveness and mercy must never be confused. Every day the atheist enjoys the benefits of health and strength, beauty and pleasure; this is all part of God's mercy—his universal grace as we saw in chapter two. But that is not forgiveness. The little ditty found in some gardens well expresses this confusion:

> The kiss of the sun for pardon;
> The song of the birds for mirth.
> One is nearer God's heart in a garden
> Than anywhere else on earth.

The kiss of the sun and the song of the birds is God's universal grace of mercy, but it is not pardon for sins; it is not forgiveness. No one is reconciled to God through a good day's gardening.

To overlook the essential element of reconciliation in forgiveness denies all that this word forgiveness means in the Bible. This truth is perhaps best seen in a passage that is so often used to support forgiveness regardless of response. In Matthew 18 Peter complains to our Lord about his brother and asks how often he must forgive him; our Lord's reply is often held up to us as a clear lesson of forgiveness without regard to reconciliation. But this entirely overlooks the context of Peter's question. Peter did not ask his question 'out of the blue'. His question and our Lord's answer in Matthew 18:21–35 immediately follows Jesus' teaching on what to do when 'your brother sins against you' (vs 15–17). Here our Lord requires us to 'go and tell him his fault, between you and him alone', and if he 'listens to you' then you have won him over. That 'listening' must imply at the very least an admission of guilt, because if he refuses to hear what is being said, the offended brother must report him to the church; if he refuses to listen to the church then he must be treated 'as a Gentile and a tax-collector' (v 17). Whatever that means it does not sound much like forgiveness!

At this point in the narrative Peter came up with his question: 'Lord, how often will my brother sin against me, and I forgive him? As many as seven times?' The parable that our Lord told in response to Peter's question clearly portrays a debtor who pleads for compassion (vs 23–35). On another occasion Jesus made this very clear when he repeated the same teaching and added, 'If your brother sins, rebuke him, *and if he repents, forgive him, and if he sins against you seven times in a day, and turns to you seven times, saying, "I repent",* you must forgive him' (Luke 17:3–4). It could hardly be clearer that Jesus is not teaching unconditional forgiveness. Our Lord is expecting reconciliation: but only on the back of repentance by the offender and forgiveness by the offended— any number of times. This is our pattern.

It is surely against the background of this clear teaching that Matthew 6:14–15 must be interpreted, 'If you forgive others their trespasses, your heavenly Father will also forgive you, but if you do not forgive others their trespasses, neither will your Father forgive your trespasses.' As God will always and only forgive us when we repent, so we *must* forgive others when they repent. Similarly the phrase in the Lord's prayer: 'Forgive us our debts as we also have forgiven our debtors' (Matthew 6:12) must be understood in the same way; the very offering of this prayer implies an admission of guilt and a sorrow for it.

Never did God forgive and still allow those forgiven to remain his enemy

But someone may suggest that the teaching in Matthew 18 and Luke 17 refers to the domestic quarrels in a family or a church and can hardly be extended to the terrorist atrocity or gang rape. As a matter of fact there would be even more reason to forgive my unrepentant brother than the unrepentant murderer. But where will we turn to find an example of forgiveness in those more extreme circumstances? Some find it in the story of Joseph and his forgiveness of the heartless brothers who all but murdered him when they sold him into slavery. The story of their return to Joseph in the land of Egypt is told in Genesis 43 to 50, and the closing order of events is very instructive.

Chapter 8

When Joseph first realised who these travellers from the distant land of Canaan were, we are not told that he forgave them—and it is not for us to implant our reconstruction into the mind of Joseph. But he did show them mercy. In fact he proceeded to test their integrity before he revealed his identity to them. And even when at last he told them that he was their brother, there is still no word of forgiveness in the biblical text. Forgiveness came much later in the story. It is not until Genesis 50:16–17, after the death of their father, that the brothers fully own up to the enormity of their sin and plead for forgiveness (v 17). At this point Joseph was committed to forgive, and not before. However, it is evident from the whole story that Joseph had long before divested himself of any bitterness and anger at his brothers' action, so that when they turned up on his doorstep many years after their murderous treatment of him, Joseph could instantly show them mercy. That distinction between mercy and forgiveness must never be overlooked or else we downgrade the word forgiveness.

Fourthly. In Scripture forgiveness always implies repentance as a condition and reconciliation as a consequence
This point is, of course, proven by the previous two. If repentance is understood as a hatred and rejection of sin, and if forgiveness is understood in the vigorous way that we have seen earlier in this chapter, then reconciliation between the two parties follows inevitably. It always does when God forgives us, and we cannot assume any different meaning to the three words—repentance, forgiveness and reconciliation—when *we* are called upon to forgive. God, in Christ, is our pattern. But where did the Father or the Son ever forgive without any interest in repentance, a changed life or reconciliation? He said to the woman found in the act of adultery, 'I do not condemn you', but this was followed by an insistence upon a repentant life: 'Go and stop your life of sin.'

There is a striking pastoral illustration of this in Paul's letters to the Corinthians. In 1 Corinthians 5 Paul refers to a serious moral issue in the church that the leaders had apparently overlooked; an issue that even the pagans would not tolerate: 'a man has his father's wife' (v 1). The apostle demanded rigorous discipline: 'Deliver this man to Satan … Purge the evil person from among you' (vs 5, 13). From 2 Corinthians 2:5–11 it would appear that this action had its hoped-for effect and the man repented of his sin, because Paul refers to his 'excessive sorrow' (v 7). The issue now was how should the Christians respond to him? There can be no doubt at all. However grave his wrongdoing and however serious the scandal, there could now be only one response from the church: 'For such a one, this punishment by the majority is enough, so you should rather turn to forgive and comfort him, or he may be overwhelmed by excessive sorrow. So I beg you to reaffirm your love for him' (vs 6–8). This love would be displayed in wholehearted *forgiveness*—a word that Paul uses three times in verse 10— and that would mean full reconciliation. Significantly there was also repentance on the part of the church for tolerating the sin in the first place; and their repentance is described in 2 Corinthians 7:9–13.

Where there is repentance on the part of the offender there must always be willingness on the part of the offended to forgive and be reconciled. And we have already seen just how bountiful and extensive the forgiveness will be if it is a reflection of God's forgiveness. This is exactly what our Lord taught Peter in Matthew 18:15–35 in the impossible 'seventy times seven'. Both in the teaching (vs 15–20) and the illustration (vs 23–35) repentance was essential in order to obtain forgiveness. Full forgiveness and reconciliation in such a case cannot be doubted. It may not always be easy, but it is essential; it is a reflection of the unlimited grace of God. True repentance on the part of the offender must be immediately and unconditionally followed by free, full and for ever forgiveness by the offended; it must reflect the forgiveness of God which will lead to total reconciliation.

Where there is repentance on the part of the offender there must always be willingness on the part of the offended to forgive and be reconciled

Fifthly. Therefore, forgiveness is not appropriate where there is no repentance—but something more valuable must take its place

If I do not have to forgive where there is no repentance, do I have to stay bitter and resentful with a poisoned heart like the Warsaw ghetto leader who said, when he had seen such brutality by the Nazi regime, 'If you were to lick my heart it would poison you'? Is that how we are to remain? Of course not! C S Lewis wisely commented that: 'Everyone says that forgiveness is a lovely idea until he has something to forgive.' Forgiveness is not always easy or pleasant, but it is made so much more easy and pleasant when the condition is fulfilled and the prize is reconciliation. And when the condition is met, the injured party is under a divine obligation to forgive in exactly the same way that God in Christ has forgiven us—joyfully, wholeheartedly and entirely.

If I do not have to forgive where there is no repentance, do I have to stay bitter and resentful with a poisoned heart?

Corrie ten Boom, the Jewish Christian who spent much of the war in a concentration camp wrote, 'You never so touch the ocean of God's love as when you forgive and love your enemies.' And she should know. Years after the war Corrie met one of her prison guards. At the close of a meeting the man approached her: 'You mentioned Ravensbruck in your talk', he began, 'I was a guard there; but since that time I have become a Christian. I know that God has forgiven me for the cruel things I did there, but I would like to hear it from your lips as well. Fraulein, will you forgive me?' Corrie recognised him at once as one of the most cruel guards in that terrible camp. She hesitated as all the vivid memories of those dark days leading to her sister's death flooded back into her mind and she admitted, 'I stood there with the coldness clutching my heart.' Then, woodenly, mechanically, she put out her hand and grasped his, 'I forgive you, brother. With all my heart.' That is precisely what our Lord wanted her to do; that is exactly what he does when we come in repentance and faith. That is abundant, forgiving grace. At that moment—confronted with the repentance of the prison guard—Corrie ten Boom *had* to forgive. But she did not have to forgive until her prison guard was repentant.

In place of forgiveness

I am aware that by now some are angry and others are smug. The angry readers believe that I am allowing hurt and wronged people to remain bitter and resentful; and the smug readers are pleased to believe that they can go on feeling just like that. Both are wrong.

So, when there is no sorrow or repentance on the part of my enemy—when they do not want reconciliation and cannot see that they have done anything wrong—what does God expect of me then? To exercise a massive effort of will and forgive may help *me*, but it actually does nothing for the offender. He may continue to scoff at God and revel in the misery he has caused. To forgive is meaningless to him. It is as meaningless as the vicarious repentance that is so popular by well-meaning people today who repent on behalf of the crimes committed during the Crusades against the Moslems in the eleventh and thirteenth centuries, by the Conquistadors against the South American Indians in the sixteenth century, by the British Empire against its colonies in the nineteenth century, by the whites against blacks from the eighteenth to twentieth centuries and by men against women from time immemorial. To repent on behalf of those who may never have been sorry for what they did, and to forgive those who are still not sorry for what they are doing, are pleasant little gestures but they are without meaning and, worse still, they devalue the words repentance, forgiveness and reconciliation.

What then should be our response? Remember, the Lord is our pattern in this subject as in all things. So what do we learn from him? When he looked out over the crowds, we are never once told that he forgave them; but what we are told is that he was moved with 'compassion' for them (Matthew 9:36; 14:14; 15:32). That is a very strong word because it refers to him being moved with all his inner being. The result of this compassion was that he healed their sick or fed them, as the occasion demanded. That was mercy. This is exactly the distinction that we have already made. Interestingly, in that parable of the unforgiving servant recorded in Matthew 18, the word 'pity' is used in v 27, but the result in v 33 is described as 'mercy'; some English translations have 'compassion' in both verses, but this is not accurate because two distinct words are used. That gives us the answer we are looking for. Our response must be one of compassion or pity and this will lead to mercy. Mercy is compassion in action. The Oxford English Dictionary defines *compassion* as 'pity inclining one to help or be merciful', and it defines *mercy* as 'the quality of compassion'.

This pattern is set for us so beautifully in the story of Christ at the cross in Luke 23:33–34. Throughout his ministry, when he was spitefully abused—verbally and physically—never once do we read of him forgiving his enemies. When Dr Kendall in his book pleads for unconditional forgiveness, even he recognises that at the cross Jesus did not say 'I forgive you', and he explains that omission in this way: 'Such words would have been misinterpreted and wasted. It would also have been casting his pearls before pigs' (Matthew 7:6). That is a wise understanding, but such an admission undermines his whole argument that there should be forgiveness without repentance. It is precisely for this reason that we are not expected to forgive the unrepentant terrorist—or brother. To forgive those who do not want to be forgiven and who are unconcerned about reconciliation, devalues the meaning of 'forgiveness' and throws pearls before pigs.

Our response must be one of compassion or pity and this will lead to mercy

So, if our Lord did not forgive, what did do? He prayed for them. And he could only do that if he had a heart of compassion. That is our model when we are sinned against and when repentance is entirely lacking. To pray for our enemies is far more valuable both to us and certainly to them than to announce a public forgiveness. This is exactly what our Lord taught his disciples. He did not promise, 'Blessed are those who forgive' but 'Blessed are the merciful' (Matthew 5:7). In the same way—though this fact may be very surprising to some—the Bible nowhere commands us to 'Forgive your enemies'. Our Lord commanded his disciples to 'love your enemies and pray for those who persecute you' (Matthew 5:44) and 'Love your enemies, do good to those who hate you ... pray for those who abuse you' (Luke 6:27–28 and 35–36). So much is said about loving and doing good to our enemies, but not a single word about forgiving them. Is this an oversight or what?

Significantly, in 1 Corinthians 13—a whole chapter devoted to Christian love—the word forgiveness does not occur once. In the long list of qualities of true Christian love: patience, kindness, humility, selflessness, endurance, not seeking revenge, or rejoicing in the calamity of the wrongdoer, or harbouring a grudge—nothing is said about forgiveness. This absence is not because all these virtues are the inevitable result of forgiveness but because they must be present even if the conditions for forgiveness are not met. According to Paul they reflect the character of God: 'Do you presume upon the riches of his kindness and forbearance and patience, not knowing that God's kindness is meant to lead you to repentance?' (Romans 2:4). And that makes it all very clear. Just as God's compassion and mercy are intended to lead *us* to repentance for forgiveness, so our compassion and mercy on those who sin against us are intended to lead *them* to repentance. The words 'love' and 'compassion' are much greater words than 'forgiveness', because that is where forgiveness begins.

To pray for our enemies is far more valuable both to us and certainly to them than to announce a public forgiveness

It was this very compassion in the Father that formed the foundation of our Lord's expectation that his disciples would learn to love their enemies and show mercy, however hard that would be. They must be prepared to love, do good and lend, even when they could expect nothing in return; in this way they would show themselves to be 'sons of the Most High' (Luke 6:27–35). The reason for this is that God himself is, 'kind to the ungrateful and the evil'. They must be merciful: 'Even as your Father is merciful' (vs 35–36). Again, there is nothing here about forgiveness but much about kindness, mercy and compassion.

The more I read about and discuss this question of forgiveness in its current debate, the more I realise that today, the big reason to forgive is because it makes the victim, and the rest of us, feel better. But that surely should not be the object of forgiveness. Does God forgive repentant sinners in order that *he* might feel better? The object of forgiveness is to make the *sinner* better, and he never will be better until he repents. I may say, 'I forgive you' with a smile on my face and a feeling of spiritual superiority because I have risen to the saintly height of being able to forgive in spite of the dastardly deed done against me. But there is something far better than that.

Compassion sheds tears. Healing for the Christian comes not from forgiving those who have sinned against you, but by trusting in the wisdom and the love of God, humbly accepting his wise ways, and yearning with a compassion that leads to prayer, for the forgiveness by God of those who have wronged you. If we can learn anything from the psalmist on this subject it is that not once did he forgive his enemies; on the contrary, he left them to the mercy or judgement of God (for example Psalm 1:5–6; 6:8–10; 7:6). There is still such a thing as divine retribution, and it is remarkably odd to imagine that I am required to forgive someone for an offence for which God promises them only judgement. Do I really have to forgive those whom God himself will not forgive?

So, the opposite of forgiving is not bearing a grudge, seeking revenge, remaining bitter, nursing a hatred or storing up a list of wrongs done. It is asking for a compassionate heart that pities those who have been so cruel; a compassion that leads to prayer, and action that leads to their repentance so that I may forgive them. As the proverb reminds us: 'Hatred stirs up strife, but love covers all offences' (Proverbs 10:12).

At the cross our Lord's prayer, 'Father, forgive them, for they know not what they do' (Luke 23:34) was probably not for the crowds that bayed for his blood, but specifically for the centurion and his cohort who hammered the nails into our Lord's hands and feet and then cast lots for his clothes. If this is so, and if his prayer was for the Father to bring them to repentance that they might know forgiveness, then we can expect to meet them in heaven. According to Peter this is the pattern that our Lord set us: 'When they hurled their insults at him he did not retaliate. When he suffered he made no threat, instead he entrusted himself to him who judges justly' (1 Peter 2:23 *New International Version*). Stephen, at his own martyrdom, followed his Master's example almost to the letter when he prayed, 'Lord, do not hold this sin against them' (Acts 7:60). It was not for Stephen to forgive them; he knew that was not his prerogative, but he offered a final compassionate prayer for those who crushed his skull. Forgiveness is not the same as asking God to forgive those who have wronged us. That is an expression of compassion and mercy, not forgiveness itself.

Do I really have to forgive those whom God himself will not forgive?

God's grace is undeserved, unending, unlimited, invincible and eternal—but not unconditional. 'Repentance' is our part, and to miss this is to misunderstand the character of God, the nature of true conversion, and completely to misread what forgiveness is; and this in turn places a burden on people that should never be there. Repentance starts only when I am able to say with a full heart and with tears in my eyes: 'Christ Jesus came into the world to save sinners of whom I am the foremost.' And then abundant grace and unlimited forgiveness is found in the cross of Christ, and it is ours for free, for good, and for ever.

NOT WHAT THESE HANDS HAVE DONE
can save this guilty soul,
and nothing that this flesh has borne
can make my spirit whole.

2 Not what I feel or do
can give me peace with God;
not all my prayers or sighs or tears
can bear my awful load.

3 Your work alone, O Christ,
can ease this weight of sin;
your blood alone, O Lamb of God,
can give me peace within.

4 Your love to me, O God,
not mine, O Lord, to you,
can rid me of this deep unrest
and all my heart renew.

5 Your grace alone, O God,
speaks pardoning love to me;
your power alone, O Son of God,
can set my spirit free.

6 I bless the Christ of God,
I rest on love divine,
and with unfaltering lip and heart
I call this Saviour mine.

HORATIUS BONAR 1808–89
Praise! 701 © in this version Praise Trust

Eternal grace

'Now may our Lord Jesus Christ himself, and God our Father, who loved us and gave us eternal comfort and good hope through his grace, comfort your hearts and establish them in every good work and word'
2 Thessalonians 2:16

The church at Thessalonica made Paul's heart sing. With all the problems and pressures of the first century world and the tragic failure of many young Christian communities, this was one church that Paul had constant cause to be grateful for. Partly he was grateful to God for their decisive conversion. All the churches were talking about how the Thessalonians had turned to God from their idols (1 Thessalonians 1:8–9), and how they had immediately recognised the authority of the gospel not as the words of men but as the word of God (2:13). These were certainly marks of true conversion. But Paul was grateful also for their hard work which he refers to as their 'work of faith and labour of love' (1 Thessalonians 1:3). Hardworking Christians are always an encouragement to their leaders. He was also grateful to God for their beautiful relationship together. Paul knew that the 'love of every one of you for one another is increasing' (2 Thessalonians 1:3); it was a love that spilled over to all throughout Macedonia, and Paul had experienced it himself (1 Thessalonians 4:9 and 3:6). Equally, Paul was glad because of their endurance in suffering. He could tell them that he boasts about them among all the churches because of their: 'Steadfastness and faith in all your persecutions and in the afflictions that you are enduring' (2 Thessalonians 1:4).

But there was something more that encouraged Paul and which probably underlined all else. It was their 'steadfastness of hope' that he refers to in 1 Thessalonians 1:3. And it is that very thing that is explained more fully here in 2 Thessalonians 2:16–17. As in all his letters, Paul is very specific in his prayer here in vs 16–17. There was nothing vague about Paul's praying for the churches. He knew precisely what he wanted God to do for them and he went directly to it. He prays that the Father and the Son will *comfort* their hearts and *establish* them in every good work and word. Notice carefully what Paul says here; there is no sloppy thinking with Paul. He is always very specific in what he writes because he knows that these young Christians will pick it up and take it as truth. Paul only prayed for things that may or may not happen—he never prayed for that which is a certainty. That would be both unnecessary and unbelieving. So, when Paul prayed that God would comfort and establish them in every good work and word, it is because he knew only too well that you can be a Christian and not experience and enjoy those two things.

Paul only prayed for things that may or may not happen—he never prayed for that which is a certainty

There is a world of difference between the *reality* of something and the *enjoyment* of it. There have been and there still are some very rich people in this world. They have all that money can buy and all the money to buy more—but many of them are not happy. They are rich, but they gain no pleasure in their wealth. Sometimes they live miserably fearful lives. One of the saddest examples of this was Howard Hughes. When Hughes died on Sunday 4 April 1976 at 1.27 pm, he left behind an estate worth an estimated $2.3 billion. But for all his wealth and power, he lived his closing years, as one reporter described it: 'a sunless, joyless, half lunatic life … a virtual prisoner walled in by his own crippling fears and weaknesses.' That was sadly too true. Hooked on heroin, distrusting everyone, and with a pathological fear of contact with the world of germs, Hughes died miserable and alone—yet the boss of an empire more wealthy than many African states. You see the difference between the reality and the enjoyment of the reality?

Many Christians are exactly like Howard Hughes. You say, 'I don't know any Christians who are *that* wealthy.' Yes you do. Every Christian is infinitely more wealthy than Howard Hughes ever was—or ever will be. Notice carefully that Paul does not pray that the Thessalonians might *have* eternal love, comfort and good hope. He knows very well that, as true Christians, they each have all that. But what he prays for is that they may be *comforted and established* in those three things.

Let's be sure that we understand what those three things are:

Every Christian is loved by the Lord Jesus Christ himself and God our Father

That is not just *how* we came to salvation, it is the reason *why* we came to salvation. That was a love that was both eternal and invincible. I mean by that, it was a love that not only chose us to be saved—and Paul refers to that in v 13—but his love conquered our rebellion when he called us through the gospel (v 14). That's invincible grace. In the distant corridors of eternity, the Father and the Son and the Spirit—all three are here in vs 13 and 14—planned your salvation. What an incredible privilege. What a glorious security that should give us. Don't argue about it, enjoy it!

If you want to know the measure of God's love, you will find it in these words: 'God so loved the world that he gave his only Son ...' (John 3:16). If a Christian ever doubts God's love or wonders whether they really matter to God; or if they ever question their personal value in the scheme of eternity and infinity and among the billions of people who have already lived on this tiny planet Earth, then they have only to look again at that cross on the hill Golgotha on which the great Prince of Glory died, and at the same time recall, 'The son of God, *loved me* and gave himself *for me*' (Galatians 2:20). Could God express his love any more powerfully than that?

Every husband wants to be loved by his wife, and every wife by her husband; every child wants to be loved by their parents and every parent wants to be loved by their child. And good families find a thousand ways to express their love to each other. The privilege of every Christian is that they are loved by Christ. It is our privilege if we are trusting Christ alone for salvation. We don't have to pray for it, long for it or hope for it. To be loved by Christ is our most prized possession because it is our most valuable possession—it is beyond price. It is worth more than all the worldly wealth of all the earthly billionaires together. But the question is, do I enjoy it? That is what Paul is praying for here.

Every Christian also has eternal comfort

The *Oxford English Dictionary* defines 'comfort' as 'relief in affliction', and that fits quite well the word that Paul uses here in 2 Thessalonians 2:16, though the word 'encouragement' found in some translations might be better. Actually the word is from the noun *parakletos*. It was a strong word used largely, though not exclusively, of tribunals and law courts. It is made up from two Greek words that together mean: 'called to the side'. For the Greeks, the *paraklete* was the one who accompanied the accused person to the tribunal and supported him by testifying and interceding on his behalf. He was their relief in affliction and was something equivalent to our barrister today. It was quite natural therefore, that the Jews should use the same word in their synagogue worship to refer to the daily sacrifice that secures divine forgiveness; it became their advocate to pacify the anger of God against their sin.

To be loved by Christ is our most prized possession because it is our most valuable possession—it is beyond price

That is exactly the word we would expect to be used of Jesus, who stands before God the Father on our behalf and meets the just demands of God's holy anger against our sin. So, we are not surprised to find that John used the word in just this way when he refers to our 'advocate with the Father, Jesus Christ the righteous' (1 John 2:1). The word 'advocate' is this same word *parakletos*. Our eternal comfort and encouragement is that Christ is in heaven for ever as a perpetual reminder to the Father that everything necessary for our salvation has been done. In fact *he himself* is our eternal comfort, our relief in affliction and our advocate with the Father. Christ is our barrister who wins every case that he presents to the supreme Judge of the whole earth; he has never lost a case yet—and he never will. Paul uses another, though similar word when writing to Timothy: 'There is only one mediator (an arbiter or surety) between God and men, the man Christ Jesus' (1 Timothy 2:5).

When we sin, what will we do? Will we allow the devil to accuse us or will we, in the words of that well-loved hymn by Charitie Bancroft: 'look to heaven and see him there, who made an end of all my sin'? He is our eternal advocate. In non-legal jargon, he is our backer, our sponsor, our supporter; and with Jesus Christ at our side we just cannot lose—not ever. Only once did the Father turn his face away from his Son, when Christ hung on the cross guilty with our sin and rebellion and in that hour of terrible abandonment cried out: 'My God, my God, why have you forsaken me?' But he will never reject his Son again. Our security lies in the fact that Christ is our perfect and eternal advocate with the Father.

However, what is of particular interest to us is the fact that four times in John's Gospel the same word *parakletos* is used of the Holy Spirit: John 14:16, 26; 15:26; 16:7. Since it is such an appropriate word to use of Christ as our advocate with the Father, it may seem strange to apply it to the Spirit. But the Holy Spirit can also be said to be an advocate. Jesus himself tells us that the Spirit, as our *parakletos,* has come 'to convict the world concerning sin and righteousness and judgement' (John 16:8). Lord Hailsham died on Sunday 7 October 2001. He had been a leading lawyer in England for half a century and had served under six Prime Ministers. Not long before his death he commented, 'I hope, when I stand before my Maker, that I shall have sufficient skill to plead guilty and cast myself on the mercy of the court.' Only the Spirit can make a man wise enough in this life to realise

As an honest attorney the Holy Spirit persuades us that our case is hopeless, ... and that the course of wisdom is to cast ourselves wholly upon the mercy of the court

that his only hope is to cast himself wholly upon the mercy of God and discover in Christ complete salvation. In other words, like a representative of the law, the work of the Spirit is to convict the guilty of their sin and its terrible consequences by convincing them of the nature of true righteousness and the fearful judgement of God. As an honest attorney the Holy Spirit persuades us that our case is hopeless, that we have nothing to plead in our defence, and that the course of wisdom is to cast ourselves wholly upon the mercy of the court. He is the King's Counsellor.

But the Spirit does more than this as our advocate. He first brings us to that condition where we know our desperate need of Christ and forgiveness, but we are so unfamiliar with the language of prayer that we often cannot find the words to offer to God. It is at this point that the King's Counsellor tells us just what to say—or how to say it: 'The Spirit helps us in our weakness. For we do not know what to pray for as we ought, but the Spirit himself intercedes for us with groanings too deep for words' (Romans 8:26). These are not his groans, but ours. It is the Spirit breaking our spirit until we cry, desperately and at times incomprehensibly: 'Oh God!' These are some of the most profound prayers we will ever utter. Our King's attorney has persuaded us to cast ourselves entirely at the mercy of God, and the King himself stands there to present our case to the Father with his own guarantee of the secure outcome. Those are two powerful advocates.

That is my privilege as a Christian. I do not have to pray for this. It is unquestionably, undeniably and eternally mine. That is something that, sadly, Howard Hughes knew nothing about, in spite of all his vast financial empire. But do I live in the happy enjoyment of it?

Every Christian also has a 'good hope'
This can only be the expectation of heaven based upon the sure foundation of the reliable promises of a completely reliable God. 'Good hope' is about the most minimal way Paul ever described heaven. But what a hope! When this earthly, perishable, painful, life is over, Christians will be forever like their Saviour for they will see him face to face and the mortal will be swallowed up in immortality. There will be joy and peace and an appreciation of God's grace and all his created beauty in a way

unimaginable here. And the promise of that for every true Christian is unconditional and is guaranteed by the character of God himself. If that is not wealth, what is? Riches that far surpass the total of all the wealth that the entire history of this world has ever known. But are we enjoying the expectation of that now?

Those three things: God's love, God's eternal advocates in Christ and the Spirit, and God's good hope, are all certainties for the Christian. We need not pray for what we already have. The Thessalonians entered into the reality of all that the very moment they were converted. And so does every Christian. This is why there is no need to pray for those things. And notice that they all came through grace (v 16). That is the whole point. We deserved nothing but received everything.

So what *does* Paul pray for? He prays that God would help this young church to experience the 'comfort' of those three great truths and therefore 'establish' them in all that they do and say for Christ (v 17). The word 'establish' is used of our Lord himself when: 'He *set* his face to go to Jerusalem' (Luke 9:51). Some translations have 'steadfastly set', and that well emphasises the idea of a clear and definite purpose.

But what is particularly interesting is the word 'comfort'. It is the verb from our noun *parakletos*—comforter, encourager or advocate! In other words, Paul is praying that God will help these young Christians to experience the reality of those three great facts—God's love, God's eternal advocacy and God's good hope—in such a way that in any and every situation those three eternal facts will themselves act as advocates, reassuring them that they are safe in Jesus, and thus making them stable, strong and steadfast. Comfort is sometimes offered with

God's love, God's

eternal advocates in

Christ and the Spirit,

and God's good hope,

are all certainties for

the Christian. We

need not pray for

what we already have

empty or even deceiving words and assurances; in bereavement; too many false comforters are ready to offer vacant hope in vain words. But there is nothing empty or vain in the reassurance that comes from God's love, God's eternal advocates and God's good hope.

Just as the great work of Jesus was to die on Calvary so that he could stand beside us at the tribunal and, as our advocate, present our cause as his own and so assure us of acquittal, so one great work of the Spirit is to remind us of that powerful advocate. And this, together with the knowledge of God's love for us and our ultimate good hope of heaven, will provide all the relief we need in affliction. It is an incredible privilege to know that grace is eternal, and a great joy to live in the light of it—and what strength to work in the confidence of it!

These young Christians in Thessalonica urgently needed to be reassured of all this. Paul had just finished writing to them about the Man of Lawlessness who, with his power and false signs and wonders, and with his wicked deception, will make life very hard for those who believe in Jesus (2 Thessalonians 2:1–12). I doubt whether the Thessalonian Christians speculated or argued about who this Man of Lawlessness was or when he would come or how they would recognise him. They just knew that they must be ready for him—whoever and whenever—and the best way they could be ready was to be living in the daily enjoyment of the certainties of their Christian faith. In other words: to be happy in the reality of eternal grace. But not all either believe or enjoy this great truth that grace is eternal, and that is why Paul prays as he does.

There are some whose theology of human effort will not allow them to believe in eternal grace

They believe that it is not possible to have assurance, and they conclude that only the proud and self-confident will express certainty in ultimate salvation. This is true of all the cults as well as the Roman Church. We should not be surprised at this because for those who believe that salvation, one way or another, depends significantly upon human action or endeavour then I agree it would be blatant arrogance to claim that we are sure of a place in heaven. Who, on earth, could ever be *that* certain? Who, on earth, has ever lived *that* consistently and cleanly?

John Newton once wrote against this theology of self-effort in what was for him an unusual understatement: 'To have nothing to trust to for our continuance in well-doing, but our own feeble efforts, our partial diligence and short-sighted care, must surely be distressing.' But for those who believe that we are saved by grace through faith and that this is not our own doing but it is the gift of God, not a result of works, so that no one may boast (Ephesians 2:8), it is the most sincere act of humility to lay claim to eternal grace. Everyone has to decide whether they will try to earn their way to heaven and live with the uncertainty of knowing whether or not they have ever gained sufficient merit, or whether they will accept the reality that they can never gain heaven by merit and that faith in Christ alone is the only hope.

It is the most sincere act of humility to lay claim to eternal grace

In 1788 Newton was asked to give evidence against the slave trade before the Privy Council in the British Parliament. Few men knew that miserable trade better than Newton since he had been a trader himself for nearly ten years. On that day he surveyed his life and his salvation and wrote, 'O Lord, it is all thy doing; to thee be also the praise. To me belongs the shame and confusion of face, for I am a poor vile creature to this hour.' A man like that clearly was not relying upon his own efforts to provide him with eternal comfort! His only confidence was in the eternal love of God, his advocate in Jesus Christ, and the promise of a good hope for the future.

There are some whose theology lays all the stress upon their own perseverance

They do not trust in any human merit or effort for salvation; for that they rely upon Christ alone. However, they believe that it is possible for us to lose our salvation. This was the theology of John Wesley, the founder of Methodism. What this means is that whilst I may have complete assurance of salvation at the moment—because I am trusting wholly and only in the death of Christ for my forgiveness—I cannot be sure that I will not lose my faith tomorrow and fall away from grace. There cannot be any 'eternal comfort' for me. Life is a constant round of watching, waiting and striving for fear that I may finally lose my salvation. Of course the weakness here is discovered in the whole doctrine of beginnings: if I come into my faith largely through my own effort, so I may go out again in the same way.

That may be a strong doctrine to encourage my diligence as a Christian, but it is no comfort when I fall. As a young teenage Christian no one had told me that salvation once gained could not be lost or, which is more likely, if they had I wasn't listening; as a consequence, whenever I sinned I would come back to God and pray, 'Lord, if I have never been a Christian before, I want to become one now.' My intentions were sincere but my theology was poor. It was good that I really hated my sin, but it was hardly the way to progress in my Christian life: every time I sinned I felt I had to start all over again.

Our Lord promised, 'The one who endures to the end will be saved' (Matthew 10:22), but that is to be taken as an encouragement to keep on, rather than as a warning against falling away from eternal grace. *Those who have received eternal grace will endure to the end* grace. Those who have received eternal grace *will* endure to the end. After all, it was the same Lord who promised, 'I give them eternal life, and they will never perish, and no one will snatch them out of my hand. My Father, who has given them to me, is greater than all, and no one is able to snatch them out of the Father's hand' (John 10:28–29). But the real confidence is that if God has chosen those who are his, and has given them to Christ as the trophy of his Calvary sacrifice, then he cannot and will not lose even one of them.

There are some who think that this doctrine will make us careless

Well, it may. But if anyone thinks that they can take advantage of the promise of eternal grace and live as they please then they are only proving that they have never truly met with Jesus Christ in a saving way. Salvation is far more than a detached theology. It is a radical and far reaching change.

Conversion means precisely that: nobody converts their mortgage, their house or their shares, and leaves everything just as it was before. Conversion is a transformation.

Paul met this very challenge when he wrote to the Christians at Rome: 'What shall we say then? Are we to continue in sin that grace may abound? By no means! How can we who died to sin still live in it?' (Romans 6:1–2). He went on to explain that the Christian is someone who has died with Christ and has been raised to a new life with Christ; as a result we live in 'newness of life' (v 4), our old self has died (v 6), we are set free from inevitable slavery to sin and we are under the Lordship of Christ from now on (vs 7, 12–14). Far from the enjoyment of eternal salvation providing an excuse for sloppy living, the New Testament constantly sees it as an incentive for holiness.

There are some who think that the doctrine of eternal grace is too good to be possible

To which my best reply is that it would be—if anything was impossible for God! It is understandable that in this world of transience, where nothing lasts for long, we find it hard to believe in a promise of salvation that is eternal and that can never be lost or taken from us. But let God himself reassure us with his own promise: 'Lift up your eyes to the heavens, look at the earth beneath; the heavens will vanish like smoke, the earth will wear out like a garment, and its inhabitants will die like flies. But my salvation will last for ever, my righteousness will never fail' (Isaiah 51:6 NIV).

There are some who are always timid and uncertain about their faith

They have a natural timidity of character and every decision of significance in their life sends them into a panic. They are never sure about anything. So when it comes to the subject of faith, they are always analysing their faith and examining their lives to see whether they have sufficient faith to justify assurance. How often I have been asked, sometimes almost despairingly: 'How do I know whether I have enough faith to believe?' It is as if faith is some kind of good work that is rewarded by salvation. I can tell such people immediately that they need not trouble to examine their faith any more—I can assure them that they certainly *do not* have sufficient faith.

The Bible is far less concerned about the *quantity* of faith as it is about the *object* of faith. It is not a matter of whether you have sufficient faith but who you put your faith in. I may be facing major heart surgery, and I am naturally very anxious about it. But when they tell me that the country's leading heart surgeon and his entire specialist team will undertake my operation then I am somewhat relieved and have far more confidence and less fear. I have no confidence in myself, but significant confidence in my physician. However, my apprehension will soon return if I am informed on the morning of the operation that my consultant is unavoidably sick and that his team have been drafted to another case—I will have a junior houseman in charge of my surgery after all. I had no more confidence in myself either way, but understandably I had much more hope when I knew the excellent reputation of my physician. You surely know the excellent reputation of your great spiritual physician.

You surely know the excellent reputation of your great spiritual physician

It matters more than anything *where* you place your confidence for eternity. We have all seen the evidence of those who, with massive faith in their religion, will carry out the most despicable actions. They are so convinced that by giving their lives for the cause of Allah, they will certainly receive instant admission into paradise and enjoy all the sensuous pleasures that their imams promised them. I am quite sure that they have far more certainty and less doubt than many Christians have. But it is tragically misplaced. It is unswerving faith in a false religion.

You may be beset with doubt—'fighting without and fear within' as Paul describes it in 2 Corinthians 7:5—but if you are trusting in Christ alone, he has promised you eternal salvation. What matters most of all is not how strongly you are on the side of God, but how certainly he is on your side. Christ is the one who defeated Satan on the cross and made an open show of him (Colossians 2:15). Christ promised his disciples that all those he called he would keep. Like sheep following the shepherd, they would hear his voice and they would 'never perish, and no one will snatch them out of my hand' (John 10:28–29). What is more, he gave the reason for this certainty: 'My Father, who has given them to me, is greater than all, and no one is able to snatch them out of the Father's hand. I and the Father are one.' Have you watched a small child holding the hand of its parent in a crowd? Whose grip was the most firm—that of the child or that of the parent?

The faint-hearted and timid have only to keep in mind a well-worn promise of Paul. Having dealt with the great theology of justification by faith alone in the death of Christ alone, and having reassured the Christians at Rome—who may at any time be hauled off to the butchery of the arena—that the Spirit will help them in their weakness and that there is a glorious new creation waiting for them ahead, the apostle then laid out a question and answer: 'If God is for us, who can be against us?' Paul was utterly convinced that nothing can ever separate us from the love of God in Christ so he ran through a list of possibilities: tribulation, distress, persecution, famine, nakedness, danger, sword, death, life, angels, rulers, things present, things to come, powers, height, depth, or anything else we can imagine in all creation, and then he concluded that none of this 'will be able to separate us from the love of God in Christ Jesus our Lord' (Romans 8:31–39).

Is Christ no more reliable that the careless parent who allows a child to wander off and get lost in the crowd?

Is there any argument against this? The response that suggests the only exception to this list is my own weak faith is a remarkably weak argument. Can we really believe that Jesus Christ went through hell on Calvary in order to reconcile us to God and fit us for heaven, only to let us slip through his hands at the last? Is Christ no more reliable than the careless parent who allows a child to wander off and get lost in the crowd? Is that what we think of him?

Few men were more aware of their wicked past than John Newton. As a blasphemous infidel who had deliberately abandoned the faith his mother taught him, he worked hard to undo the faith of others; as a debauched, drunken sailor he threw himself into the vile slave trade. Even after his conversion he was only too aware of the weakness of his own heart. But here was his conclusion on the matter of eternal grace when he wrote a letter on the subject: 'While Christ is the Foundation, Root, Head and Husband of his people, while the word of God is yea and amen, while the counsels of God are unchangeable, while we have a Mediator and High Priest before the throne, while the Holy Spirit is willing and able to bear witness to the truths of the gospel, while God is wiser than men and stronger than Satan—so long the believer in Jesus is and shall be safe. Heaven and earth must pass away, but the promise, the oath, the blood, on which my soul relies, afford me a security which can never fail.'

Finally, there are those whose conscience plagues them with guilt

Understandably, some believe that either before or since their conversion, they have committed something so bad that God cannot possibly forgive them. These people are usually tortured with the conviction that they have committed the blasphemy against the Holy Spirit. To this I can only respond by asking this question: 'Would you claim that during his earthly ministry Jesus Christ was in league with the prince of demons?' I think I can fairly anticipate the response! Well, that is precisely the context of our Lord's warning about the blasphemy against the Holy Spirit in Matthew 12:31.

One of the earliest verses I learnt soon after I became a Christian was Hebrews 7:25, 'He (Christ) is able to save to the *uttermost* those who draw near to God through him, since he always lives to make intercession for them.' I remember that it was common at that time to explain the verse like this: 'Christ can save from the guttermost to the uttermost.' It was one of those slick little phrases that at least had the merit of being memorable. In reality there is some disagreement among the commentators about the meaning of that Greek word, *panteles*. Does it have to do with time or completeness? William Gouge took it as completeness and likes the translation 'uttermost'—and he should know because in the first half of the seventeenth century he spent thirty-three years and one thousand sermons expounding this book of Hebrews to his congregation at Blackfriars, in London. On the other hand, John Calvin prefers a reference to time and translates the word as 'for ever'—and he should know because he was the great Swiss Reformer and theologian. But perhaps a poor disabled woman can help us here, because the only other occasion this word is used in the New Testament is in Luke 13:11 where the crippled woman 'could not fully straighten herself'; here the word 'fully' is our word *panteles*, and it must mean 'completely'.

Either way, there is a for ever fullness—an eternal completeness—about our salvation. Back in Hebrews 7:25 the apostle gives us the reason why our salvation is so complete and for ever: 'Since (because) he always lives to make intercession for (us)'. Our confidence that God's forgiving grace can embrace the foulest, and for ever, is in the fact that Jesus Christ is alive and his presence in heaven guarantees our safe arrival. This is exactly why Paul tells the Corinthians that if Christ did not rise from the dead then all the preaching since Calvary and all our feeble faith has been in vain; we are still lost in our sins (1 Corinthians 15:14, 17).

There is a for ever fullness—an eternal completeness—about our salvation

The Puritans in the seventeenth century used to say that sometimes God puts his children to bed in the dark. There is hardly a clearer and sadder example of this than the experience of our national poet, William Cowper. Suffering throughout his life from manic depression, his conversion to Christ only brought a temporary respite for his tortured mind. Although he wrote some of his finest poetry during his period of extreme spiritual depression, this was little comfort for the man who considered himself to be, in his own words 'buried above ground'. Before his conversion Cowper had more than once tried to take his own life and he thought that this must be a sin God could never forgive. John Newton, his faithful friend and pastor, spent many hours trying to help him, and at one time he and Mary had Cowper living with them for eighteen months. The poet was convinced that Christ had died for everyone except himself. But John

Newton knew that the poor suffering bard had trusted Christ alone for salvation and he was sure that Cowper would arrive in heaven by the secure grace of God. He told William this many, many times.

Sadly, Cowper was not alone in his fears. There have been, and still are, many Christians who would love to enjoy the assurance of salvation and find strength in the experience that Paul was praying for on behalf of the Thessalonians; but somehow they can't. They stagger round in a never ending circle of doubt finding a little hope here and there but unable to grasp the full benefit of all that Christ has done for them as their advocate.

The enjoyment of confidence in eternal grace depends upon the great unchanging certainties of the gospel

Are you one of these? There are many reasons. Perhaps it is because the way the gospel was first presented has left you with the idea that you must never be certain, or that salvation can so easily be lost. Or perhaps your own hesitant, brooding personality never allows you confidence in anything. On the other hand, it may be that you can never forgive yourself for some particular sin you have committed in the past, and you are always doubting whether God can therefore forgive you either. For this very reason John encouraged us that 'whenever our heart condemns us, God is greater than our heart' (1 John 3:20).

The enjoyment of confidence in eternal grace depends upon the great unchanging certainties of the gospel. Not upon how you felt when you woke up this morning; or what kind of week it has been in the factory, office, workshop or classroom; or whether you feel a complete failure as a parent or husband or wife right now; or whether you messed-up your Christian testimony yesterday.

William Cowper died cheerless and hopeless on Friday 25 April 1800 in East Dereham, Norfolk. John Newton was now seventy-five, and when he heard the news of his friend's death, John picked up his pen and wrote a few lines imagining that he himself had just arrived in heaven and found, as he expected, that William was already there. Looking back over the long years during which he had tried to convince the doubting poet that God's eternal grace could be trusted, John could not resist saying, 'I told you so'. Here are the closing two verses as John meets William in heaven:

My friend, my friend! and have we met again,
Far from the home of woe, the home of men;
And hast thou taken thy glad harp once more,
Twined with far lovelier wreaths than e'er before;
And is thy strain more joyous and more loud,
While circle round thee heaven's attentive crowd?

Oh! let thy memory wake! I told thee so;
I told thee thus would end thy heaviest woe;
I told thee that thy God would bring thee here,
And God's own hand would wipe away thy tear
While I should claim a mansion by thy side,
I told thee so—for our Emmanuel died.

That is eternal grace. Trust it, believe it, be comforted, strengthened and encouraged by it—and enjoy it.

SOVEREIGN GRACE AND LOVE ABOUNDING
over sin and death and hell!
Sing its depth that knows no sounding;
who its breadth or length can tell?
On its glories,
on its glories
let my soul for ever dwell.

What from Christ that soul shall
bound by everlasting bands?
Once in him, in him for ever,
thus the eternal covenant stands.
None shall tear us,

none shall tear us
from the Strength of Israel's hands.

Heirs of God, joint-heirs with Jesus,
called and chosen in the Son!
To his name eternal praises
for the wonders he has done!
One with Jesus,
one with Jesus,
by eternal union one.

On such love, my soul, still ponder,
love so great, so rich, so free;
say, while lost in holy wonder,
'Why, O God, such love to me?'
Hallelujah!
Hallelujah!
Grace shall reign eternally.

JOHN KENT 1766–1843
Praise! 671 © in this version Praise Trust

Purposeful grace

'To me this grace was given, to preach the unsearchable riches of Christ' Ephesians 3:8

Paul had good reason to consider himself 'the least of all the apostles' because he knew that he had been a Christ-rejecting rebel. From his past he deserved nothing, and if he was now an apostle—with the added privilege of seeing Christ after his resurrection and ascension—then he knew it was only by the grace of God. This undeserved grace was enjoyed by Paul only when he abandoned every effort to save himself and trusted in Christ alone. He had first to admit that his greatest sin was in rejecting Christ.

But even when Paul had come to that conclusion, he still had nothing to be proud of. Five years after writing to the Corinthians from Ephesus, Paul was under house arrest in Rome and was now writing to the church at Ephesus, and at the beginning of his letter he addressed them as 'the saints who are in Ephesus' (1:1). In his ministry as an apostle, Paul considered himself to be the last of all and the least of all, but he addressed the *saints* in Ephesus. Who are they? This is not the only time Paul used that word in his letter. The Greek word in the singular is *hagios* and it refers to one who is religiously holy or clean. In the first century it was a common word used chiefly as a description of the gods who were different from the commonplace; they were set apart from that which was ordinary. The only other beings who could claim this word were the priests whose ministry brought them into touch with the holy gods. As he did so often, Paul clothed this common word with a very special Christian meaning.

Who are the saints?
Both 'saints' and 'grace' were devalued words in the middle ages. The church imagined that certain Christians of the past had lived more holy lives than was necessary and therefore had accumulated a hoard of good works into which ordinary mortals could dip in order to add to their own

diminishing supply of righteousness—this was 'grace'. Those long dead pious celebrities were adorned with the title 'saint', and tragically that use of the word spoiled it for the true meaning of the New Testament word.

The Roman Church had decided that these 'saints' could be of use to us since it was thought that they had amassed a fund of good works that were above what was required of them. The church even invented a word to explain this: they were known as works of 'supererogation' which came from two Latin words *super* and *erogare*—which meant 'beyond requirement'. In practice it came to refer to what we may loosely call 'the big payout'. This meant that the penitent could use the super abundance of righteousness by the saints to help pay off their own debt of sin—and that was thought to be grace. As the years and centuries rolled by, the church selected certain figures of the past and honoured them with this exalted title of 'saint'—even Mary the mother of our Lord was included among them. Eventually these saints were seen as intermediaries between Christ and the sinner, and Mary was elevated above all because as the 'Mother of God' and as a woman, she was thought to be more tender-hearted even than her own son. Praying to these saints became a significant practice up to the time of the Reformation in the sixteenth century.

In fact, it is still a common practice within the Church of Rome and was underlined by a decision of Pope John Paul II as recently as November 2000. The story behind that decision began back in the sixteenth century when Thomas More was Chancellor to King Henry VIII. More was executed by the King for his refusal to back Henry in his struggle to wrest authority over the church in England away from the hands of the Pope. Four hundred years later, in 1935, the Pope of the day declared that Thomas More was to be regarded as one of these saints. This was especially interesting since More had once declared that if he could get his hands on evangelicals he would put them 'in the frying pan'. In fact he did get his hands on some of them and he did put them in the frying pan. Some 'saint'! However, in November 2000 Pope John Paul announced that Thomas More was now the patron saint of politicians! That requires no comment except to add that Sir Thomas More knew nothing of democracy as we know it, and the only politics he understood was scheming and scaffold. He won most of his battles by the first and lost his final tussle with the King by the second.

More was executed by Henry VIII in 1535, which is an interesting date because it was just one year before William Tyndale himself was strangled and burnt at the stake for his crime of translating the Bible into English—and his most distinguished opponent was none other than 'Saint' Thomas. It is now generally conceded by historians of all persuasions that More's greatest mistake was to take up his pen against Tyndale.

But why this history lesson? Because this view of the word 'saint' was a complete reversal of Paul's message in the New Testament and totally overlooked its true meaning. As a result of history, saints are now understood to be a special kind of super-Christian; they are depicted in stained glass windows and jockey for the honour of becoming patrons of this or that. This false use of the word is heard whenever someone explains the misdemeanours of another with the comment: 'He is no saint'.

For the apostle Paul 'saint' referred to all who have received the undeserved grace of God by faith, having the righteousness of Christ alone reckoned to their account; and on that ground they are declared holy. In other words, every true Christian is a saint in New Testament terms. For Paul there are two clear implications of the word. First, it refers to those who have been declared righteous by God on the ground of Christ's death alone, and secondly it implies that these people have been set apart for the service of God. It is this second meaning that is so important for our present chapter.

Every true Christian is a saint in New Testament terms

In his letter to the Ephesians Paul uses the word saint five times (1:1, 15, 18; 2:19; 3:8). Read those verses and imagine that the word refers to a club of superior Christians, and test your reaction. Sometimes Bible translators have lost their nerve and insert 'God's people' instead of the word 'saints' (see for example the NIV at 2:19 and 3:8). It is true that all the saints are God's people, but Paul deliberately used the word *hagioi* to demonstrate that all Christians, without a single exception, are holy in the sight of God and set apart for his service. This was as surprising to the first century pagan world as it is to parts of twenty-first century Christianity, for in both cases the word was reserved for a special class of religious people above the normal, and Paul was now applying it to all Christians.

Less than the least of all saints?

If you did not appreciate the short history lesson on the word 'saint', then you probably will not enjoy the lesson on grammar that is about to follow! In his attempt to explain how he sees himself, Paul threw together a comparative formed on the back of a negative superlative! In verse 8 he wrote, 'I am less'. That word is a comparative word. He is comparing himself with others, and he says 'I am looking at the other saints (Christians) and I want you to know that I am less than them.' But Paul had not finished, he went on to say, 'I am less than the least'. The word 'least' is a superlative, and I call it a negative superlative because he did not say I am the best, he said, I am the least, I am the worst. You can be less without being the least but when you are the least you cannot be any less. However, that is exactly what Paul claimed to be: 'less than the least'! That he was a Christian—a saint—is not in doubt; but he felt so strongly about his unworthiness that he could not be content merely to say that he is less than any, or even that he is least of all; instead he breaks all the rules of grammar and claims to be less than the least.

In his attempt to explain how he sees himself, Paul threw together a comparative formed on the back of a negative superlative!

In some respects John Newton and Saul of Tarsus had similar testimonies. You may recall that the only significant difference between the spiritual condition of the two men was seventeen hundred years. In 1764, when he was curate in charge at Olney in Buckinghamshire John Newton published his autobiography, *The Narrative of a Surprising Conversion*. Now, at last, everyone could read the incredible story of this Church of England clergyman who had once been a drunken, debauched, hardswearing sailor, impressed onto a man-of-war in His Majesty's navy, beaten for deserting his ship and finally a slave dealer in Africa before his remarkable conversion to Christ, during a violent Atlantic storm that almost wrecked his ship. Shortly after the publication of his biography, Newton discovered that people were travelling to Olney, a small out-of-the-way village, to meet this strange man, and he claimed that he felt like a monkey in a cage as people came to view this amazing sight. 'They find me a mystery', John declared and then added, 'I am a mystery. I am a mystery to others, I am a mystery to myself.' He could not understand how God could have loved him or how it could be possible for such an unclean man to be become a saint. Saul of Tarsus faced the same dilemma himself; he could not understand how God could have loved him.

Those who do not look back in shame cannot look forward with hope

Here is part of Paul's testimony: 'I persecuted the followers of this Way to their death, arresting both men and women and throwing them into prison ... I went (to Damascus) to bring these people as prisoners to Jerusalem to be punished' (Acts 22:4–5 *New International Version*). And elsewhere: 'Many a time I went from one synagogue to another to have them punished, and I tried to force them to blaspheme' (Acts 26:11 *New International Version*). That is precisely what John of Wapping did; on each ship he served before his conversion to Christ, he encouraged young sailors to profane the name of God and to sing bawdy and blasphemous sea shanties. He taught them to abandon whatever faith they came on board with and to join him in freethinking and free-living. For his part, Paul had an obsession with persecuting Christians and even went from city to city to hound them. Both men looked back in shame. Those who do not look back in shame cannot look forward with hope.

John Newton was converted after a violent storm at sea. While the ship was wallowing in the Atlantic he spent hours with an agony of conscience and heart searching before he found grace and his life was transformed by the power of God's Spirit through the word of God. Some years ago I read a book called, *A short history of Sierra Leone* by A P Kup. In his survey of the history of the west coast of Africa the author had little alternative but at some point to mention John Newton. Kup obviously knew something about John Newton's conversion, but equally obviously he didn't understand it, so he dismissed it in one pithy sentence: 'Newton was caught in a violent Atlantic storm, threw a fit and entered the ministry.' Newton's own description of what happened was inscribed on his memorial plaque: 'preserved, restored, pardoned'. Seventeen hundred years earlier, the Apostle Paul was on trial before Herod Agrippa and the Roman Governor Portius Festus. As always, he gave his testimony and eventually came to the incredible fact that Jesus rose from the dead. That was just too much for Festus, and the Governor broke in: 'Paul you are out of your mind, your great learning has driven you insane.' Or to borrow the words of A P Kup: 'You have thrown a fit.' For his part, Paul called it, 'God's grace through the working of his power.'

Saints are not static memorials of God's grace, but living examples for his service

Both Paul of Tarsus and John of Wapping knew that, undeserving as they certainly were, they were now through Christ clean in the sight of God and, what was just as amazing, they were made holy for the purpose of serving God. From now on, every circumstance in their life would be with the one chief end that God would be served whether by their life or their death (Philippians 1:20).

Purposeful grace

Paul was keenly aware that the word 'saint' that he had minted for the purpose of instructing the young Christians, not only referred back to the undeserved grace of God, but it looked on to the purposeful grace of God. Saints are not static memorials of God's grace, but living examples for his service. To put it simply: saints are declared holy by God so that they may serve wholly for God. What amazed Paul, and what never ceased to amaze John Newton, was that God's plan was to make use of a man like him—and that is true of every saint. Towards the end of his life Paul wrote, 'God saved us and called us to a holy life, not because of our works'—that is undeserved grace—'but because of his own purpose and grace which he gave us in Christ Jesus before the ages began'—that is purposeful grace (2 Timothy 1:9). Two verses later Paul described that purpose: 'I was appointed a herald and an apostle and a teacher' (*New International Version*).

Paul was told at the outset of his new spiritual life that he was God's chosen instrument: 'to carry my name before the Gentiles and kings and the children of Israel' (Acts 9:15). Here in Ephesians 3, Paul picked up on that, and having received the undeserved grace of God he now recognised that he was a servant (v 7) and a servant is chosen to serve. A servant has a ministry, a duty, something to do—that is purposeful grace. The precise purpose for Paul he explained as, 'to preach to the Gentiles' (v 8). That is not preaching in our formal sense of the word; it is the word from which we get our English 'evangelise'. What Paul was claiming was that he was saved and received the undeserved grace of God so that he might evangelise the nations. When Paul wanted to write about preaching in a more formal sense, he used the word 'herald' (see for example 1 Timothy 2:7 in the *New International Version*).

Clearly, the purpose of anyone receiving grace is that they may bring glory to God; but the issue here is *how* do we bring glory to God? When God gave Paul undeserved grace, it was accompanied by purposeful grace. Grace that would enable him to serve God and fulfil God's plan for his life in any and every circumstance. His purpose in being saved, his purpose in receiving undeserved grace was that he might evangelise the nations with the gospel. But that was not an end in itself. To suggest that the purpose of the church, and therefore of the Christian, is mission, is only the first half of the answer to the question: 'What is the purpose of the church?' *The* great purpose of the church, and therefore of every saint, is to glorify God. But how do we do that?

The content of our gospel is described in verse 8. Paul called it the *unsearchable* riches of Christ. That word is used in only one other place in the New Testament when, in Romans 11:33, Paul moved to his wonderful doxology: 'Oh, the depth of the riches and wisdom and knowledge of God. How unsearchable [that is not the word] are his judgements and how *inscrutable* his ways'—there is the word 'unsearchable' that we have in Ephesians 3:8. The content of our evangelistic message, the content of our good news that we have to share with the nations is beyond discovery! We can never fully explain it. It is the 'riches of Christ'. Notice that it is not the riches *in* Christ, but the riches *of* Christ. If they are riches found in Christ then we may preach about the riches, but if they are the riches of Christ, then we have to preach Christ himself. And what is that? It is the wealth of undeserved grace.

Undeserved grace is not just to be personally enjoyed, it is to be prodigally shared

Paul went on to record that these riches of undeserved grace were hidden at the beginning by the Old Testament types and symbols of the sacrifices and the offerings, and by the visions and prophecies of the ancient seers. Throughout the Old Testament they were slowly revealed, little by little and step by step. The Old Testament was God's progressive revelation and even the prophets longed to understand the full meaning. In fact Peter tells us that these are 'things into which angels long to look'(1 Peter 1:12); apparently the angels themselves did not fully understand the gospel. Paul continued in Ephesians 3:9 by reminding us that ours is the privilege of throwing the switch and turning on the light of the gospel that had been so long hidden. The good news is now an open secret and there is a universal fellowship among those who know God's undeserved and purposeful grace.

What must be clear from this is that undeserved grace is not just to be personally enjoyed, it is to be prodigally shared. The moment we receive undeserved grace we receive purposeful grace. We have to do something with the grace we have received; we have to evangelise the nations by being a witness. We have the privilege of making known the fact that there is a wonderful community resulting from the undeserved grace of God. The task of the church is to reveal the otherwise undiscoverable riches of Christ which are described in verse 10 as 'the manifold wisdom of God'. The word 'manifold' means 'many sided', and poetically it has the meaning of colourful or variegated.

So, how did Paul, and how do we as individuals and as a church, throw light upon the many sided and variegated wisdom of God, to entice men and women into the community of those who enjoy the undeserved grace of God? As a matter of fact that is easier than we could ever imagine. God has already done it for us, and if we are true Christians—saints—we are the answer to our own question. Each one of us is a story of God's many-sided wisdom and grace. The kaleidoscope of our lives in the infinite diversity of his dealings with us is all part of God's manifold wisdom. The way he prepared us for the gospel and the providence that preserved our life for the moment when we found Christ as our Lord and Saviour; and the way that he has led us every step of our life since then; all this should be a sparkling story of God's wisdom and grace. That is why Paul could write, 'Oh the depth of the riches of the wisdom and knowledge of God'. Our story—our quality of life, miracle of conversion, transformation from rebel to servant and from Christ-rejecter to Christ's disciple and discipler—is all part of God's purposeful grace; that kaleidoscope of his wisdom and his love. That should be our best evangelism. And every saint—without a single excuse of age or infirmity—can evangelise like that.

This must surely be what Paul is referring to when he wrote to the Corinthians and assured them that, 'in Christ (God) always leads us in triumphal procession, and through us spreads the fragrance of the knowledge of him [Christ] everywhere' (2 Corinthians 2:14). The preaching and verbal witness of Christians, however vital that is, cannot spread the attractiveness of Christ in this world half so effectively as the kaleidoscopic beauty of the wisdom of God lived out in the lives of a countless myriad of Christians in the cities and farmlands, deserts and jungles, offices, factories, workshops, classrooms, and neighbourhoods of this world.

When Paul encouraged the Christians at Rome with the assurance that 'for those who love God, all things work together for good, for those who are called according to his purpose' (Romans 8:28), he went on to say precisely what that purpose was. The purpose of our election and calling—invincible grace—is that we might become, 'conformed to the image of his Son'. In other words, everything that happens in the life of the Christian is for the purpose that we might become moulded more into the likeness of Jesus Christ, God's Son, *so that* others will be brought into the fellowship of the unimaginable grace of God, *so that* God will be honoured by more and more people.

This may make us feel a little uncomfortable in the knowledge that God should stake the knowledge of his glorious undiscovered wisdom upon people like us. In fact this may also help us to understand why the apostle Paul could call himself 'less than the least of all saints'. Perhaps we are beginning to jockey with him for that position! There is so much to do, but so little done. Such a life to live, but so poorly lived. I am less than the least.

A new twist to the purpose of purposeful grace

If the purpose of purposeful grace is for every saint to bring the light of the gospel to those who are in darkness, and by this means to bring glory to God, have we said all? Typically Paul adds an unexpected twist to his argument. Instead of leaving us with the obvious conclusion that the more people who are saved the more glory there is to God, Paul takes us one step further. In verse 10 he informs us that 'through the church the manifold wisdom of God might now be made known to the rulers and authorities in the heavenly places.' Who are these? We might expect him to refer to the town council at Ephesus, and no doubt he was concerned for them. On the other hand, since he is imprisoned at Rome, Paul may be thinking of the imperial household of the Roman Emperor Nero. But that is clearly not his conclusion here. These 'rulers and authorities in the heavenly places' are referred to earlier in Ephesians 1:21, and whilst some suggest that this is the demonic realm—and there can be no doubt that to their shame they will see the glorious grace of God in the lives of his saints—that is unlikely to be Paul's reference here. Paul appears to be speaking of all the host of heaven; those angels we referred to earlier when Peter informed us that all through the history of God's redemption, right up until the coming of Christ, even the angels longed to understand what the message of the prophets was all about (1 Peter 1:12). Now they understand fully because at last in the church they can see the wonderful undeserved grace of God.

Some proof of this is found in the words of our Saviour: 'There will be more joy in heaven over one sinner who repents' (Luke 15:7), and immediately our Lord repeats himself: 'there is joy before the angels of God over one sinner who repents' (v 10). It is as if the angels wipe their eyes and say, 'Oh, we see it now'. With the conversion of every saint the angels worship the Lord God for such wonderful, undeserved and purposeful grace. Therefore purposeful grace brings glory to God not only because the transformation of a sinner into a saint demonstrates his grace on earth, but because it demonstrates it to all heaven as well. Whenever a sinner is saved, all heaven explodes with worship and adoration of such a God who planned such a way of salvation. The theology of the angels, and therefore their worship, is greatly enhanced by the grace of salvation. This is Paul's plus factor in purposeful grace.

Whenever a sinner is saved, all heaven explodes with worship and adoration

But let's take a broader look at purposeful grace. It would be quite wrong to assume that purposeful grace is found only in those good things that happen in the life of the Christian; still less that it is to be identified only in the life of Christians. There is purposeful grace in everything that happens to everyone in this world. That is certainly a massive claim, but it has to be true or else there are circumstances that we can only attribute to blind chance or the wheel of fortune.

Purpose in natural suffering

Not even the most grotesque events or circumstances are beyond the purposeful grace of God. Here is one hard example: Over the next twenty years it is estimated that AIDS will claim two hundred million lives—most of these across the beautiful yet sad continent of Africa. AIDS is referred to as the 'silent holocaust' and it is an international emergency of pandemic proportions; tragically many innocents suffer, including widows and orphans. The fact is that obedience to the law of God would eradicate the HIV virus within that same twenty year time scale; even the World Health Organization recognised in 1991 that the most effective way to prevent the spread of AIDS was for two uninfected partners to remain faithful to each other.

HIV is not a nasty virus that God drops in on godless lifestyles, any more than he manipulates liver failure for the alcoholic, lung cancer for the smoker, brain damage for the heroin addict or heart failure for the obese. Rather, any immoral, God-defying lifestyle will bring tragedy, because when we refuse to operate according to the Maker's instructions, pain and misery always result. And too often others get hurt—as we have learned so sadly with AIDS. When Achan disobeyed the command of God: 'He did not perish alone for his iniquity' (Joshua 22:20 and see 7:1–5, 24–26). This was a terrible lesson that Israel would never forget. The tragic results of natural suffering like this are not beyond the knowledge or control of God; they are part of his purposeful grace. AIDS did not begin by infecting millions; it began small and limited as a serious warning. But the warning was ignored—and it still is by far too many—and as a result the terrible virus spread. It was so simple to prevent and it would be so easy to eradicate, but the world has chosen a lifestyle against the revealed purpose of God and it is reaping the consequences. If ever there was an example of sowing the wind and reaping the whirlwind (Hosea 8:7), HIV and AIDS is that example.

The world has chosen a lifestyle against the revealed purpose of God and it is reaping the consequences

In a similar way, we will have to learn the hard way that when a nation chooses to set aside God's wise law concerning one day of rest in seven, it triggers a natural law that the health of the people will suffer in every respect. And when we are content for our marriages to break up at the current alarming rate and parents drift in and out of relationships, we need not be surprised that our children will grow increasingly wild and lawless. There are natural laws that govern all these results. Imagine a society composed of homes where God is first, where husbands and wives keep themselves only for each other, where children honour and respect their parents, and where parents love and care for their children, where gossip is unheard, blasphemy unknown, lies are never told, coveting and stealing always resisted, and where love reigns. Is that an impossible dream? Perhaps, but it would certainly be the blessing of conformity with the master plan of God. Let no one blame the Creator if we do not enjoy the fruit that would follow from obedience to his laws.

In chapter three when we considered sovereign grace, we saw that there is a purpose even in natural disasters that may appear at first to have no connection with human delinquency. When the earth cracks open, when mountains spit fire with molten rock, when cruel oceans engulf towns, and when violent winds devastate crops and homes, few pretend to identify the particular sins that gave rise to such dreadful curses; but frequently they are precisely that: judgement against sin and a warning of future judgement. In that chapter on sovereign grace we established that God is in control of all events on earth; but much more than this, that he has a purpose behind all those events that he controls. When the psalmist recorded, 'The nations rage, the kingdoms totter; he utters his voice, the earth melts' (Psalm 46:6), this was far more than a statement about the ultimate control of God; it was a commitment to the fact that God has a plan behind all his control.

God never closes

a case on

unforgiven sin

Purpose in spiritual suffering

When King David, against the command of God, ordered a census of his fighting men, God allowed him to choose his own punishment: famine, military defeat or plague. We do not always connect sin and its punishment, but God warns that he will always punish sin—sooner or later. His punishment is not always immediate. Adam was warned that the day he disobeyed the command of God he would die, and he did—though the process took another 930 years to complete! God never closes a case on unforgiven sin.

Similarly, the blessing of obedience does not always come at once. It is a lie when 'prosperity' preachers promise immediate health, wealth and happiness for all who trust Christ. That is untrue to the Bible and to two millennia of Christian experience. The second generation of children out of Egypt suffered forty years for the unfaithfulness of their parents before they themselves could inherit the Promised Land (Numbers 14:33); and in Hebrews, the apostle listed some of the great heroes of faith, none of whom received the promised blessing but 'greeted them from afar' (Hebrews 11:13). God frequently delays reward just as he defers judgement. Let no one take advantage of this—it always comes.

Christians ... can bask in the sunlight of God's evident grace, but ... they are a people who can also see in the dark

Paul wrote of being 'utterly burdened beyond our strength (so) that we despaired of life itself' (2 Corinthians 1:8) and of being 'afflicted in every way, perplexed, persecuted and struck down' (2 Corinthians 4:8). But he understood the purposefulness of grace; he knew that even at such times there were lessons to be learnt, not least the provision of God to help in times of need so that the experience of God's purposeful grace can be passed on to others (2 Corinthians 1:4, 9). Once I was asked at the close of a meeting: 'Do you believe there is always health and prosperity as a result of obedience?' I replied, 'Yes—but not in this life.' There are natural laws that bring blessing and pain from obedience and disobedience, but there are spiritual laws also that may often override the natural.

The reality of purposeful grace

At one time armies fought set piece battles during the day. The opposing forces would line up facing each other, and at a given time battle would commence. If there was no result by sundown, the two sides would generally retreat to their camp and continue to sort it out in the morning. Armies rarely fought at night simply because no one could see in the dark. Today, with his electronic communications, global positioning and night sights, the modern soldier is as well equipped to fight at night as in the day. He can see in the dark. If physical suffering taught Paul to trust more in Christ, he also learnt that imprisonment opened new doors for the gospel. It is this ability to watch for the unfolding plan of God when all around is dark that is the Christian's unique privilege. Christians are a people who not only can bask in the sunlight of God's evident grace, but when it is not so evident, they are a people who can also see in the dark.

Let me show you how this works. In Romans 15:4 Paul encouraged the young converts in the great metropolis of the empire that 'Whatever was written in former days was written for our instruction.' This means that all Old Testament events are with this purpose in view, though not all the Old Testament characters recognised this fact. For example, Joseph was sold into slavery by his brothers and when towards the end of the story, they came grovelling to him in sorrow, repentance and fear, Joseph came up with that magnificent statement of faith: 'You meant evil against me, but God meant it for good' (Genesis 50:20). Joseph had no idea of the full significance of what he was saying. He thought, and rightly so, that the story of his time in Egypt was good for his family, and good for Egypt—and so it was. But the purpose was far bigger than this. Countless generations have learned from the story of Joseph's integrity and purity, as well as from the aggressive cruelty of his brothers. Just so, with Moses' anger, David's tragic moral slide, Jonah's disobedience, and Hezekiah's pride, all of these have a greater purpose than any of them understood. Their story was meant to teach *us*. The same is true with the successes and triumphs recorded in the Old Testament: Joseph's honour, Ruth's loyalty, Samuel's faithfulness, Nehemiah's courage—all these have a purpose well beyond the immediate life of the character involved.

This is exactly how Paul saw his own life. And so can, and so must, every Christian. Even in sickness and the death of a loved one; there is purpose in our weakness and in our failure; there is purpose when our plans crash and when our circumstances fall out the 'wrong' way. For those who will only listen, they will hear the reassuring voice of God: 'I will instruct you and teach you in the way you should go; I will counsel you with my eye upon you' (Psalm 32:8). We do not always discover the purpose, but we must always believe there is one. When Jesus was told that Lazarus was ill, he responded 'it is for God's glory'; *we* know that, because we can read the end of the story. But when Paul left 'Trophimus, who was ill, at Miletus' (2 Timothy 4:20), we still do not know the purpose in this, but there certainly was one. The well-worn promise of Jeremiah 29:11 had been comfortably applied by generations of Jews before Christians took it over: 'I know the plans I have for you, declares the LORD, plans for wholeness and not for evil, to give you a future and a hope.'

We do not always discover the purpose, but we must always believe there is one

Let me take you a little further. One of the most quoted verses from Paul's letters must surely be: 'We know that for those who love God all things work together for good, for those who are called according to his purpose' (Romans 8:28). That phrase 'according to his purpose' is crucial. Paul believed that was the purposeful grace of God. He meant that in everything—everything—there was a plan and purpose designed by God for the ultimate benefit of his people and the certain honour of his name through the proclamation of the message of Jesus. But did Paul really believe this? Most certainly he did.

Writing from house arrest in Rome about the same time as his letter to the Ephesians, Paul wrote, 'I want you to know, brothers, that what has happened to me has really served to advance the gospel' (Philippians 1:12). Paul had the audacity to write about 'advance' when he was actually confined to quarters! And later he told the Philippians that he had 'learned in whatever situation ... to be content' (Philippians 4:11); this was not a reluctant resignation that 'whatever will be will be', but a confidence in the fact that God had plans—better plans—than immediately appeared. For this reason he was always on the lookout to see how those plans would be fulfilled.

But did this really work for Paul? Yes, it did. Being under house arrest in Rome could have been utterly frustrating for the itchy feet of a pioneer evangelist who longed to reach the unreached with the good news of Christ. Yet, writing to the church at Philippi he revealed that he had discovered at least a two-fold purpose in his confinement: 'I want you to know, brothers, that what has happened to me has really served to advance the gospel, so that it has become known throughout the whole imperial guard and to all the rest, that my imprisonment is for Christ. And most of the brothers, having become confident in the Lord by my imprisonment, are much more bold to speak the word without fear' (Philippians 1:12–14). His imprisonment had not only taken the gospel into the very centre of the Emperor's palace guard, but it had put new courage and new life into some of the wavering converts. Besides this, Paul was able to write encouragingly to Philemon that Onesimus 'whose father I became in my imprisonment' was now on his way back to his master as a valuable servant (Philemon 10).

For this reason, Paul prayed that whenever he spoke on behalf of his King, he would fearlessly make known the gospel of Christ 'for which I am an ambassador in chains' (Ephesians 6:20); an ambassador in chains? So much for diplomatic immunity! Similarly, he urged the Christians at Colossae to pray that 'God may open to us a door for the word, to declare the mystery of Christ, on account of which I am in prison' (Colossians 4:3); it is certainly an expression of Paul's confidence in purposeful grace that he can write in the same sentence of an open door whilst he is in prison! Backed by the example of his own faith and experience, Paul expected the young churches to follow the same route. To the Philippians he urged: 'Whatever happens (to me or to you), conduct yourselves in a manner worthy of the gospel of Christ' (Philippians 1:27 *New International Version*).

There can therefore be no excuses. For all who are saints—declared holy by God to serve wholly for God—God has a purpose to bring honour to his name, and what is more, we can fulfil that purpose. We may try to excuse ourselves by the plea that we are not gifted, lack strength, are not muscular in faith, or that we are elderly, frail, or alone. But we can do all that he plans for us because he gives purposeful grace to all his saints, just as he gave to

Chapter 10

Paul: 'to me, grace was given to preach'. When Paul claimed, 'I can do all things through him who strengthens me' (Philippians 4:13), he was not so stupid as to believe that this meant he could swim the Mediterranean Sea backstroke or rid it of pirates! What he meant quite simply was that he could accomplish all that God had purposed for him.

William Carey is well known as the 'Father of modern missions' and the Baptist pioneer in India who sailed from England in 1793 and died forty-one years later without ever returning home. His prodigious contribution to India—and the world beyond—in the realms of botany, engineering, economics, medicine, communications, literature, education and social reform were eclipsed only by his outstanding work of Bible translation. Carey was responsible for overseeing translations of the Bible or parts of it into forty Indian languages and dialects. Which was not bad for a Northamptonshire cobbler who once earned fifty pence a week making and mending shoes!

But it is the story of one of his sisters, Mary, which is even more significant for us here. Mary was born with a diseased spine and few expected her to live very long. William led her to Christ and she was cared for by her sister Ann. All through his time in India, William sent money home to help towards Mary's support. By the age of twenty-five, Mary was paralysed, and for the next fifty years she was confined to her room. For eleven years she could not speak, and her right arm became the only limb in her body that she could move. Yet, we are told that her face shone with the joy of Christ, and she taught Ann's children the Bible by writing on a slate; in fact for years she led a Bible Class this way.

When Carey went to India, Mary wrote letters to him regularly. She told him all the family news—all the things distant missionaries really want to know. But best of all, she was described as the mission's chief priest whose ceaseless prayer was a fragrant offering to God. One nephew learnt the heart of mission work from his Aunt Mary, and in 1828 a niece wrote, 'Aunt's sufferings were a few weeks ago very distressing; yet we could not give her up. We do all love her so dearly; to part with her would tear us asunder. Her late affliction was enough to kill a person in good health. She is merely skin and bone, and not much of that, and so weak as to be hardly able to sit pillowed up in her chair, while her bed is made. Yet she continues the same sweet-tempered, humble Christian she ever was, feeling for others more than for herself, and always fearful lest mother should debar herself anything for her comfort.'

Incredibly, Mary lived to the age of seventy-four. In her own way her work was as great as that of her illustrious brother. His achievements belonged to her. Only eternity will reveal just how much Mary accomplished in India by her prayers. Without a doubt she had learnt the meaning of purposeful grace by discovering God's plan for her life.

What he commands we can do. Where he sends we can go.

This is how saints are to see their lives and circumstances. What he commands we can do. Where he sends we can go. What he brings we can endure. Because purposeful grace is the ability to do what God's purpose has planned. Why then do we duck his claims, avoid his call, hold back from his work, and make excuses? He has a plan, and purposeful grace will be given to fulfil it, abundant grace for an abundant purpose. In a superb expression of this Paul wrote to the church at Corinth: 'God is able to make all grace abound to you, so that having all sufficiency in all things at all times, you may abound in every good work' (2 Corinthians 9:8). This is one of Paul's many extravagantly precise claims: all grace for all things at all times providing all you need for all your work. That is purposeful grace for all his saints.

What he brings we can endure. Because purposeful grace is the ability to do what God's purpose has planned

YOUR WAY, NOT MINE, O LORD,
whatever it may be;
lead me by your own hand,
choose out the road for me.

2 Smooth let it be or rough,
your path will be the best;
direct or winding, still
it leads me to your rest.

3 I dare not choose my life,
I would not if I might;
choose for me, O my God;
your choice is sure and right.

4 Then fill my cup, O Lord,
according to your will,
with sorrow or with joy;
choose all my good or ill.

5 And choose my friends for me,
my sickness or my health,
choose for me my concerns,
my poverty or wealth.

6 Not mine but yours the choice
in things both great and small;
Lord, be my guide, my strength,
my wisdom and my all.

HORATIUS BONAR 1808–89
Praise! 874 © in this version Praise Trust*

Sufficient grace

'My grace is sufficient for you' 2 Corinthians 12:9

W e will leave the commentators to argue over the precise nature of Paul's 'thorn in the flesh' that he refers to in verse 7—their views range from poor eye-sight to a poor choice of wife! Whilst it is true that the phrase almost certainly refers to a physical ailment, it doesn't matter to us what it was. For Paul it must have been the effect rather than the cause that especially troubled him.

Paul had work to do: important work and lots of work—and it was all gospel work. And this 'messenger of Satan' as he saw it, threatened to hold him back. That it was a serious hindrance is clear from the fact that Paul had been through any number of dangers and beatings, some of which he describes in 2 Corinthians 11:23–33, and through it all he could claim to have worked harder than most (v 23). A lacerated back, an empty stomach, threats from bandits, and shivering, aching limbs from near drowning and exposure never stopped Paul from preaching the good news of Christ. But this one, whatever it was, seems to have come into an altogether different category for Paul.

He calls it simply his 'thorn in the flesh', and three times he pleaded with God to take it away. Clearly he was not coping, and he knew that he could do a lot better without it. Paul felt that it came directly as a satanic attack and he was 'harassed' by it. That is the same word used of the fist-beating that our Lord suffered (Matthew 26:67). Paul was not one of those simple-minded Christians who identify demons in every irritating fly that buzzes round their head whilst they are trying to study, so when he referred to a problem as a 'messenger of Satan to harass me', it must have been something out of the ordinary. However, each time Paul pleaded with God—with unselfish but insistent prayers—he knew that the same answer was coming back to him: 'My grace is sufficient for you.' Whatever this grace was, Paul clearly did find it to be sufficient, because to these same Christians at Corinth he promised that God was able to provide ample grace: 'So that having all sufficiency in all things at all times, you may abound in every good work' (2 Corinthians 9:8).

Some people can talk about sufficient grace very smoothly, and with the ease of evangelical jargon that we become so familiar with. But when anyone talks to me about sufficient grace, I want to know what he or she has experienced in their Christian life that has enabled them to prove the reality of sufficient grace. Do they really know what suffering is? Have they confronted the hard realities of life and death? Are the disappointments and heartbreaks and the frustrations and failures of this world part of their own experience? If this man Paul preaches to me about sufficient grace, I want to know exactly what he experienced and whether he really found grace sufficient. And if those two things marry—his experience of life and the sufficiency of grace—then let me discover what this grace is that he found so abundantly available and so sufficiently helpful.

Paul's physical pain

Let me introduce you to Paul's sufferings. At one level much is discovered in 2 Corinthians 6:4–10 and 11:23–27.

Paul, how many times have you been imprisoned?

'Oh, I've lost count—many times.'

And the thirty nine lashes when that cruel whip made of four leather thongs was brought down on your back thirteen times, then across your chest and once more on your back until deep, bleeding furrows were cut into your flesh? How often did you endure this for the gospel?

'Five times as I recall.'

And have you been beaten with rods?

'Yes, three times.'

Stoned by angry mobs?

'Only once. It happened at Lystra after the lame man was healed; the mob who responded by worshipping Barnabas and myself soon turned to stone-throwing when the Jews spread rumours against us. I was left for dead, but as the young converts gathered round, God wonderfully restored me.'

So you are no stranger to the threat of death?

'Not at all, And you can see the evidence in my broken body, lacerated back and the limp that I will carry with me to my grave.'

I read that you were shipwrecked once?

'Ah, that's because my dear friend Luke only mentions one occasion. In reality it was three times—including a night and day adrift in an open boat.'

So, what other danger have you faced?

'Danger from floods, bandits, Jews and Gentiles, and even false Christians.'

Where, Paul?

'Oh, all over. In cities, in the country, on the high seas.'

Anything else?

'Well, if I were to summarize my experiences I can say that I know the meaning of endurance, afflictions, hardships, calamities, beatings, imprisonments, riots, labours, sleepless nights, dishonour, slander, exhaustion, hunger, thirst, and exposure; and I understand the meaning of being poor and living constantly close to death.'

Now, I will listen to a man who has experienced all this for the sake of Christ. That is an impressive list of suffering for thirty years of missionary work, and if he really found the grace of God sufficient then he has something to teach me. But at this point Paul would interrupt our conversation and insist that he had not even begun to tell us about his real pain and suffering; apart from other things, there was the daily pressure on him of his anxiety for all the churches. When they were suffering and weak, he felt weak also; and when they were led into sin and error, he burned with anxiety and anger (2 Corinthians 11:28–29). That word 'anxiety' referred to a distraction from the main task.

Painful churches

What were those churches that distracted Paul?

The churches in Galatia were among some of the first to be won for Christ and among the first to be led astray by error. Paul experienced his first beating from the authorities with those vicious leather whips whilst he was in Galatia. At considerable personal risk he returned to make sure the new converts were well established and thoroughly grounded in the truth. But no sooner was his lacerated back turned than the 'Judaeizers' came among them and told them that as Gentile (non-Jewish) converts they had to submit to some of the old Jewish ceremonial laws if they wanted to be real Christians. And they swallowed this line! They were bewitched by false teaching. All that Paul could do as he inwardly burned with anger at the heresy being spread among them was to write an urgent letter and plead for them to come to their senses and not reject the Saviour who had paid the price for their salvation.

There were other churches, like the Christians at Colossae and Laodicea, who were in danger of being enticed away by fine-sounding but empty philosophy and futile religious observances—even the worship of angels! In addition there had been petty squabbles at Ephesus and Crete; and the Hebrew Christians, who knew their Old Testament perfectly, were making very little progress in their faith and still needed to be taught the elementary things of the Truth when, by now, they should be teaching others. Then there was the church at Corinth. Divisions and party spirit in the church, toleration of heresy, immorality that would even make their heathen neighbours blush (and that took some doing in the first century), lawsuits among the Christians, a lack of love and care for one another—these are just a few of the tragic problems at Corinth. It took Paul at least three letters and one very painful visit—during which the church told him to mind his own business and stop pulling apostolic rank on them—finally to sort them out.

No wonder Paul was distracted from the main task. There were better people in the world than some of those in the church

No wonder Paul was distracted from the main task. There were better people in the world than some of those in the church.

Painful people

Painful above all were those individuals who either caused so much trouble or who could not be relied on when the pressure mounted. There were men in Asia who seemed only to be preaching in order to parade their superior gifts against Paul (Philippians 1:15–18) and some in Greece who did all that they could to assassinate his character with barbed innuendos against him (2 Corinthians 10:2, 10). Paul wrote sadly to Timothy that in Asia everyone had deserted him when he needed them most, including Phygelus and Hermogenes; whoever they were, their failure to stand by him was a particularly painful experience (2 Timothy 1:15). Then there was Demas, who had once been so eager and who always asked Paul to add his own greetings to the churches; now he too had deserted the gospel because of the attractive pull of the world (2 Timothy 4:10). Hymenaeus and Philetus were claiming that the resurrection was past, and their beguiling message acted like gangrene in the body of the church (2 Timothy 2:17); and Alexander was well known as the troublesome blacksmith who hammered away at Paul and did him so much harm (2 Timothy 4:14). That final letter to Timothy, with its catalogue of Christian failures, was enough to frighten off any young man in the Christian ministry.

It was a lonely role for Paul as the spearhead of gospel expansion

Writing from house arrest in Rome in AD 62 Paul was clearly feeling abandoned by many when he informed the church at Philippi that so many: 'Seek their own interests, not those of Jesus Christ' (Philippians 2:21); and this added to his disappointment that he had had to send Epaphroditus back to the Philippians and Timothy would soon be on his way also—at the time they seemed to be his last two loyal colleagues (2:19–20, 25–26). We can sense his disappointment in the lament to the Colossians that of all the converts from Judaism, only Aristarchus, John Mark and Jesus Justus were currently with him (Colossians 4:10–11). It was a lonely role for Paul as the spearhead of gospel expansion.

Paul used the Greek word *catastrophe* in 2 Timothy 2:14 to describe the effect of 'quarrelling about words'. And not even the women were exempt from some of the trivial quarrelling in the churches that could do such severe damage. At Philippi, Euodia and Syntyche would work hard, long and fearlessly—just so long as they were not working together! Euodia had a beautiful name that means 'sweet smell'—but her relationship with Syntyche stank (Philippians 4:2–3).

The sharp disagreement with Barnabas over John Mark was hurtful enough (Acts 15:36–40), but nothing like the issue that forced him to confront Peter and 'even Barnabas' a few years later over the heresy of the 'Judaeizers' (Galatians 2:11–21). Peter had been so determined in his resolve to preach to the non-Jews that the gospel of salvation was by faith in Christ alone; in fact he had little alternative after his very clear commission at Joppa (Acts 10). But he became uncharacteristically fearful of the Judaeizers and before long he was refusing to eat with the Gentile converts unless they became Jewish proselytes first. By his action he was forcing the Gentile Christians to live like Jews (Galatians 2:14)—and that, for Paul, was unforgivable. Happily it all ended with Peter and Barnabas admitting their error, but it was a very painful experience at the time. Paul wrote his strong and appealing letter to the Galatians shortly after this episode when that church was facing the same error.

There were even workers who, through no fault of their own, caused Paul anxiety. Poor Trophimus was so ill that he bravely offered to be left behind at Miletus rather than hinder the missionary advance (2 Timothy 4:20); Epaphroditus nearly died in Rome, and when he eventually recovered Paul felt obliged to send him back to his home church; partly no doubt for convalescence but also to reassure his fretting family that he really was sufficiently well to travel (Philippians 2:27).

Suffering did not take Paul by surprise, though the relentless scale of it might have done. He was warned right from the start: 'How much he must suffer' for the name of the one who has saved him (Acts 9:16), and in turn he warned the young churches he established that, 'After my departure, fierce wolves will come in among you, not sparing the flock' (Acts 20:29). Paul sadly knew that many of these wolves who would cause so much devastation in the church would come from among them: 'From among your own selves will arise men speaking twisted things, to draw away the disciples after them' (v 30).

Who has suffered more than Paul's physical, spiritual and pastoral pain? So, when Paul writes about sufficient grace, I will listen carefully to such a man. He must surely know what he is talking about.

Sufficient grace

But how do we know that Paul found grace to be sufficient? Have you never wondered at some of the extravagant statements of Paul in his letters? He assures the Philippians: 'I have learned in whatever situation I am to be content. I know how to be brought low, and I know how to abound. In any and every circumstance, I have learned the secret of facing plenty and hunger, abundance and need. I can do all things through him who strengthens me' (Philippians 4:11–13). To the Corinthians he writes, 'We are afflicted in every way, but not crushed; perplexed, but not driven to despair; persecuted, but not forsaken; struck down, but not destroyed' (2 Corinthians 4:8–9). And to these same Christians who caused Paul so many headaches, he can assure them: 'Thanks be to God, who in Christ always leads us in triumphal procession, and through us spreads the fragrance of the knowledge of him everywhere' (2 Corinthians 2:14). The church at Rome is reminded that, 'We are more than conquerors through him who loved us' (Romans 8:37). The Philippians are given the seemingly impossible command: 'Rejoice in the Lord always' (Philippians 4:4), and an even more impossible example: 'I can do all things through him who strengthens me' (4:13).

What is the bridge that spans the gulf between all that suffering and disappointment among the churches and Christian workers on the one hand, and Paul's incessant optimism on the other? It is called, sufficient grace. Paul described it in 1 Corinthians 15:10, 'I worked harder than any of them, though it was not I, but the grace of God that is with me'. Whatever this grace was, it enabled Paul to be glad in his weakness, and to delight in insults, hardships, persecutions and difficulties. He says it was grace that enabled him to be strong when he was weak, to accomplish all that God wanted him to achieve and to glory in his confidence in God to such an extent that he felt that he had slipped into the foolish boasting of the super pseudo-apostles going the rounds of the churches at that time (2 Corinthians 12:11). So, what was this sufficient grace that Paul clearly found all-sufficient?

Paul's belief in the passion of God was sufficient grace

When God said to Paul, 'My grace is sufficient', that was a very intimate and personal promise. No man ever had a greater understanding of the character of God than Paul, yet his God was not remotely distant. His was a God who *felt*. An issue being debated today is how far we can speak of God feeling, even to the point of suffering, with his people. The *Westminster Confession of Faith* of 1643, which has been such a bulwark against error from the time of the Puritans onwards, describes God as, 'infinite in being and perfection, a most pure spirit, invisible, without body, parts or passions, immutable ...' The intention here is to avoid any idea that God is governed by irrational outbursts of emotion. But language changes, and the word 'passion'—and its derivative 'passionately'—does not need to have a negative reference. It certainly refers to strong emotion, but to suggest that God does not express strong emotion is altogether false. The word 'immutable' comes from a Latin word that means unchangeable. When the *Westminster Confession of Faith* later describes God as, 'most loving, gracious, merciful, long-suffering ... hating all sin', it is describing a God who, though unchangeable in the essential nature of his character, can nevertheless feel and express strong emotion. Not only does God express his love in warm and compassionate terms, but he expresses his hatred of sin in equally strong terms.

His God was not remotely distant. His was a God who felt

The Old Testament pictures a God who is grieved, concerned, and angry. He is a loving husband (Jeremiah 31:32), a caring mother (Isaiah 66:13), a compassionate father (Psalm 103:13), a watchful shepherd (Psalm 23:1), and a faithful friend (2 Chronicles 20:7). These are all pictures of a God of compassion. God cares, and cares deeply. Paul knew this, and therefore he could write to the Corinthians: 'No temptation has overtaken you that is not common to man. God is faithful, and he will not let you be tempted beyond your ability, but with the temptation he will also provide the way of escape' (1 Corinthians 10:13). The hymn writer Thomas Chisholm beautifully expressed it like this:

'Great is thy faithfulness, O God my father,
there is no shadow of turning with thee;
thou changest not, thy compassions they fail not;
as thou hast been, thou for ever wilt be.'

To speak of strong emotion or passion in *us* always implies a change; our moods shift just as the weather changes, and whilst occasionally the sun shines through a downpour, that is not normal. But this is not so with God. He does not change in any way. There are many aspects of the character of God: He is holy and just, wise and all-knowing, present everywhere, trustworthy and merciful, pure and all powerful. If we knew it, we would discover that the list is endless. But unlike us, God is always all that he is. We may sometimes observe his wrath and at other times his mercy, but still he is always both. This is why we must never suggest that one attribute or characteristic of God—like love for example—is more significant than another. Charles Wesley is both correct and incorrect when he suggests in his hymn: 'Is not all thy nature love?' The nature of God *is* wholly love—but it is wholly everything else that he is as well!

God is the most perfect expression of all true emotion, and ours is the pale sin-spoiled reflection of this

When such words as passion, compassion, love, anger and mercy are used of God, in order to avoid the danger of suggesting that God is fickle, it is common to assume that they must be what is called 'anthropomorphisms'—that is, attributing human emotions to God only as a picture to help us understand God. But there is no need for this defensiveness. These words of emotion tell us something profound about our God. To assume that just because words of emotion imply change in us they are therefore not appropriate to use of the unchangeable God, is to view them the wrong way round. In reality God is the most perfect expression of all true emotion, and ours is the pale sin-spoiled reflection of this. We are created in *his* image and likeness, he does not express himself in *our* image and likeness. Therefore all that is good in us is perfect in him, because that is where our goodness comes from. It is this very fact that makes humankind distinct from animals. In other words, it is not that God's passion is unlike ours, but it is ours that is a poor and tainted reflection of his. Viewed like this, we can certainly talk of God's passion—his ability to feel and experience.

But this begs the vital question: could God really appreciate Paul's pain? Could God suffer? To say 'no' means that Paul went through experiences of which God himself had no understanding. To say 'yes' appears to bring God to the level of flinching in agony with each lash across Paul's back! But neither of these responses is quite true.

There are two important dangers to avoid when we think about God. One is to think of God as so different from us that he is remote and unconcerned; whilst the other is to see him as so close to us that he becomes vulnerable to our own changes. This is the twin danger of extreme *transcendence* (apart from us) or extreme *immanence* (near to us). The first was expressed in deism that riddled the formal church of the eighteenth century prior to the evangelical revivals, and the second reveals itself in what is known as 'process theology' today—with its evangelical wing of 'open theology'. Open theology maintains that love is the most important attribute of God, and this means that he is sensitive and responsive (open) to us, to the extent that he does not always have his way with us and so he allows his plans to be, as Clark Pinnock expresses it: 'only possibilities of his intentions'. God has plans, but since he does not know infallibly what our response will be, he can only wait to see before he decides his next move. This is understood to be God's beautiful and sensitive relationship with his people in which he enjoys this meaningful interaction with us. It has been referred to enthusiastically as 'the weakness of God'.

These two opposite extremes—deism and open theology—have misapplied the wholeness of the character of God as both transcendent and yet immanent, unchangeable and yet moved, unaffected and yet passionate. There are many other aspects of our Christian belief that we hold in this kind of paradoxical tension: such as divine sovereignty and human responsibility, the deity and humanity of Christ, the existence of the mass of evil in the world with a God of sovereign power and infinite love. The passion of God is just such a paradox.

It was one great and glorious purpose of the coming of Christ into this world (the incarnation) to show us how human nature was intended to be; he alone was wholly without sin (Hebrews 4:15). It is in Christ that the transcendent God reveals that he is immanent. God did not *become* immanent in the incarnation he simply *demonstrates* his immanence; in the same way that God did not *become* love when he sent his Son into this world, he *shows* his love (Romans 5:8)—a love that was always there. God has always been and always will be closely and immediately active in his world.

Another great purpose of the incarnation was so that we could focus upon the Father; the Son would help us to understand what the Father is like, so that when we have seen and understood him, we have seen and understood the Father (John 14:9). Our Lord was always, unchangeably both God and Man. We may at times see more plainly his deity (when he raised Lazarus) and at other times his humanity (when he slept in the boat), but he was always and consistently, both God and Man. Of course this leaves open the mysterious wonder of the incarnation and crucifixion, as Wesley so powerfully expressed in his hymns,

> 'Our God contracted to a span,
> incomprehensibly made man.'

And,

> 'The immortal God for me has died!
> My Lord, my Love is crucified.'

But, and this is vital to grasp, Christ did not come to earth in order to experience our suffering and then return to heaven to tell the Father what suffering is like; on the contrary, he came here to tell us what God is like. So the real physical suffering of Christ expresses the real understanding of the Father. God the Father cannot suffer physical pain, but as God he fully understands physical pain and can enter into our experience of it *perfectly*.

Christ was not the Father's experiment of passion, on the contrary he was the Father's expression of passion. The Catholic theologian, Weinandy, in a detailed discussion of this issue, concludes that it is only in the incarnation that we can truly say that God suffers. This may be close to the truth, but we must avoid the conclusion that the Father's experience of suffering is only a vicarious suffering, that is to say, learnt through Christ.

Christ was not the Father's experiment of passion, on the contrary he was the Father's expression of passion

God is most certainly a passionate God. Compassion, which is the ability to pity others, necessarily implies passion, which is the ability to feel emotion in oneself. The psalmist claimed that God is a 'merciful and gracious God, slow to anger and abounding in steadfast love and faithfulness' (Psalm 86:15 see also 103:8; 111:4; 112:4; 145:8). And when Isaiah promised Israel that, 'In all their affliction he was afflicted' (Isaiah 63:9), he was telling them something profoundly relevant. Paul would have been little helped by the knowledge of a God who was not affected by his own personal suffering, or even by a God whose concern was only an intelligent response and a benevolent attitude. When Christ wept at the tomb of Lazarus, that did not only reflect what the incarnate Word felt, it was a true expression of the heart of God. Perhaps we will never understand how much God felt the agony of Job who cried out in his torment of body and spirit:

'Why is light given to him who is in misery,
And life to the bitter in soul,
Who long for death, but it comes not,
And dig for it more than for hidden treasures'
(Job 3:20–21)

Is this whole subject of the passion of God a mystery? Of course it is, and we must beware of trying to explain our Christian faith so adequately and scientifically that there are no more mysteries left. Equally we must be aware that we can so protect the revelation of God's character that we deny the very things that he wants us to enjoy. It *is* possible to believe in a God who feels and understands our suffering and pain to the fullest extent of his passionate compassion, and at the same time to maintain a God who knows and plans all things beforehand and who is sovereign and unchanging in his character. Only in heaven will we resolve all mysteries. Meanwhile, Paul found sufficient grace in the passion of his God who understood perfectly all that he suffered.

The grace that Paul

found sufficient was,

The grace that Paul found sufficient was, among other things, the knowledge of a God who was neither too distant to care nor too intimate not to be in total control. When he claimed, 'We do not have a high priest who is unable to sympathise with our weaknesses, but one who in every respect has been tempted as we are, yet without sin', he knew all this from the example of his great Friend whom he once persecuted. Therefore Paul could conclude, 'Let us then with confidence draw near to the throne of grace, that we may receive mercy and find grace to help in time of need' (Hebrews 4:15–16). The word used of Christ: 'When he saw the crowds he had *compassion* on them' (Matthew 9:36 for example), is a powerful word that expresses our Lord's passion; it means being moved with all his inner being.

... the knowledge of a

God who was neither

too distant to care nor

too intimate not to be

in total control

Sufficient grace was to know that Christ was also whipped and beaten; that he was once misunderstood by his brothers, deserted by his disciples and betrayed by a close friend; he also knew what it was to be accused of doing the devil's work, of deceiving the people and being a no-good friend of sinners; he knew what it was to be insulted and humiliated; he knew the pain of a breaking heart. And all this was more than simply an example for Paul to follow; it was his great comfort also. It was sufficient grace. But even more than this, the apostle knew that because God is perfect in his compassion and pure in his passion, he could feel with Paul even when Paul's own experience was not mirrored in the life of Christ. Paul was perfectly understood by a God who was infinite in his compassion and eternal in his watchful care.

The apostle reasoned that Christ did not come to earth in order to help the angels, but to be able to help the 'offspring of Abraham'. And it was for this reason that 'he had to be made like his brothers in every respect, so that he might become a merciful and faithful high priest in the service of God'. (Hebrews 2:16–17). Of course it was his death as a sacrifice for sin that qualified him to turn away the anger of God against us, but all that he suffered enabled him to help us when we are tested and tried.

Paul was perfectly understood by a God who was infinite in his compassion and eternal in his watchful care

I was away from home and took with me my laptop to work on; I also packed a CD containing an important programme that I needed to help me in my work. Unfortunately, every time I inserted the CD, my computer threw up a message informing me that there was insufficient memory to run the programme and I was advised to close down one of the other programmes I was running. What was infuriating was the fact that I was not running any other programmes and on checking, I discovered that there was plenty of free memory. Obviously my computer had taken it into its RAM that it had more than enough to do and could manage no more. Or, to change the picture to one familiar to all parents, how often we have responded to a child's continued harassing with the plea: 'I have only one pair of hands. I can't do everything at once.' But God's memory is never overloaded and his hands are never too full to be of assistance to any of his people, anywhere and at any time. Or, in the words of Hanani the prophet, 'The eyes of the LORD run to and fro throughout the whole earth, to give strong support to those whose heart is blameless towards him' (2 Chronicles 16:9). Many know the experience of Job in those long nights of pain when we long for the morning to come, 'When I lie down I say, "When shall I arise?" But the night is long, and I am full of tossing till the dawn' (Job 7:4). The Lord understands that perfectly for he knows how we feel. The passion of God is sufficient grace.

Paul's trust in the promises of God was also part of this sufficient grace

Contrary to the schoolboy's definition of faith as, 'Believing in what you know isn't true', Paul reassured the Christians that faith is 'the assurance of things hoped for, the conviction of things not seen' (Hebrews 11:1). Other translations emphasise that faith is the 'Substance of things hoped for, the evidence of things not seen' (AV and NKJV). Faith in God's word is both substantial and evidential. Paul believed that every promise of God was true and reliable, and he lived in the reality of that.

When Paul wrote to Timothy and sadly commented that at the first hearing before the Emperor Nero everyone deserted him, he added, 'But the Lord stood by me and strengthened me … (2 Timothy 4:17). What Paul does not tell us is just how the Lord stood beside him. Whether he felt, saw or heard anything we can only guess; but what we do know for certain is that Paul held to the promises of God. Writing in Hebrews 13:5–6 the apostle refered to both Deuteronomy 31:6 and Psalm 118:6 to remind the Christians that God will never abandon them and that with the Lord as their helper, they need never fear whatever man does to them. It was on this ground that Paul was firmly convinced that the outcome of his trial meant that either way, God would 'rescue me from every evil attack and bring me safely to his heavenly kingdom' (2 Timothy 4:18 NIV).

Like Daniel and his three friends five hundred years earlier and in a not too dissimilar culture and predicament, the outcome of the threat of fire or lions was guaranteed to bring them safely into heaven. The stories of Hananiah, Mishael, Azariah and Daniel are certainly stories of courage and victory, but they are primarily stories of faith in the trustworthiness of God. The accounts of their daring defiance of pagan persecution would have been equally well-worth telling even if the three friends had been burnt to ashes and if Daniel had been ground to meal—except that we would not have been so eager to recount them to the Sunday School! Their trust was in God to keep them safe, though not necessarily to deliver them from death. They knew that if he wished, their God would deliver them through death safely into heaven; that is exactly what lies behind those remarkable words of the friends: 'But if not ... we will not serve your gods' (Daniel 3:18). It was this trust that enabled the psalmist to declare without a fear of contradiction, 'Many are the afflictions of the righteous, but the LORD delivers him out of them all' (Psalm 34:19).

Blind unbelief will assume that God will always run to dry up the flood and douse the fire

That bold promise of God recorded in Isaiah 43:1–3 has presented a problem to some Christians: 'Fear not, for I have redeemed you; I have called you by name, you are mine. When you pass through the waters, I will be with you; and through the rivers, they shall not overwhelm you; when you walk through the fire you shall not be burned, and the flame shall not consume you. For I am the LORD your God, the Holy One of Israel, your Saviour'. In reality, Christians do drown and they do burn to death; so what of this promise then? That is exactly the point. Blind unbelief will assume that God will always run to dry up the flood and douse the fire. He may do this and at times he has done it for his people, but more significantly it is a promise that flood and fire will never have the final word for the Christian. God will always bring his people safely through—one way or the other.

In the middle of the nineteenth century John Paton left Scotland to preach to the cannibals on the Pacific island of Tanna. Before he left, one elderly Christian tried to dissuade him with the repeated and dire warning: 'The cannibals! You will be eaten by cannibals.' Eventually Paton silenced his protector: 'Mr Dickson, you are advanced in years now, and your own prospect is soon to be laid in the grave, there to be eaten by worms; I confess to you, that if I can but live and die serving and honouring the Lord Jesus, it will make no difference to me whether I am eaten by cannibals or by worms; and in the Great Day my resurrection body will arise as fair as yours in the likeness of our risen Redeemer.' To his credit the old man retreated with the concession: 'After that I have nothing more to say.' That is the deeper meaning of Isaiah 40:1–3.

Paul must have been aware of some of the most reassuring words of our Lord just before he left the disciples: 'I am with you always, to the end of the age' (Matthew 28:20). On this verse David Livingstone, the great missionary to Africa, commented in typical Victorian fashion: 'Those are the words of a gentleman of the highest honour.' However, it is disappointing that these words of our Lord have rarely been rendered in English translations with all the strength and colour of the way Matthew recorded it. Literally our Lord said, 'And behold I (emphatic) am with you all the days until the consummation of the age.' William Hendriksen paraphrases it: 'I am with you day in day out to the close of the age.' Paul lived in the light of that promise—day in and day out. He took Christ at his word, and so can we. But there was nothing new in this promise. It had always been a commitment by the Sovereign God to his people, Jacob received the promise 'I will not leave you', and Joshua was reassured as he took over from Moses the unenviable task of leading Israel into their promised land, 'Just as I was with Moses, so I will be with you. I will not leave you or forsake you' (Joshua 1:5. See also Genesis 28:15).

John Newton's wife, Mary, died on Wednesday 15 December 1790. The following Sunday the heartbroken pastor entered his ornate pulpit at St Mary Woolnoth in the City of London and announced his text: 'Although the fig tree shall not blossom, neither *shall* fruit *be* in the vines; the labour of the olive shall fail, and the fields shall yield no meat; the flock shall be cut off from the fold, and *there shall be* no herd in the stalls: Yet I will rejoice in the LORD, I will joy in the God of my salvation. The LORD God *is* my strength ...' (Habakkuk 3:17–19 *Authorised Version*). In all his ministry John had never preached on this verse before, but thirty-six years earlier, as a Customs Officer in Liverpool, he had written a letter to a friend in which he explained a serious illness of Mary for which they had little hope of her recovery; she was so weak that at times she could not bear anyone to walk across her room. However painful it was for him to see his loved one suffering like this, he wrote that he knew God to be perfectly in control and, 'What he chooses for us must be best.' He believed also that his faith was being strengthened by this suffering and that he was learning more about his own insufficiency 'and the vanity of all things about us.' More importantly, 'We discover more of the power, faithfulness and nearness of a prayer-hearing God.' John then referred to these verses from Habakkuk and concluded, 'Oh the name of Jesus when we can speak of him as ours; this is the balm for every wound, the cordial for every care; it is an ointment poured forth, diffusing a fragrancy through the whole soul, and driving away the hurtful fumes and fogs of distrust and discontent.' By the grace of God Mary was to live for another thirty-six years and when she was finally called home, this was John's text. He held to the promise of God.

My own experience similarly proved the value of his word. When in 1998 the Lord took away from me the one whom I loved more than anyone else on earth, I wanted to be reassured that she was safe with Christ. I longed for just a brief glimpse of Barbara in heaven. My knowledge of the Bible told me that this was not possible, but I caught myself explaining to the Lord that in the light of just such a brief reassurance I could wait patiently until he called me home also. I discovered that I was not alone in that longing because I came across a hymn by Newton on the same theme. It was published in the *Olney Hymns* (1779) and part of it reads like this:

> In vain our fancy strives to paint
> The moment after death,
> The glories that surround the saints
> When yielding up their breath.

> One gentle sigh their fetters breaks;
> We scarce can say, 'They're gone';
> Before the willing spirit takes
> Her mansion near the throne.

Faith strives, but all its efforts fail,
To trace her in her flight;
No eye can pierce within the veil
Which hides that world of light.

Thus much (and this is all) we know,
They are completely blessed;
Have done with sin, and care, and woe,
And with their Saviour rest.

But even as I thought about this, I knew the answer. I heard the Lord saying to me, 'Let not your hearts be troubled. Believe in God; believe also in me. In my Father's house are many rooms. If it were not so, would I have told you that I go to prepare a place for you? And if I go and prepare a place for you, I will come again and will take you to myself, that where I am you may be also' (John 14:1–3). His word was clear, and through it he said to me: 'Brian, that is all you will have to sustain you until it is your turn to come home. Are you asking for some new revelation, or some out-of-this-world experience? Is my word not enough for you? You trust the Father, then trust me.' As one who had never doubted God's word and the security of my salvation from the day of my conversion as a teenager, I sometimes think that I never knew what it was to walk by faith until the Lord took Barbara away from me. My sole evidence that she is safely at peace and joyfully with her Saviour, is his word. And since the Lord assures us that nothing is more secure than his word, then that must be sufficient grace.

Since the Lord assures us that nothing is more secure than his word, then that must be sufficient grace

It is incredible how many Christians claim to believe that the Bible is God's sufficient revelation, and yet spend so much of their time looking for additional revelations. At the close of a meeting, a man came to me and related how hard the previous year had been for him; he explained a few of the tragedies and traumas that had been part of his experience and then he added that at the start of the year someone had given him a word of prophecy that included the promise of God's help; he concluded, 'Without that prophecy I really do not know how I would have got through the year'. Well I do! He might have relied upon the promises of God in his word. To look for a twenty-first century promise to reassure us that God will never leave us and that nothing can separate us from his love or pluck us from his hand, is to suggest that the first century promises have somehow lost their credibility and reliability over the passage of two millenniums. According to Peter, God has given us all that we need for 'life and godliness' (2 Peter 1:3), and he describes part of the 'all' as the 'precious and very great promises'. With that Paul would fully agree, since he assured Timothy that the God-breathed Scriptures were sufficient to equip a man for every good work (2 Timothy 3:16–17). Paul's confident trust in the promises of God was for him a major part of sufficient grace.

Paul firmly believed

that he could

accomplish all that

God had planned for

him to do

Paul's confidence in the purposes of God was grace

Because Paul believed in purposeful grace as we saw in the previous chapter; he was convinced that all that God had called him to do, he would be able to accomplish. That is exactly what he meant when he told the Philippians, 'I can do all things through Christ who strengthens me'. We have said before that he was not so foolish as to imagine that he could swim the Mediterranean back-stroke or rid it of all the pirates that Rome was battling against with its galleys, but Paul firmly believed that he could accomplish all that God had planned for him to do. He knew that he had been called according to God's 'own purpose and grace' (2 Timothy 1:9).

However, for us all there are times when our circumstances change—often suddenly, unexpectedly and radically. It is not always to our liking or to our understanding and, like Paul with his 'thorn in the flesh' we argue that there is surely a better way; how much more useful we could be if … I have argued that way myself, for too long and too often. Sufficient grace is when I accept his wisdom in place of mine and his plans instead of mine—and go on with the work he has given me to do. Paul also believed that in all the circumstances of his life there was a higher purpose than may appear immediately. It was precisely this that led John Newton to claim during Mary's severe illness that through it, 'We discover more of the power, faithfulness and nearness of a prayer-hearing God.'

Writing to the first century Christians the apostle expressed his confidence like this: 'Therefore, let us be grateful for receiving a kingdom that cannot be shaken, and thus let us offer to God acceptable worship, with reverence and awe' (Hebrews 12:28). God alone can give us grace to accept the purposes of God in our life and to believe that whatever our situation or suffering he has a plan for us and therefore a place for us in the work of his Kingdom. In the words of Samuel Medley, God is 'too wise to be mistaken and too good to be unkind.'

Like Paul, we often longed for a way out, but like Paul also we learnt that it was more valuable to find a way through

There is always purpose in life. More than once Paul struggled with the dilemma of longing to be away from this world of injustice and pain and be with Christ which is 'far better'; but he checked himself with the knowledge that for the sake of the churches it was better that he should remain here a while longer (Philippians 1:23–24). He learnt in Asia that the severe suffering that caused him to despair of life was always for a purpose and would teach him to rely more upon the Lord and less upon himself (2 Corinthians 1:8–10). Even the frustration of a closed door at Mysia proved to be the means of an open door to Philippi (Acts 16:6–10).

With a degenerating disease that eventually left Barbara confined to a wheelchair for twelve years, we had to learn that each new downturn was not to be seen only as an inevitable decline in mobility, but an opportunity for a new experience. Like Paul, we often longed for a way out, but like Paul also we learnt that it was more valuable to find a way through. Expecting light at the end of a tunnel is living in hope, but finding light *in* the tunnel is a far better reality. The experience of a deepening love for each other, the joy of Christian friends who cared, the more than sufficient provision of God for our needs, the opportunity of expressing our trust in God when life ran against us, and the certain hope of a heaven, were what we called, 'the better side of worse'.

Every rock thrown at his head, every lash that ploughed across his back and every chain that chafed his wrists and ankles had a meaning in the purposeful grace of God

Across the world today there are tens of thousands of Christians who are persecuted for their faith: Fathers taken away from their families and daughters taken away from their parents; brothers and sisters in Christ denied justice and tortured. Harassment, arrest, interrogation, imprisonment, fines, torture and death are some of the ways that religious and atheistic governments pursue their vain attempt to stamp out the Christian faith. In two thousand years of Christian history such methods have failed entirely to do more than dent the community of which Christ promised that the gates of Hades would not prevail against it (Matthew 16:18). Yet still persecution and injustice appear to prevail. Paul experienced this, but in his own case the persecutor became the persecuted. Every rock thrown at his head, every lash that ploughed across his back and every chain that chafed his wrists and ankles had a meaning in the purposeful grace of God.

Paul was convinced that packed into his almost unbearable suffering in Asia was not only benefit for himself as he experienced the comfort that

Christ could give, but also benefit for the Corinthians as they too learnt from him how to find consolation in Christ, 'For as we share abundantly in Christ's sufferings, so through Christ we share abundantly in comfort too. If we are afflicted, it is for your comfort and salvation; and if we are comforted, it is for your comfort, which you experience when you patiently endure the same sufferings that we suffer' (2 Corinthians 1:5–6).

Paul's pleasure in the people of God was sufficient grace

In 1783 John Newton, with a small group of fellow evangelical ministers, commenced a regular meeting to discuss matters of common concern. They called it 'The Eclectic Society' and John kept a notebook of the issues they discussed. In December 1795 one of the subjects on the agenda was, 'How may we best introduce religious conversation in company?' There was a history behind that question. When John had arrived to begin his ministry in the City of London in 1780 he soon discovered that his evangelical views were not at all acceptable among many in the fashionable society of his new parish. He wrote sadly to a friend that he received very few invitations into homes, and when he did, the conversation was simply polite and no more; it seemed almost impossible to steer the conversation onto profitable subjects, and yet he was dissatisfied simply to be there and be of no value to them. To join in their trivial conversation in order to bring them up to his, 'would be a rather hazardous experiment'. He felt very much alone.

Sooner or later every Christian will know what it means to be on the edge of a crowd

Paul also knew what it was to be alone. He often found himself in aggressive company; deserted even by those who shared the same message. Sooner or later every Christian will know what it means to be on the edge of a crowd, outside the chattering conversation, snubbed by colleagues because their views do not fit the current topic. Or else there is the loneliness of being the only one in the home to serve Christ, the only one in the office to refuse the lottery, or the only one in the lecture hall not sleeping with her boyfriend.

We began with a very black portrait of people in the first century church: those who reneged on the truth, quarrelled over trifles and abandoned Paul in his need. But not all were like this. One of Paul's greatest joys was the fellowship he had with Christians, and their progress in the gospel. Here is Paul writing to some of the churches:

'Because I have heard of your faith in the Lord Jesus and your love towards all the saints, I do not cease to give thanks for you' (Ephesians 1:15–16).

'I thank my God in all my remembrance of you, always in every prayer of mine for you all making my prayer with joy, because of your partnership in the gospel from the first day until now' (Philippians 1:3–5).

'We always thank God, the Father of our Lord Jesus Christ, when we pray for you, since we heard of your faith in Christ Jesus and of the love that you have for all the saints' (Colossians 1:3–4).

'We give thanks to God always for all of you, constantly mentioning you in our prayers, remembering before our God and Father your work of faith and labour of love, and steadfastness of hope in our Lord Jesus Christ' (1 Thessalonians 1:2–3).

'We ought always to give thanks to God for you, brothers, as is right, because your faith is growing abundantly, and the love of every one of you for one another is increasing. Therefore we ourselves boast about you in the churches of God for your steadfastness and faith in all your persecutions and in the afflictions that you are enduring' (2 Thessalonians 1:3–4).

Ah, that's better! There is much to encourage us, providing we keep our eyes on the faithful Christians who work so hard, so long and so loyally for Jesus Christ. The doctor who assesses the whole of society by the people he meets in his surgery each day will have a miserably jaundiced view of life; let him go out to the local sports field on a fine Saturday morning and he will gain an altogether different and far more encouraging perspective. So Paul, ever the model of balanced Christian theology and experience, was sufficiently realistic to admit both the tragedy of fallout and the encouragement of faithful workers. They are all part of sufficient grace.

In the course of my ministry I see so much petty squabbling, unnecessary divisions, harsh criticism, and downright sinful behaviour among Christians. Sometimes those who have been battered and bruised by 'brothers' tell me it is always like this—sadly that's just the way Christians are. But I can tell them that it does not have to be like that. For nearly forty years I have been part of a caring and united local church where love and a happy respect for leadership reigns; and there are many others like it across the nation—and beyond.

Let me introduce you to some of Paul's best encouragements.

There was 'My dear friend Epaenetus', who was the first convert to Christ in the province of Asia (Romans 16:5), and hard-working Epaphras 'A dear fellow servant and faithful minister' who, like Aristarchus, was prepared to stand by Paul even when it meant that he became a 'fellow prisoner' (Colossians 1:7; 4:10), and Epaphroditus Paul's 'brother, fellow worker, and fellow soldier' who nearly gave his life for Paul's sake and who should be held in high esteem by everyone (Philippians 2:25–30). Then there was Luke 'the beloved physician' (Colossians 4:14), and Onesiphorus, the prison visitor who searched all over Rome until he found where Paul was being held and, at great risk to himself, so often encouraged Paul (2 Timothy 1:16–18), and even Onesimus who, as a runaway slave had forfeited his life, found Paul, got converted and was now on his way back to his master as a valuable 'brother' from now on (Colossians 4:9; Philemon 8–20). Even John Mark, that first-term failure who caused such a rift between Paul and Barnabas, became so useful to Paul (2 Timothy 4:11) and, as Peter's assistant, wrote out one of the gospel stories. Paul spoke so highly of Tychicus, 'a beloved brother, faithful minister, and fellow servant in the Lord' (Colossians 4:7), and Apelles who was 'approved in Christ' (Romans 16:10).

To counterbalance those two at loggerheads in Philippi, there were many women who served the gospel with encouraging zeal, like Phoebe who had been such a help to so many, not least to Paul himself (Romans 16:1–2); and Tryphaena and Tryphosa—presumably two sisters—and 'the beloved Persis' who 'worked hard in the Lord' (v 12). The mother of

Rufus was like a mother to Paul himself; we can imagine her fussing over his welfare—and this in a church he had never yet visited (v 13); and Nympha opened her home regularly as a meeting place for the believers (Colossians 4:15).

Then there were the husband and wife teams that gave Paul such hope for the future of the church. Priscilla and Aquila appear constantly in the story of the young church; firm in their grasp of the truth they always opened their home for a church to gather, risked their lives often for the sake of Paul and, especially noteworthy since they were converted Jews, took similar risks also for 'all the churches of the Gentiles' (Romans 16:3–5; 1 Corinthians 16:19). His relatives, Andronicas and Junia were converted before Paul himself and obviously prayed him into the kingdom (Romans 16:7); their loyal support was well known among the apostles, though it clearly got them into trouble and they were at one point 'fellow prisoners' with Paul himself.

The grace of the

Christian community

is a privilege we

should never neglect

We can be so distracted by the fools and failures that we overlook the army of men and women who ensure that the church remains strong, healthy and true to the gospel. Paul knew there would be hard times ahead, but he was confident that there were sufficient wise heads and stout hearts to guide and guard the church when he had been taken into that 'Heavenly kingdom'. Even when Paul felt alone, and when he was in reality isolated in his prison cell, he could thank God for the family to which God had called him three decades before. And when he knelt friendless in the execution yard with only the buzz of the flies, the distant sounds of the city about its work, the rough scrape of steel on leather as the soldier drew his sword from its sheath, and the clink of harness as the legionary lifted his arms for a powerful thrust, Paul was not alone. Like Stephen, whom he had watched die with a face like that of an angel, Paul knew himself to be surrounded by the testimony of a great cloud of witnesses who had gone before him, and innumerable angels in their joyful gathering (Hebrews

12:1, 22). And, as always, the Lord stood at his side. He was not alone even then.

To be part of this magnificent and universal family here on earth, with all the privileges of that—and to know that we shall spend eternity with such people all made perfect in Christ—is all part of God's grace to his people. The grace of the Christian community is a privilege we should never neglect.

Sufficient grace in any and every time of need is the grace of a God who cares, his promises that will never be broken, a purpose that he will always fulfil and his people who will always be ours.

HOW FIRM A FOUNDATION, YOU SAINTS OF THE LORD,
is laid for your faith in his excellent word!
What more can he say than to you he has said,
to all who for refuge to Jesus have fled?

2 In every condition—in sickness, in health,
in poverty's grip or abounding in wealth,
at home or abroad, on the land, on the sea—
as days may demand shall your strength ever be.

3 Since Jesus is with you, do not be afraid;
since he is your God, you need not be dismayed:
he'll strengthen you, guard you, and help you to stand,
upheld by his righteous, omnipotent hand.

4 When through the deep waters he calls you to go,
you will not be drowned in the rivers of woe;
for he will be with you in trouble, to bless
and work for your good through your deepest distress.

5 When through fiery trials your pathway shall lie,
his grace all-sufficient shall be your supply;
the flames shall not harm you: his only design
your dross to consume and your gold to refine.

6 The soul that in Jesus has found its repose,
he will not, he cannot, desert to its foes;
that soul, though all hell should endeavour to shake,
he'll never, no never, no never forsake!

'K' IN RIPPON'S SELECTION 1787
Praise! 877 © in this version Praise Trust

Chapter 12

Community grace

'Grace was given to each one of us according to the measure of Christ's gift' Ephesians 4:7

A t 11.00 pm on 9 November 1989 East German border guards threw open the gates of the Berlin wall and crowds surged through. Excited German citizens from the West tore at the wall with their bare hands and carried off pieces of the old way of life as souvenirs. This twenty-eight mile barrier—a symbol of half a century of division—was at last coming down. Those on the eastern side had been *separated* from all the benefits of the west, *alienated* from West German citizenship, and were *strangers* in their own land. Because they were members of an atheistic state they were, in theory at least, *without God* in the world, and although geographically they were in close proximity to their neighbours, they were in reality *far away*; the relationship between the two states was one of *hostility* and *alienation*, and, under the harsh boot of communism they were *without hope*. Suddenly everything changed and they were now, at long last, together with their friends and relatives. The world talked excitedly about the 'unification' of Germany. Scenes of union and togetherness were flashed across the media. The whole world watched and rejoiced. It was as if a miracle had taken place.

Paul in his letter to the Ephesians was writing about a far greater and a real, not imagined, miracle. Ten years earlier there had been no Christians in Ephesus: only a ghetto of Jews meeting in their synagogues, pagan philosophers debating in the Hall of Tyrannus, profiteering bankers, merchants in their money changing dens, and devotees of Diana the goddess worshipping at her magnificent temple situated on the hill some one and half miles northeast of the city. To describe what these people were Paul used in Ephesians 2 all the words I have just employed to describe the East Germans before the great barrier came down. The Ephesians were *separated* from Christ (v 12), *alienated* from citizenship in the Kingdom of God (v 12), *strangers* to God's promises (v 12), *far away* from him (v 13),

Grace—amazing grace **241**

and *hostile* (v 14) and *strangers and aliens* from God himself (v 19). In fact they were *without God* in the world and consequently *without hope* (v 12). To shift anyone from there to somewhere else requires a miracle—and only God can do miracles. That miracle was God's undeserved saving grace towards the Ephesians which brought them into all the benefits of community grace.

But everything that was true of the Ephesians is equally true of all who have become Christians. Like them, whoever we are and whatever our background, we were separated from Christ, excluded from citizenship in the Kingdom of God, foreigners to God's promises and, as Christ rejecters, we were alienated from God and often from each other. We were hopeless, godless and far off. Then came the miracle. As in Ephesus two thousand years ago, today people from widely different interests and education, temperament and personality, religions, languages and cultures are converted to Christ; his righteousness is reckoned to their account and those who were without hope and without God become united not only to him, but to each other also. Across the world at any moment in time there are hundreds of thousands of congregations of Christians meeting to worship and serve their Friend and Saviour, Jesus Christ. Clearly Paul was incredibly impressed by the fact that God can turn all this aggressive diversity into a remarkable unity. This is his constant theme throughout this letter to the Ephesian Christians. It was all part of the beautiful word 'grace'. Grace for community is expressed in the phrase: 'Grace was given to each one of us according to the measure of Christ's gift.' The context is gifts for sharing in the church. The apostle felt exactly the same when he wrote to the Philippians: 'You are all partakers with me of grace' (Philippians 1:7).

There are many things that threaten this unity, but Paul did not begin by addressing the problems; in his letters he always set out first to remind the Christians what they are and only then did he tell them how to live. Let me show you what I mean by community grace by drawing attention to something you may never have noticed in this letter to the Christians at Ephesus.

Paul's 'together' word

There is a small three letter word in Greek that means 'together' or 'with'.

The Greek word *sun* often stands on its own, as it does in 3:18, '*with* all the saints'. This little word is very important and has been described as the 'aristocrat' among the prepositions. Paul had another more common word for 'with' that he could choose from, and he used that one over four hundred times. But he employed this word *sun* on its own sparingly—only around forty times in his letters. *Sun* often carries the idea of union, or what we may call 'togetherness'. In Romans 6:4–8 the word occurs three times to describe our relationship with Christ: we are 'buried *with* him by baptism' (v 4), 'united *with* him in a death and in a resurrection like his'(v 5), and we are 'crucified *with* him' (v 6).

However, more importantly for us, Paul used this little word in Ephesians as a prefix: that is, as a word bolted onto the front end of another word—either a noun or a verb—to give it the meaning of being or behaving *together*. On no fewer than eleven occasions in this letter Paul chose a word with the prefix *sun* attached to it. Find them with me.

In 2:5–6 Paul used three verbs as descriptions of what Christ has done for us. He has, 'made us alive' (v 5), 'raised us up' and 'seated us with Christ' (v 6). But each verb has this prefix *sun* so that what Paul was emphasising is that we are, 'made alive together with Christ', 'raised up together with him', and 'seated together in the heavenly places in Christ Jesus'. It might be argued that the emphasis, as some translations imply, is simply upon us being made alive *with* Christ, raised up *with* him and seated *with* him—all of which is true of course. But if that was all that Paul wanted to say, he need not have chosen a verb with *sun* as the prefix; instead he could have allowed the word to stand on its own. This is especially clear in Colossians 3:1, 3 and 4, where Paul wrote that we are 'raised with Christ', 'hidden with Christ', and will 'appear with him in glory'; in each case *sun* stands as a word on its own and not as a prefix. So here in Ephesians 2:5–6, by bolting it on to the front of a verb Paul wanted to emphasise the fact that Christians share together in the action. This is made more certain by the following uses of our little prefix.

In Ephesians 2:19–22 there are five nouns to describe what we are as Christians: Citizens (v 19), a household (v 19), a building (v 21), a temple (v 21), and a dwelling (v 22). Three times in those verses Paul chose a word with our prefix; so, we are, 'citizens together', 'joined together', 'built together'. And whilst the word for 'household' does not have our prefix, it hardly needs it because the word literally means 'belonging to a family'. In Ephesians 3:6 there are three more nouns to describe the local church: heirs, members, sharers. Once again each word carries our prefix, so we are, 'heirs together', 'members together' and, 'sharers together'. Sadly, most of our translations (the NIV excepted) fail to express this clear intention of Paul. Finally in Ephesians 4:16 Paul used two verbs to describe the church in its activity and each has our prefix; we are, 'joined together', and 'held (united) together'.

So, there are eleven words in this letter with the prefix 'together', and twice it is used as a stand alone (3:18 and 4:31). Thirteen times in all.

Here, then is a summary of Paul's use of our small aristocratic preposition: At conversion we are made alive in Christ—together; we are raised up from death—together; we are seated with Christ in heavenly places—together. And what are the benefits of that? We are citizens together, joined together, built together, heirs together, members together, sharers together, and united together.

Butterflies and bulldozers

That should all be very clear and the broad implications will be obvious. When I receive the undeserved grace of God for salvation, it brings me into all the privileges of the people who belong to God—the Christian community. Undeserved grace is also community grace and one application of this is that the New Testament never recognizes a Christian who is not joined to a local congregation of Christians—what we call 'a church'. That is very important. It is not to say that someone cannot be a Christian unless they belong to a local church, but that the New Testament simply does not recognize such a thing as a Christian who is not actively part of the family. The letters of Paul are all written to churches or leaders of churches; Philemon was host to a church in Colossae (Philemon 2) and Timothy and Titus were leaders of the churches in Ephesus and Crete respectively.

There are some things in the New Testament that are considered as possible but not permissible. One example is an unholy Christian; it is certainly possible to take Christ as Saviour and yet not acknowledge his lordship over every area of life, but the New Testament does not allow such a contradiction—it is simply not recognised. Similarly it is possible to be a Christian but not baptized, since salvation does not depend upon any sacrament or ceremony; but, again, the New Testament never records an unbaptized Christian. In just the same way, nowhere in the record of Acts or the letters of Paul is there any acceptance or even recognition of someone converted and baptized but not joined to a local church. These things are all possible, but they are not permissible—they are not allowed.

Nowhere in the record of Acts or the letters of Paul is there any acceptance ... of someone converted and baptized but not joined to a local church

There are many reasons why some Christians remain permanently on the edge, standing alone and apart from a local church. A few are like delicate flowers that have been damaged in one garden and believe their wisest course is never to put down their roots anywhere; in this way, they will not be hurt again. Occasionally they will talk darkly about having met 'too many hypocrites in the church'—as if the rest of us haven't. Their position is perhaps understandable but it is certainly not excusable. Christianity is always at risk from the world and from false Christians. Our Lord himself was betrayed by a friend and abandoned by the others; Paul was deserted by Demas, hammered by Alexander the blacksmith, and offended by the quarrelling spirit of Euodia and Syntyche. But neither Jesus not Paul abandoned the church—on the contrary, the one laid its foundation and the other built on it.

Closely aligned with those who keep clear for fear of being hurt, are the more 'spiritual' who so enjoy good preaching that they would hate to be tied to the same man week after week. They attend all the best conferences and know all the best preachers—they have become connoisseurs of the finest rhetoric—but no one in their locality quite matches the big men on circuit. Some of these drifters may even attend a local church regularly, but they make no public commitment, no corporate promise, no declared loyalty, and best of all, they can get out easily. It is their form of ecclesiastical cohabitation. Others simply coast around from church to church, conference to conference, preacher to preacher. There is something even worse than cohabiting—but I will leave you to press my analogy. A more generous description is that they are spiritual butterflies: a little nectar here and there is what they are after. Butterflies often look impressive—but they have a very short lifespan.

There are also lazy Christians who stay on the fringe simply to avoid anyone expecting anything of them. They will often find some 'principle' that keeps them out of joining a local church, but in reality they prefer to stay in the comfort zone of Christianity; taking up a cross daily to follow Christ is not very appealing.

A traditionalist is one who mistakes the customs of his church for the laws of God

Others hold to such a narrow theology and demand agreement on so many details that there are few Christians left with whom they can have a meaningful relationship. They are like bulldozers that are quite incapable of distinguishing between a concrete slab and a Ming vase. They cannot tell the difference between the rigid phantom truths of their own preference or tradition and the beautiful and vital truths that are essential for giving or maintaining true spiritual life. Consequently there is almost no one who quite fits into their constricted mould. They draw a small circle around themselves and effectively defy anyone to squeeze in beside them; they alone are 'faithful to the truth'. From their splendid isolation they can demolish just about everyone else. This is inexcusable and sinfully schismatic—and too common. I discovered a wise saying of the humanist George Bernard Shaw: 'A barbarian is one who mistakes the customs of his tribe for the laws of nature.' If I may turn that a little to my own end I would say that a traditionalist is one who mistakes the customs of his church for the laws of God.

John Newton wrote to a young man on the subject: 'On hearing sermons'. It might equally have been entitled, 'On choosing a church'. Having outlined the various kinds of preaching, and admitting that probably no one preacher embodies all the gifts of 'Christian advocacy', Newton then encouraged his reader to find the man 'where your soul may be best fed'. Having found such a preacher, the converted sea captain who once preached no more eloquently than to harangue his insolent slave trading crew, advised, 'You will do well to make a point of attending his ministry constantly … the seldomer you are absent the better.' Newton offered his reasons for this advice: 'It encourages the minister, affords a good example to the congregation, and a hearer is more likely to meet with what is directly suited to his own case, from a minister who knows him, and expects to see him, than he can from one who is a stranger.' The wise pastor warned his reader: 'Especially I would not wish you to be absent for the sake of gratifying your curiosity to hear some new preacher, who you have perhaps been told is a very extraordinary man.' John had his own analogy from Scripture for those who run about after new preachers; they reminded him of Proverbs 27:8, 'As a bird that wandereth from her nest so is the man that wandereth from his place.' He then summed up these wanderers perfectly: 'Such unsettled hearers seldom thrive: they usually grow wise in their own conceits, have their heads filled with notions, acquire a dry, critical, and censorious spirit; and are more intent upon disputing who is the best preacher than upon obtaining benefit to themselves from what they hear.'

By his eleven times use of the word 'together' as a prefix, Paul was clearly insistent on the value of corporate grace. So, just what is its value? Let me give it to you under three of the pictures Paul uses in 2:19–21. He wrote of our privilege as fellow citizens, God's household, and a holy temple.

Fellow citizens with the saints (Ephesians 2:19)
Ephesus was the most important city in the Roman province of Asia and financially the most secure; to be a citizen of Ephesus was to be a citizen of Rome also, with all the *Pax Romana* security and privileges of that, including a fair trial and strong leadership. But many of these young Christians were slaves who had no rights of citizenship, and others, who

would later refuse to worship the Emperor, would soon be stripped of theirs; a number were not Israelites before their conversion, therefore they could not even boast a great ancestry among the chosen nation of God. So, in the early dawn before they went off to their daily work, some of the recent converts who sat on the hard benches of their meeting place in Ephesus must have wondered what they had let themselves in for as they listened to one of the elders reading Paul's newly arrived letter. Just as they had not belonged to Israel so they did not belong to Rome either. They knew only too well that since following Christ they had been excluded from citizenship and treated like foreigners and aliens—often even in their own home. They no longer worshipped at the temple of Diana or at the synagogue of the Jews, so where did they belong? Where was their security? They were strangers where once they felt at home. And worse, having abandoned the gods of their fathers and the state, they were ridiculed as *atheos*—atheist.

This has been the common experience of true disciples of Christ throughout the two millennia since Tychicus brought Paul's letter to the church at Ephesus. Christians should never feel comfortably at home in society. The jarring conversation and language, the crude *double entendre*, the loss of credibility because they choose not to see the most recent movie, the refusal to follow all that is 'politically correct'; these all contribute to an alienation from the very society in which they were born. One hundred years before Paul wrote this letter, Cicero, the Roman philosopher and statesman, had written of: 'The beach parties, dinner parties, drinking parties, musical parties, concert parties and boating parties' in connection with what he called, 'orgies, cohabitations and adulteries'. Nothing much had changed up to the time of the early church—and nothing much has changed since.

In the eighteenth century John Newton experienced this alienation from his society very early in his Christian life. When anchored in St Christopher's in the West Indies, the captains would spend the evenings entertaining each other on their ships. This unusual captain put up with a good deal of banter and even abuse from the other captains. They could not understand a man who prayed, read his Bible and wrote letters to his wife. 'They *think* I have not a right notion of life', John wrote in one of his letters to Mary, 'and I *am sure* they have not. They say I am melancholy; I tell them they are mad. They say, I am a slave to one woman, which I deny; but can prove that some of them are mere slaves to a hundred. They wonder at my humour; I pity theirs. They can form no idea of my happiness.' John was certain of this last point and confessed that he would have been ashamed if such men, who 'can be pleased with a drunken debauch, or the smile of a prostitute', could understand his joy.

But mere ridicule is paltry compared to the suffering of thousands of Christians across the world today. For the sake of Christ many are thrown out of their homes and employment, experience their wife and children turned against them, suffer imprisonment, torture and death. Governments driven by the religions of atheism and Islam—of which North Korea and Saudi Arabia are only two of the more obvious examples—openly forbid anyone to convert to Christ; with the threat of torture or death, and mostly with the full support of their society. It is sadly too easy to point to the modern parallels of first century Rome.

What comfort would these young Christians find in Paul's letter before they moved off into the routine of their tedious daily work? Some of them looked across the meeting hall to where their master sat, and wondered what their new found faith had to offer them to break down this terrible social barrier where two thirds of the population owned the remaining one third and often treated them as nothing more than vocal implements? It was a miserable existence to own nothing—not even your wife and children— and to have no citizenship, no rights, no future and no hope.

The words 'You are fellow citizens with the saints', were calculated to jerk young Demosthenes awake and to fix his eyes on his owner across the way. The elder was explaining what Paul meant here. Our true and lasting citizenship is in heaven and for now, Jews and Gentiles, philosophers and pagans, senators and schoolmasters, slaves, serfs and freemen, bankers and merchants, are all one in Christ—citizens together. The elder pointed out that just as Roman citizenship was obtained either by birth or at a cost, so both were true of the Christian's citizenship. Our great Emperor has paid the price for our peace with God at the cost of his own life, and by a new birth we became citizens of heaven. There is an immediate cessation of hostilities between us and God—and between us and each other!

When we become a Christian we are not like an illegal immigrant with all the stigma attributed to that, on the contrary we are welcomed immediately as a fellow citizen—and by the King himself. This incredible truth would register well with Demosthenes. He who was stateless and perhaps did not even know who his parents or country of origin were, was assured of an eternal citizenship that no one could take away from him. It was, as Peter would write some years later: 'An inheritance that is imperishable, undefiled and unfading, kept in heaven for you' (1 Peter 1:4). This was like music to the ears of our imaginary servant Demosthenes.

If we will be with these people in heaven, however can we walk out on them here?

We are citizens of the same king—and what a king! We are under the same protection—and what a divine protector! We are heading for the same destination— and what a glorious goal that is! At the very least we must consider that if we will be with these people in heaven, however can we walk out on them here? And if we will be in perfect fellowship and harmony in eternity, how can we spend our time in petty squabbling now?

Members of the household of God (Ephesians 2:19)

If Demosthenes had slipped in his concentration because of his early morning church attendance, this expression would bring him back to reality. Aristotle viewed slaves as little more than animals in value; the old and infirm were often sold off like broken beasts and the philosopher accurately concluded that, 'Three things make up the life of a slave: work, punishment and food.' Admittedly it was not all like this, and some slaves were treated well and eventually purchased their own freedom. But it was a pure lottery which way your ownership fell. All slave revolts failed, and tens of thousands of slaves were killed in the aftermath. In the year AD 61, the very year in which Paul most likely sent this letter to Ephesus from his house arrest in Rome, the City Prefect in the capital, Lucius Pedanius Secundus, was murdered by one of his slaves. Custom required that every slave under the same roof—in this case four hundred men, women and children—should be executed. A riot to oppose such severity forced the Emperor Nero to line the route to their execution with troops to prevent disorder. News of such enormous barbarity soon found its way down to Ephesus and, as was intended, fear spread across the slave population. Others sitting around Demosthenes, though serfs or freemen, had been thrown out of their homes when they became Christians. The riot over the great goddess Artemis (Diana) was still fresh in everyone's memory.

Paul was putting a new spin on these relationships: we are all 'family'. In fact, there was living proof among them that Paul meant what he said. Tychicus not only carried this letter from Paul to Ephesus (Ephesians 6:21) but on the same journey he carried a letter to the church at Colossae (Colossians 4:7) and one to Philemon in whose home the church at Colossae met (Philemon 1–2). However, what is even more significant is that Tychicus was accompanied by Onesimus who, some time before, had stolen from his slave master and run. Philemon was that slave master. Onesimus had found his way to the great metropolis—possibly to hide—but perhaps in a panic he made contact with Paul about whom he had heard during his time in Philemon's house. The runaway slave was converted and was now on his way back to his master. With the example in mind of what happened to the slaves of Lucius Pedanius Secundus, we can imagine how Onesimus was feeling!

The journey from Rome to Colossae would naturally stop off en route at Ephesus to deliver the letter to that church. So when the elder read Paul's words: 'You are members of the household of God', all eyes would turn to Onesimus. In fact, since Tychicus would have known the content of the letter he carried for Philemon, he could have confirmed to the congregation at Ephesus that Paul really meant all that was implied. In this very letter Paul informed Philemon that he was sending Onesimus back: 'No longer as a slave but more than a slave, as a beloved brother—especially to me, but how much more to you, both in the flesh and in the Lord' (Philemon 15). And Paul was hoping to make a follow-up visit to Colossae to check out that Onesimus had been treated as a brother.

Demosthenes felt more at ease; he was now a member of the very household in which he was a slave! This meant that his master sitting opposite was a brother—or at least a father—from whom he could expect far better treatment than before and to whom he would render far more diligent service than ever.

The church as a family is a beautiful description and one of the most appealing. Today we are told that concepts like God as Father and the church as family are of little meaning in a society where so many hate a cruel father—or do not know who or where their father is—and few know anything of the harmony and security of a good family. But that is precisely why these pictures are so relevant. The first century view of God and experience of families was even less 'Christian' than today's society. Many in the congregation at Ephesus had no idea what 'family' meant; they had lost contact with their father and mother years ago, even if they ever knew them. Their brothers and sisters were sold into slavery nations apart. And this is precisely why Paul introduces the idea of the church as a family. He wants the church to live and behave as a family, so that others can come among them and learn what family is all about. If the world does not learn about family from the local church—both through its individual families and its corporate life— where else can it expect to learn about it?

When a local church behaves like a true family it is the most beautiful society on earth

A family has all ages, and a good family enjoys clear leadership and warm relationships. As in any family there may be upsets and differences, but when there are we must remember who we are. This is God's family. Families care, show interest and support the weak. In healthy families there is conversation between young and old and relationships across divides. By our new birth we are born into the family of God. We have no choice in that. Neither do we have a choice in who our brothers and sisters are! We may not like them all the time, or agree with them all the time, but they are part of the same family, and when a local church behaves like a true family it is the most beautiful society on earth.

Family is the great leveller. Within the context of leadership, family reminds us of the value and dignity of each member. The father is not more important than the son, nor the mother more significant than her daughter; older and younger brothers and sisters are of equal value. A good family thrives on the fact that we all care for one another; however costly this may be. Writing to the Galatians, Paul reminded them of their duty as Christians to do good to everyone as much as they were able, but 'especially to those who are of the household of faith' (Galatians 6:10). Onesimus would still be a slave to his master, but now the relationship would be wholly different. Philemon must model to his society what a slave owner should be like, and it would be so much easier since his returned slave was a brother. Philemon's neighbours would be scandalized by his response to a runaway slave, and even more so to hear this talk of 'brother'. This was radical in first century society. And a good family is almost as radical today.

With all our prayers for success, conversions, power or whatever else we think we need most from God, there can be little doubt that some of our greatest prayers should be that our church should live and work together as a model family. We should be able to say to a confused society: look at our church and see what the word 'family' means.

This a theme that Paul places at the centre of so much of his writing. Whenever he writes of gifts and leadership it is in the context of this family. The grace for the community that he writes of in Ephesians 4:7 is all about one another. Gifts are never meant to impress but encourage; and they are not merely natural but spiritual. The very word for 'gift' (*charisma*) is derived from the word grace (*charis*). The gifts that are given to each member by the Spirit are distributed for the sake of one another (Romans 12:6). Even our conversation is to be for the benefit of this community grace: 'Let no corrupting talk come out of your mouths, but only such as is good for building up, as fits the occasion, that it may give grace to those who hear' (Ephesians 4:29). Even the insistent giving of the church in Macedonia for the famine relief of Judea is described three times by Paul as an act of grace (2 Corinthians 8:1–7). Peter picks up the same theme: 'As each has received a gift, use it to serve one another, as good stewards of God's varied grace.' (1 Peter 4:10). The word 'steward' refers to the manager of a household. All this is part of community grace.

A holy temple (Ephesians 2:21)

As Paul moved away from his picture of the family he arrived at the symbol of the Christians as a 'holy temple'. Perhaps our young Demosthenes had been converted from the pagan worship of Artemis. Regularly he would have made his way up the hill to the great Temple of Diana. With its one hundred massive columns, thirty-six of which were elaborately sculptured, it was one of the seven wonders of the ancient world. Once there, the intricate decorations and the precise and mysterious ritual of the priests made a massive impact on the mind of our young slave whose education had been suddenly ended when he was dragged away from his home during some local conflict with the legionaries of Rome. But since his conversion to Christ, those regular visits to the magnificent Temple of Diana had gone, and he now sat on a hard bench in the courtyard of the largest home available among the Christians in the city.

In an idle moment Demosthenes gazed around him. He was uncomfortably aware that he no longer had a great building to worship in; no marble pillars with ornate carvings at their base; nothing impressive to invite his friends to. If he told them where he had been they would laugh at him. After all, Ephesus was the centre for Diana worship; the city was the custodian of her religion, and pilgrims travelled across the Empire to admire this magnificent structure and bring their offerings to the goddess who had entrusted her honour to the Ephesians. Demosthenes had been so proud of all this. If only the Christians had a beautiful temple.

Perhaps Paul anticipated thoughts like this and his reply to Demosthenes would have been immediate: 'But you do have a temple. It is magnificently beautiful, far beyond that of Diana. The building has a firm foundation, a reliable cornerstone, and each part is so carefully constructed that as the blocks are fitted together the whole becomes a glorious holy temple; and, unlike the temple of Diana, this one is eternal.' And if Demosthenes questioned, 'Where is it then?', Paul would reply with a sparkle in his eyes: 'You are it!' And to punch his theme home Paul would add, 'Yes, and just as the pagans believe that their god lives in their temple—so do we! Demosthenes, you are a dwelling place for God by the Spirit' (v 22). Our Lord himself had promised his disciples: 'If anyone loves me, he will keep my word, and my Father will love him, and we will come to him and make our home with him' (John 14:23). The Holy Spirit lives in the life of every Christian to create the community of grace and the grace of community.

A mark of the Protestant Reformation in the sixteenth and seventeenth centuries was to emphasise the 'priesthood of all believers'. This meant that to discover the great gift of salvation we need no organization or human mediator, no re-sacrifice of Christ, and no earthly ritual. Nor do we need these things to maintain our relationship with God. On the contrary, believers can approach God for themselves through the merits of Christ alone. However, it is easy to abuse this privilege as we have seen already when we surveyed the reasons why some Christians remain outside the local family of the church. Notice how Paul countered this danger.

In Ephesians 2:12 he refered to the Christians before their conversion as 'without God'. The word is *atheos*, from which we get our word, 'atheist'. It referred equally to those who had abandoned the gods or who had been abandoned by the gods. This was one of the accusations levelled against the Christians in the first century: they had abandoned the traditional gods and were therefore considered to be *atheos*. Paul said, 'On the contrary, in spite of all your religion, you were atheists before your conversion; but now you are a beautiful holy temple in which God is pleased to live by his Spirit.' But notice how Paul described this temple. He reminded the Ephesians that the whole structure is 'joined together' and they are being 'built together' (vs 21, 22).

The Holy Spirit lives in the life of every Christian to create the community of grace and the grace of community

When people enter an impressive church building or cathedral there appears to be a quiet, a stillness. They talk in whispers and walk softly. This often reflects more an attitude to a building rather than to God himself. If only we could understand that when the community of believers worships together they are engaged in the most beautiful thing on earth; they are the holy temple worshipping the holy God. Significantly, one of the only two occasions when

Paul used the word *sun* on its own in this letter is in 3:18 where he prayed that they may have power: 'To comprehend with all the saints what is the breadth and length and height and depth, and to know the love of Christ that surpasses knowledge, that you may be filled *with* all the fullness of God.' That is the purpose of the holy temple, and that, therefore, is the purpose of community grace: 'that you may be filled with all the fullness of God.' Every gift that the Spirit dispenses among his church is for the purpose that together we may become more and more like Christ because that is what 'the fullness of God' means. And the fullness of God is the fullness of grace: his grace reflected through his people. Gifts are grace for the community of grace.

Goldfish on the lawn

The subject of community grace takes a much larger place in the New Testament than we often realise. When Jesus talked about 'church', he meant a lot more than just the universal conglomerate of Christians, because his apostles spent much of their time and energy organising local churches. Paul established them and wrote letters to them and so did Peter. It is hardly an exaggeration to claim that if the Gospels are about the Church, the New Testament letters are about the churches. When the apostle wrote to the Hebrew Christians, he placed this matter of church attendance high on his agenda: 'Let us consider how to stir up one another to love and good works, not neglecting to meet together, as is the habit of some, but encouraging one another, and all the more as you see the Day drawing near' (Hebrews 10:24–25). Why was this so important to Paul?

When the community of believers worships together they are engaged in the most beautiful thing on earth

First because the apostle knew that meeting together encourages one another. This was obvious in the first century because courage encourages others. Courage is contagious, as any soldier will tell you. So the opposite is true. My absence discourages the others. We all know the difference that a full or 'thin' congregation makes. In that letter of John Newton back in the 1760s, he encouraged worshippers to be regular in their attendance because: 'This encourages the Minister and affords a good example to the congregation'. Every preacher knows how Isaiah felt when he complained, 'I have laboured in vain; I have spent my strength for nothing and vanity' (Isaiah 49:4)!

But another reason why we should not neglect to meet together, is that we are created for community. The whole of God's creation is designed for community. On earth there is the family and the larger community in society, and the Bible gives regulations for the good ordering of both. There is community in heaven also; we are not to imagine the saints as a host of spirits floating around in splendid isolation with light-years separating each from their neighbours! Every reference to heaven is about community and surely on earth the best community of all is the redeemed community.

Significantly here in Hebrews 10:25 the apostle does not use the normal New Testament word for church. That word is *ecclesia* which William Tyndale wisely translated in 1526 as 'congregation'. But when the apostle refers here to 'meeting together' the word is drawn from the Jewish word 'synagogue' which literally means 'bring together' or 'gather together'; it is the verb 'to bring' or 'gather' with our little prefix *sun*—together. Our Creator and Saviour knew what is best for us when he planned the church. Since we are created for community we should value and take advantage of it. We need this community to help us grow and to care for us when we are weak. The first century Christians were all associated with a local church, and the New Testament letters were addressed with local churches in mind. The word 'encourage' that Paul uses here, is the same word that is used of the Holy Spirit in John 16:7—the *parakletos* or helper. That is exactly what the church is expected to do. No Christian will grow strong and healthy apart from the local church. You may say, 'But I know many Christians who regularly go to church and are still not spiritually strong and healthy.' That may be true but are you suggesting that if they don't go to church they will get better?

I have two ponds in my garden and they are stocked with scores of goldfish; over the years I have discovered they live and thrive best in water! Very occasionally I discover one that is sick. Would you recommend that I take him out and lay him on the lawn to see if he will recover? The local church is the natural environment for the Christian, and our churches as communities must care by teaching and instruction, pastoral oversight, mutual help and sharing with one another in love.

But here in Hebrews 10 the apostle gives one more reason why we should be together in community: 'all the more as you see the Day drawing near.' This seems to be his strongest argument, and that phrase 'the Day' is found everywhere in the New Testament letters: 'the Day of God's Grace', 'the Day when God will judge men', 'the Day is almost here', 'the Day of our Lord Jesus Christ', 'the Day will bring it to light', 'the Day of redemption', 'the Day he comes', 'the Day he visits us', 'the Day of judgement', 'the Day of God'. But how is that an incentive to meet together now? It may be pleasant to imagine that Paul simply meant that since we will spend eternity with each other we had better start getting along now—but I don't think this was his point. Perhaps he had in mind that as the Day approaches, things will get tougher so we need each other more—possibly. But I think his real thrust was to remind the readers that Christians, and not just unbelievers, are accountable to God.

God has promised community grace for the community of grace. There is nothing like it on earth

According to Paul in 1 Corinthians 3:13 every Christian must be careful how they build because 'the Day' will reveal it. In other words, we have a responsibility to each other in the local church, and the way we discharge that responsibility will be one of the issues that will stand before God on the day of judgement. How much gold, silver, and precious stones will shine from the legacy of my life to the glory of God, and how much wood, hay and stubble will be burned away as rubbish? Much will depend upon how well I have related to the community of the redeemed.

The first temple of Diana was completed in 540 BC and two hundred years later it burned down. Its replacement took one hundred and twenty years to complete and was itself destroyed by the Goths in AD 263. The glory of the temple of Diana has now gone and all that remains on its site is one column—

the base of another is in the British Museum in London. But where, today is the church of Jesus Christ? Across the whole world, on every continent and in every nation. It is indestructible until Christ returns in glory and the church finds its completeness in him. Until then, God has promised community grace for the community of grace. There is nothing like it on earth.

CHRIST, FROM WHOM ALL BLESSINGS FLOW
to perfect your church below,
Christ, whose nature now we share,
work in us, your body here.
Join our faithful spirits, join
each to each, with yours made one;
lead us through the paths of peace
on to greater holiness.

2 Move and activate and guide;
varied gifts to each divide;
gladly may we all agree,
bound by loving sympathy,
never from our calling move,
needful to each other prove,
kindly for each other care,
all our joys and sorrows share.

3 Placed according to your will,
let us all our work fulfil,
great and small, oppressed or free,
all in Christ shall equal be.
Love, like death, has all destroyed,
rendered all divisions void;
factions, names and parties fall,
you, O Christ, are all in all.

CHARLES WESLEY 1707–88
Praise! 593 © in this version Praise Trust

Sanctifying grace

'To him who is able to do far more abundantly than all we ask or think' (Ephesians 3:20)

I am certain that Paul had a sense of humour. In Ephesians 3:20 he encouraged the young Christians to believe that God is able to do 'far more abundantly than all we ask or think', and then he opened a new section of his letter in the very next sentence with the words: 'I therefore, a prisoner for the Lord'. He could expect the Ephesians to respond, 'Well Paul, if your God can do far more abundantly than all that we ask or think, what are you doing in prison?' Paul must have known that this was odd, and that is exactly why he refers to himself as a prisoner at this point in his letter. Just in case these young and enthusiastic Christians at Ephesus became too extravagant in their idea of 'more abundantly', Paul put a check on any unwise excess.

The impact of his words was designed to force the conclusion that 'more abundantly' has nothing necessarily to do with getting out of prison, being freed from slavery, improving health, reducing an overdraft, passing exams, or achieving promotion. On the other hand, it has everything to do with all that Paul had been writing about beforehand and all that he is about to write; in other words, it has everything to do with his prayer that they may know the love of Christ in its fullness (3:16–19), and that that they might live lives worthy of their calling (4:1–3).

How we apply Paul's promise of 'more abundantly' reveals a great deal about our priorities. If we long to know God and the love of Christ, and if we long to live in a way that is worthy of our calling as Christians then *that* is how we will understand 'more abundantly'. On the other hand, if the ambition of our Christian life is to find health and prosperity, excitement and a buzz, then we will apply it to that end. Therefore, one significant reason why Paul deliberately refers to himself as a prisoner is to make the Christians at Ephesus think through what he really means. It's as if he is saying, 'Does my imprisonment look ridiculous in the light of God's willingness to do more abundantly than all we ask or think? Of course it does—so, reflect on it; perhaps your application is not what God intends it to be.'

But there is another reason why Paul refers to himself as a prisoner at this point in his letter—and we will come to that later.

Sanctification?

But first, we had better be sure just what sanctification means, because the history of the Christian church has often confused more than clarified it. The words 'sanctification' and 'holiness' translate the same Greek word which carries the idea of being separated from the service of the world to the service of God; it is derived from that word 'saint' that we considered in chapter ten. In the New Testament the word *Sanctification is a life-* 'sanctification' is used in two distinct ways. First of all, we are sanctified by the righteousness of Christ being reckoned to *long growth into the* our account; this, as we saw in chapter five, is known as 'imputed righteousness'. Paul *likeness of Jesus* reminded the Corinthians that Christ Jesus is our 'righteousness and sanctification' (1 Corinthians 1:30), and that Christians are *Christ* 'sanctified in Christ Jesus, called to be saints, together with all those who in every place call upon the name of our Lord Jesus Christ, both their Lord and ours' (1 Corinthians 1:2). Those who are saints are sanctified. It is on the basis of this imputed (reckoned) righteousness that we are justified. This is an action that is once and for all; it will never be repeated because it will never be undone.

The second use of the word 'sanctification' in the New Testament is a progressive work of the Spirit in our lives which demands our diligent activity. Paul urges the Christians at Rome to present themselves to God: 'as slaves to righteousness leading to sanctification' (Romans 6: 19). Similarly we are to: 'strive ... for the holiness without which no one will see the Lord' (Hebrews 12:14). In this sense sanctification is a life-long growth into the likeness of Jesus Christ. One purpose of our salvation is that we might become steadily more like Christ (Romans 8:29). From here on in this chapter we will use the word 'sanctification' in this way.

But not every body sees sanctification this way. Besides the teaching of the Church of Rome—that sanctification is imparted to us through the ceremonies of the Church—some evangelicals also have their own particular views of this subject. The eighteenth century evangelist and founder of Methodism, John Wesley, taught that all the promises of God concerning holiness can be realised in this life. In a sermon on Philippians 3:12,15 called 'Christian Perfection', he claimed that a Christian can become, 'in such a sense perfect as not to commit sin, and to be freed from evil thoughts and evil tempers.' This state of complete purity is brought about by 'a simple act of faith, consequently in an instant'. He believed that there are two distinct steps of faith in the Christian life: we need regeneration and then 'entire sanctification'; this is a crisis and it was often referred to as a second blessing. From this state of purity (the quality of life) we can move on to maturity (the quantity of purity). Wesley therefore distinguished between: justified Christians, entirely sanctified Christians, and mature Christians. A development of this was the teaching of the American evangelist, Charles Finney, early in the nineteenth century; Finney believed in 'entire sanctification, in the sense that it is the privilege of Christians to live without knowing sin.' For Finney, because we are only obliged to do what we are able to do, the standard of sanctification fluctuates with our ability; for him, there were only two classes of Christians: the spiritual and the carnal.

The teaching of the 'Higher Life Movement' of William Boardman later in the nineteenth century was that just as we can do nothing for our justification, so we cannot contribute towards our sanctification either; they are two separate acts of faith. The 'second conversion' is when sanctification is infused into us and we are free from all conscious sinning. The 'first conversion'—justification—in itself is not sufficient to save, but God will always apply the second before our death. This was very popular among many Victorian evangelicals. A variation came from Hannah Pearsall Smith in her book *The Christian's Secret of a Happy Life* published in 1875. Rather like Finney, she taught that sanctification is relative to the

Christian's ability, so that, 'purity of heart may be as complete in the early as in the later experience'. However, sanctification is not *striving* to become holy but, in a well used phrase, it is: 'letting go and letting God'. Hannah Pearsall Smith maintained that, 'God can do nothing towards sanctifying a man until the man places himself in his hands for the purpose.' Sins of ignorance are not counted against us, and therefore we can be perfect this side of the grave. This became the foundation of what is known as the Keswick Message, though today Keswick does not follow this teaching. For many, such as the Church of the Nazarene, entire consecration and a baptism of the Holy Spirit are necessary for complete sanctification.

All this fails to take full account of the constant theme in the New Testament of personal warfare and struggle against sin, that God's standard for holiness is unwaveringly high, that God most certainly *does* command what is not fully attainable in this life, and that human nature even after conversion can never be entirely free from the ravages of the Fall.

Today, the whole debate on sanctification has swung in an opposite direction. It begins with the view that all you need to do to become a Christian is to believe. And to make this step of faith as simple as possible, three neat responses are offered: Step one, I have to believe that I am a sinner. Step two, I have to believe that Jesus died for sinners. Step three, I have to believe that Jesus died for me. Providing I can affirm each of these statements I am assured that I am a Christian. That may be a neat and uncomplicated way of explaining the message, but that is precisely the problem. Such a simplistic approach to the massive event called conversion is not found in the Bible. In this modern approach, nothing more is demanded or expected of me than an acknowledgement of sin and the fact that Christ died for sinners. But it is hardly a major step of faith to admit to being a sinner. I have only once met a man who told me he was completely without sin! Only a fool can come to that conclusion. Every religion in the world has some concept of sin—and an answer to it. If sin is falling short of a standard, any standard, then I cannot see how anyone should fail to admit to being a sinner; nobody has perfectly kept whatever standard they think they should be keeping! This is why we agreed in chapter five that it is not enough to list sins and then admit to failure. The real issue is that we are Christ-rejecters and that is our greatest sin.

This 'simple believism' is nothing new. Back in the eighteenth century Robert Sandeman and his son-in-law, John Glas, taught that nothing more than mental assent to the gospel was sufficient for salvation. It became known as Sandemanianism. They believed that all that was required for someone to become a Christian was for them to acknowledge the truth of the *facts* of the gospel. Recently this has become once more a big debate. On the one hand there are those who say that there is no necessary relationship between faith and good works and that to insist on the evidence of a changed life, is to deny the free and unconditional offer of the gospel. One modern writer, for example, maintains that conversion requires, 'No spiritual commitment whatsoever' and another claims that, 'There is no necessary change in your life style when you become a Christian.' As a result, repentance and commitment are not part of the evangelistic message. The claim is that God *wants* a changed life from us—no one doubts that—but he may not get it. You may take Christ as your saviour and subsequently you may take him as your Lord. On the other hand you may not. So, we are faced with the possibility of conversion without transformation and conversion without regeneration. That may be good religion, but it is not Christianity.

Paul was adamant that the only proof of faith is a changed life

Paul was adamant that the only proof of faith is a changed life; he expected that every Christian would strive to live holy for Christ and for that very reason: 'The grace of God has appeared … training us to renounce ungodliness and worldly passions' (Titus 2:11–12). Training and renouncing sound more like effort than some instant experience. James expressed it just as clearly in a verse that is often misunderstood: 'You *see* that a person is justified by what he does and not by faith alone' (James 2:24 *New International Version*). James is not saying that we are justified by our works, but that the only way justification is visible is by a changed life. According to Paul in 1 Thessalonians 4:3 our sanctification 'is the will of God'.

After a stormy and miserable relationship with the Christians at

Corinth, Paul could at last write to them that he had heard of their complete change of mind about the sins they had before tolerated in the church. He knew that their repentance was genuine not because they said so, but because he observed all the signs of what he called 'godly sorrow'. Since 2 Corinthians 7:9–11 is the clearest description of repentance that we will find in the New Testament, it is worth having the passage in front of us in full: 'I rejoice, not because you were grieved, but because you were grieved into repenting. For you felt a godly grief, so that you suffered no loss through us. For godly grief produces a repentance that leads to salvation without regret, whereas worldly grief produces death. For see what earnestness this godly grief has produced in you, but also what eagerness to clear yourselves, what indignation, what fear, what longing, what zeal, what punishment! At every point you have proved yourselves innocent in the matter.' That last expression does not mean that they excused themselves, but that they longed to be pure again on these issues that had so tarnished the testimony of the church.

Paul's plan for holy Christians

Back in Ephesians 4, Paul takes us in a different direction to understand what sanctification really means, and it is very instructive. You will notice the word 'therefore' in verse 1. That is significant because it forms a bridge between all that he has written before and what is to come. The one flows from the other. In fact, what Paul does here is to follow his usual pattern. In all his letters, Paul's invariable rule is to begin with theology and conclude with application. He tells the Christians what they should believe, and then how they should live.

One great weakness in evangelicalism has been that when someone becomes a Christian we immediately tell them what sort of life they should now live. They must give up this or that and stay away from here or there; we squeeze them into an evangelical mould of our church taboos and traditions that often have nothing to do with the Bible—but we think this will help them to grow. That is a big mistake, and it is little wonder many young converts fall back. Then we blame this on the fact that they did not do what we told them to. In reality often the reason why they fell away was because they tried so hard to become what we told them to become. They had to dress as we told them to dress, go where we told them to go, talk as we told them to talk, and even pray as we taught them to pray; in fact they had to enjoy what we enjoy and dislike everything we dislike. They soon learned that if they did not sing precisely from the same hymn book they could not maintain their relationship with us for long.

We should learn from Paul. He wanted above everything for these Ephesian Christians to go on with Christ and to live a life 'in a manner worthy of the calling to which you have been called' (4:1). That is sanctification. It took Paul three chapters before he told the Ephesians how to live because it had taken him three chapters to tell them who they are.

It took Paul three chapters before he told the Ephesians how to live because it had taken him three chapters to tell them who they are

A brief survey of Ephesians up to this point reveals that he had told them of God's great plan for them from eternity (1:4–5), of the incredible cost for their salvation through the blood of Christ (1:7), of God's lavish love poured out on them (1:8), of the Holy Spirit within them (1:13) and of the new life from death that they have received (2:1, 4, 5). Then Paul moved on to inform them of some of the consequences of all this. All barriers are broken down: whether they are Jews or non-Jews, pagans or philosophers, slaves or freemen, they are 'citizens together, a household together, and a temple together' (2:19–21). Each word is prefixed with that word 'with' that we considered in the previous chapter. This is a favourite theme of Paul in this letter and he returned to it in 3:6, where he told them that in Christ they are 'heirs together, members together, and sharers together'.

The weakness of too many Christians is not that they do not know how a Christian should live, but that they do not understand what being a Christian means. Perhaps if we had more sermons on what Christians really are, we would need fewer sermons on how Christians should live. And perhaps also there would be fewer casualties in our churches. In some of our large churches their back door is as congested as their front door. Is this why?

Look at it this way. We can tell a Christian that he must live a clean, pure, peaceable, humble and holy life, and that he must not tell lies, commit adultery, or steal. So, what's new in that? We can tell the unbeliever all this as well. The unbeliever is no less under an obligation to be holy. God does not have one standard for the Christian and another standard—conveniently a little lower—for the non-Christian. But what can we tell the Christian that we cannot tell the non-Christian? We can tell him what he is: why he is different and how he is different.

A man may invite me to book an expensive holiday, buy a lavish car and purchase a stately mansion—all three. I tell him he is a fool to talk to me like that since they are all far beyond my means. But he then tells me that he has sure evidence that I have inherited a considerable fortune. Now that is different. I have a new capacity, and all that he encouraged me to do is well within my power. That is exactly what Paul has been doing in this letter; he has been explaining the new capacity of the Christian so that when he gets round to the tough standards in Ephesians chapter 4 no one can opt out with: 'But I can't be like that.' When my boys were young, one of them decided that he would address me like others in the church. So he began to call me 'Pastor' instead of 'Daddy'. I let it continue for a few days and then I quietly informed him that he and his brother had a privilege that they alone shared; I told him that no one else in the whole wide world could call me 'Daddy' except him and his brother. He never called me 'Pastor' again! Suddenly his special relationship and all the privileges that were included in this were sufficient to encourage him to live as a son of his father.

If we had more sermons on what Christians really are, we would need fewer sermons on how Christians should live

This pattern of teaching the special relationship *before* we instruct in life-style did not originate with Paul, he was simply learning from his Old Testament. God used this approach when he gave Israel the Ten Commandments and all the laws that followed. Before he laid on them the rules to live by as outlined in Exodus 20 and following, he had told them that they were a very special people and that he was a very holy God (Exodus 19:6,17–19 and compare Deuteronomy 7:6–11). But even before this, God had given his people the Passover—which was a clear statement of forgiveness and reconciliation to God. So, God told his people about redemption and election and only then considered them ready to learn about the detailed instructions for holiness and sanctification. Or, to put this another way, God wanted his people to learn that the reason for the Ten Commandments was not simply that it was a nice way to live, but that compared to the other nations Israel was a very special and holy people, and their God was a very special and holy God (see Deuteronomy 4:6–8).

The reason why this approach has to be the best is because having explained their new privileges and capacity, when Paul laid out the high standard of Christian living he would not expect anyone to complain, 'But I can't live like that'. His reply would be immediate, 'Oh but you can. Our God can do more abundantly than all that we ask or think, according to the power at work within us.' There is always sufficient grace for living holy lives. Pascal, the seventeenth century French philosopher, mathematician and scientist once wrote, 'To change a man into a saint, grace is necessary; and he who doubts it either does not know what man is, or what a saint is.' Pascal was right. And grace for that great work of changing a man into a saint is not only necessary, it is always available from the God of all grace. This is why a chapter on sanctification comes almost at the end of this book; by now we should be understanding the privilege of the abundant grace that is ours in Christ.

The sanctified Christian

In Ephesians 4:2–3 Paul lists six dignified ways we are to live as Christians: 'With all humility and gentleness, with patience, bearing with one another in love, eager to maintain the unity of the Spirit in the bond of peace.' Put all these together and they would make an enormous difference to our churches and our neighbourhoods. And because of their new capacity Paul could expect the Christians at Ephesus to live like this. He would allow no excuses and no arguing. Years ago when I worked on the Council of a large international mission society, an awkward or insensitive member would occasionally be excused with the comment: 'It's his Latin temperament you know.' I could never accept that kindly dismissal of what was so often a downright sinful attitude. Whatever our background or personality, however hard our upbringing or circumstances, to assume that we will always have a rough, prickly or short-tempered character is a statement to the effect that God is *not* able to do 'more abundantly than all that we ask or think.' Sanctifying grace is our new capacity to live in a manner worthy of the calling to which we have been called—which is to become more Christ-like in everything.

I find this list in Ephesians 4:2–3 very encouraging, not because I am good at keeping it, but just because it is there. It was needed then and it is needed now. But more than encouraging, I find it extremely interesting. Too often we think of sanctification in terms of non-worldliness. I suppose it is, but it is much more than that. Certainly Paul wrote to Titus that the grace of God teaches us to say '"No" to ungodliness and worldly passions' (Titus 2:12 *New International Version*), but the next three words are all positive: 'self-controlled, upright, godly'. Here in Ephesians 4 the standard of holiness among Christians is equally positive. Once again, the problem with many evangelicals is that they are more than comfortable to check out a list and conclude with the young man of our Lord's acquaintance: 'All these I have kept'. What was it that distressed Paul about the church at Philippi? He made no mention of bad habits, bad thoughts, or bad interests, But he was clearly upset about bad relationships (1:15 and 4:2). Some of our churches with the most meticulous standards of right and wrong simply cannot get on together. And that is what Paul is on about here in Ephesians also.

'Be completely humble'

Humility was an attitude of mind that in the first century was uniquely Christian. The Greeks and Romans had no way of describing what Paul was thinking about here. The word he employed was never used in a good sense: *tapeinos* in classical Greek meant grovelling, low-born, slavish. A second century inscription reads, 'Do nothing *mean* or ignoble'; and the word was linked to such words as: miserable, wretched, complaining, timid. The Greeks and Romans were encouraged to think big and play the man; they must be self-confident, self-reliant and macho. Personal success was everything. The alternative was to be *tapeinos*: small-minded, feeble and weak—a despicable person. In the first century, humility was a vice, not a virtue. Two German friends of mine are working for the gospel in Papua New Guinea. One group of people they worked among had no word for 'thank you' or 'sorry'; there was just no concept of such ideas. Everything was always someone else's fault. A man would never say, 'I bumped into the door' but only, 'The door bumped into me'. The idea of *tapeinos* held no place in the thinking of that tribe. It had no place in the first century Greek or Roman culture either.

In the first century,

humility was a vice,

not a virtue

Radically, Paul took that very word and told the Ephesians this was exactly what they were to be like. They must have a deep sense of their own littleness, a modesty, an unpretentious behaviour. The word is only ever used in the New Testament in a positive sense. Paul encouraged the Philippians in the same way: 'Do nothing from rivalry or conceit, but in *humility* count others more significant than yourselves' (Philippians 2:3). And then in verse 8 he set before them the great pattern that the Lord of eternity and the universe '*humbled* himself'. He made himself low-born and despicable. In fact Jesus claimed this for himself when he said, 'I am gentle and *humble* in heart' (Matthew 11:29 *New International Version*).

Do you know a Christian who complains of being overlooked? Or one who knows everything, talks incessantly about himself, strives to build an empire, or is always pushing himself forward? Then let him go back to Calvary and look on the One who: 'Though he was in the form of God, did not count equality with God a thing to be grasped, but made himself nothing …' (Philippians 2:6). We have considered that word 'grasped' previously when looking at incarnate grace; it means to use something to our own advantage. Christ could have used his power and deity to his own advantage—but he never did. He is our perfect example of the meaning of humility. Paul followed his Master's example when he claimed to be the least of all the apostles and less than the least of all the saints. That was not pious waffle, it was sincerely how he saw himself. But if anyone declares, 'To live like that is not possible in this proud, success-driven society', Paul would respond, 'Have you forgotten the one who is able to do 'more abundantly than all that we can ask or think'? W. E. Gladstone, a British Prime Minister in the time of Queen Victoria, once claimed, 'Humility, as a sovereign grace, is the creation of Christianity'—and he was right.

'Be completely gentle'

If humility is an attitude of mind—how we see ourselves, then gentleness is our behaviour—how we deal with others. Some Christians are like hammer drills. Some pastors are as well. Why are there Christians with such a biting tongue, complaining spirit, or heavy-handed manner? We can never excuse ourselves with the defence: 'That's just who I am; I can't help it.' We can help it—or else we no longer believe in the God who can do abundantly more. Harsh behaviour, cruel words and thoughtless actions are contradictions of who we are. Paul referred to himself once as a 'nursemaid', yet by nature he was a man who did not suffer fools easily.

Harsh behaviour, cruel words and thoughtless actions are contradictions of who we are

The gentle Christian is caring and thoughtful. They give time to listen and help—like the Master himself. Because they know the love of Christ they show the love of Christ. They have a gentle tongue and a quiet manner. This does not mean that they are feeble and weak. Christ was not that. He could be angry and severe, but it was always deliberate and under control. His presence spread peace among those who listened. The great news is that any Christian can be like that! The one who said 'I am gentle and humble in heart' is able to do for any one abundantly more than all we ask or think. However abrasive our character, however hard our nature, however unyielding our personality, Christ can soften us. He did this for the vicious cruelty of both Saul of Tarsus and John of Wapping—the godless sailor and slave trader. Both became loving shepherds and gentle pastors.

'Be patient'

The word used here carries the idea of not lashing out or retaliating when wronged. Do you have a quick temper? A short fuse? Are you easily stirred to irrational anger that betrays itself in over-hasty words or actions? Patience is the quality of accepting mistreatment and abuse without retaliation. Some Christians are so prickly that you can feel the needles every time you talk with them; they are programmed always to misunderstand. Are you an angry Christian? Are you angry with another Christian or with your leaders? Even when we feel that we have a just cause to be angry, we have no reason to become impatient and resentful. Calvary, as ever, is our pattern, for 'When he was reviled, he did not revile in return; when he suffered, he did not threaten, but continued entrusting himself to him who judges justly' (1 Peter 2:23).

That last reference to Christ reminds us that patience is also accepting the hand of God with quiet serenity when it seems to be against us. It is a silent spirit with God's ways. Have you a quarrel with God? Are you arguing with him because things have not worked out as you designed, or because some great disappointment has broken into your well ordered plans? Have you forgotten his great patience with you? Or as Paul so well states, 'Do you presume on the riches of his kindness and forbearance and patience?' (Romans 2:4). He asks me to have patience with his wisdom and care, whilst at the same time he shows patience with my rebellion and indifference. Someone may say, 'If only you knew my circumstances you would not write so easily about patience.' But I don't need to know about your circumstances, I only need to know about the God of more abundant grace for sanctification.

'Bearing with one another in love'

The word 'patience' especially refers to enduring opposition, persecution, misunderstanding or simply the circumstances that God brings into my life; at least that is how Paul is using the word here. But the word translated 'bearing with', though similar because it means patiently enduring, is directed especially towards members of the church because Paul adds the word that is translated 'one another'.

Have you noticed how similar Paul's instructions are from one church to another? That is because all churches are, by and large, very similar; the problems and relationships in one are much like those in another. For this reason, when Paul wrote to the Colossians, he covered almost the same ground that we find here in Ephesians: 'Put on then, as God's chosen ones, holy and beloved, compassion, kindness, humility, meekness, and patience, bearing with one another and, if one has a complaint against another, forgiving each other; as the Lord has forgiven you, so you also must forgive' (Colossians 3:12–14).

In the household of faith we are all different from one another. We must learn to accept each other and bear with the mistakes and character traits and personality 'disorders' of others. There is a golden rule in the church that whilst we are never to excuse ourselves, we must always be ready to excuse others. To appreciate and respect fellow Christians as brothers and sisters in Christ—and to bear with their weaknesses—is the Christian dimension. So, what is tearing your church apart? Or what is simply spoiling your comfortableness with each other? Is someone demanding that everyone else comes into line with their views on phantom truth—those subjects that we make such an issue over, but in reality are our personal preference, cultural upbringing or evangelical tradition? The God of abundantly more grace can and must change these attitudes.

There is a golden rule in the church that whilst we are never to excuse ourselves, we must always be ready to excuse others

'Maintaining unity'

This humility which is our attitude of mind, gentleness which is the way we handle others, patience in opposition and circumstances, and forbearance with one another, will all lead to Paul's next encouragement: 'Eager to maintain the unity of the Spirit.' Here is Paul at his most practical. Ignore those oozy Christians who pretend that all is always well in the household of faith. We are people, and where there are people there are problems. This unity, this one-ness or together-ness in Christ is our new relationship—that is a fact. But we have to work at making the reality real. That is why some translations stiffen the phrase with 'make every effort'. The word is used variously to mean 'hurry up', 'be zealous', or 'take care'. Paul wants his readers not simply to shrug with resignation at the thought of getting on with their fellow Christians, but to do everything in their power to create family unity. He wants them to be enthusiastic about it—even excited.

In the church, unity

is enjoyed when

peace is present

The great prayer of our Lord for his disciples, that after his departure they may 'become perfectly one, so that the world may know that you sent me and loved them even as you loved me' (John 17:23), had little to do with ecumenical unity between denominations, but everything to do with the way Christians got on with each other in the family. It was the relationship between James and John, Paul and Barnabus, Euodia and Syntyche that mattered far more than how Ephesus got on with Philippi, or Asia with Macedonia. It is precisely the prayer of our Lord that Paul may have had in mind here. He wants them to fulfil the Master's plan for the church by working with every effort they can muster to maintain the unity which is the very essence of their life.

Unity is not merely something to write about, sing about, talk about or even pray about; it is to be real.

A house is not made strong by any number of new coats of paint, least of all by pretty wallpaper, but when the foundation and walls are securely built together. In the church, unity is enjoyed when peace is present.

'The bond of peace'

At the beginning of this chapter, I said there were two reasons why Paul referred to himself as a prisoner for the Lord in the context of his encouragement in the God of immeasurably more. The first was that Paul knew it would make them think: more abundantly had nothing necessarily to do with Paul being released from prison, but everything to do with the Ephesians living as Christians ought to live. The second reason is associated with his encouragement for the Ephesians to work hard to maintain unity in the church. The word that Paul used for 'prisoner' in 3:1 and 4:1 is *desmios* in Greek, and it means one who is bound or fettered. In 4:3 he uses the word *sundesmios*, the same word with our now familiar prefix *sun* meaning 'with'; it refers to a fetter—that which binds together. This is why it is translated: 'the *bond* of peace'. Paul intended that pun and did not expect the Ephesians to miss it: 'As a prisoner, I am bound to my Roman guards—in the same way you are bound together in Christ. But make sure that your shackles are fetters of peace!' As an interesting aside, the same word can refer to the ligaments that hold the body together, and Paul uses it in just this way when he wants to describe the church under the picture of a body (Colossians 2:19).

Among the descriptions of the church in Acts is the word used when Paul wanted to 'join' the church in Jerusalem (Acts 9:26). From this verb 'to join', which is *collao* in Greek, we gain our word 'collage'. When the children bring autumn leaves to school and paste them on a large sheet of paper, we have a collage. Interestingly one thesaurus I have offers as alternatives for the word collage: 'random collection, hodgepodge, clutter'. That may suit some churches perfectly, but it is not quite what Paul meant! To mix our metaphors, the church is a people bound together by the Spirit and they should form a beautiful collage. But the glue for that collage is peace; and the chemical composition of that peace is made up from five vital ingredients: humility, gentleness, patience, forbearance and unity. Paul's teaching in Colossians is the same: 'Above all these put on love, which binds everything together in perfect harmony. And let the peace of Christ rule in your hearts, to which indeed you were called in one body ...' (3:14–15).

The fierce independence of evangelical Christians has been part of their history. At best it is what has stiffened their refusal to be intimidated by the state, or to be forced into the mould of the world around. But at worst that strong spirit of autonomy has meant aggression against the family. In the Western world, many congregations and their leaders feel themselves to be under siege; few people are being converted to Christ, there is a high rate of 'falling away', and the general standard of holiness is not what we would like it to be. Too often our response to this sad scenario is to regain our sense of achievement by winning all our arguments against fellow Christians; this helps us to feel spiritual lion-hearts when in reality we are faint hearts in the world. We are not successful in spoiling Satan's kingdom, but we are very good at spoiling Christ's. We are not crusaders for the gospel in the marketplace, or even effective in holding the gospel banner in front of an unreformed and broadminded church, but our courage knows no bounds when it comes to bashing our fellow believers.

Evangelical history is not a model of unity and peace—the liberal church has always appeared more united. We may respond, 'That's because for liberals, *nothing* matters too much', which may or may not be true; but for evangelicals the opposite failure is that *everything* matters too much. We have sadly not learned to make three vital distinctions. First, there are vital truths which give or maintain spiritual life and on which we must allow no divergence. Second, there are significant truths which are important because they are in the Bible but they are not vital to spiritual life—on these we must respectfully agree to disagree. Third, there are phantom truths which have little or nothing to do with the Bible but are a mixture of our personal preference, custom or culture; this does not make them wrong, it simply means that they do not come in the category of truth. To place this last group in the category of vital truth—and therefore to make them a condition of Christian fellowship—is schismatic and therefore sinful.

John Newton was a man of peace. He gave no quarter in the battle for the truth of the Gospel, but he never looked to skirmish with those who were his true friends in Christ. He had been pastor of his flock at Olney in Buckinghamshire for four years when he described the peace that governed the life of his church: 'We are quiet and happy at Olney. We know nothing about disputes or divisions. If you pass a flock of sheep in a pasture towards evening, you may observe them all very busy in feeding. Perhaps here and there one may just raise his head and look at you for a moment, but down he stoops again to the grass directly. He cannot fill his belly by staring at strangers. Something in this way I hope it is with us. We care not who makes the noise, if we can get the pasture. If they are *talking*, they may talk on; but we had rather *eat*.' John fed his people, not with strife and dissension, but with the word of God. If only more Christian leaders would follow Newton's example.

A lack of these six vital ingredients is tearing scores of evangelical churches apart today.

Finally

Just in case the Ephesians had forgotten where Paul began, and may neglect to recall what sort of people they are, in 4:4–6 he rammed home their oneness with a quick fire list of the essential unity that belongs to every true Christian community:

One body—you, the local church

One Holy Spirit—living within each of you

One eternal hope—to which you are all called

One Lord Jesus Christ—by whom you were rescued from sin and its consequences

One faith—the faith in one salvation alone

One baptism—in the name of the Father, Son and Holy Spirit

One God and Father of all—to whom we are all ultimately accountable

Never forget these seven essential, inevitable and unavoidable facts of our unity in Christ, and never stop working at the humility, gentleness, patience, forbearance, unity and peace that keeps the church living in a manner worthy of its calling. This is the best meaning of sanctification. And it is what Peter meant when he signed off his second letter with the words: 'Grow in the grace and the knowledge of our Lord and Saviour Jesus Christ' (2 Peter 3:18). The more we know Christ, the more we will reflect his character in our lives—and that is sanctifying grace. And if anyone thinks that all this is impossible, remember that our God 'is able to do far more abundantly than all that we ask or think, according to the power at work within us' because 'Grace was given to each one of us according to the measure of Christ's gift'. There is always sanctifying grace available abundantly for his people.

> THE CHURCH'S ONE FOUNDATION
> is Jesus Christ her Lord;
> she is his new creation
> by water and the word:
> from heaven he came and sought her
> to be his holy bride;
> with his own blood he bought her
> and for her life he died.
>
> 2 Elect from every nation
> yet one through all the earth;
> her charter of salvation—
> one Lord, one faith, one birth:
> one holy name she blesses,
> and shares one holy food;
> as to one hope she presses
> with every grace endued.
>
> 3 We see her long divided
> by heresy and sect;
> yet she by God is guided—
> one people, one elect:
> her vigil she is keeping,
> her cry goes up, 'How long?'
> and soon the night of weeping
> shall be the dawn of song.

4 In toil and tribulation
and tumult of her war,
she waits the consummation
of peace for evermore:
till with the vision glorious
her longing eyes are blessed;
at last the church victorious
shall be the church at rest!

5 Yet she on earth has union
with those whose rest is won,
and shares in sweet communion
with God the Three-in-One,
whose love has made them holy!
Lord, grant to us your grace
with them, the meek and lowly,
in heaven to see your face.

SAMUEL J STONE 1839–1900
Praise! 577

Chapter 14

The grace of prayer

'For through him we both have access in one Spirit to the Father' Ephesians 2:18

In an earlier chapter we suggested that if the stars came out only once a year, the whole world would stay up all night to see them; we may add that if the birds sang their dawn chorus only once every spring, even the most disinterested among us would be up at three in the morning to hear them. But what if the opportunity of praying to the God who created those stars and birds was allowed only once a year also? Imagine the count-down among Christians: the months, weeks, days and hours would be marked off to the precious moments when we could take advantage of the great annual privilege of gaining access to God and entering into the presence of the Almighty.

Books and sermons on the subject of prayer focus chiefly on the results, value, purpose or power of prayer. Certainly Scripture is full of examples to encourage us to pray, but the greatest value of prayer is the incredible privilege of access to God. That, after all, was what was lost at the Fall, and that is what is regained through Calvary. Therefore this is not a chapter on the importance of prayer, though that is indispensible; it is not a chapter on the discipline of prayer, though that is essential; nor is it a chapter on the effectiveness of prayer, though that is irrefutable; least of all is it a tirade against the churches' current lack of prayer, though that is sadly undeniable. Only one thing is in focus in this chapter: the privilege of prayer—because that is fundamental.

In our chapter on sanctifying grace, the point was made that rather than haranguing Christians on the way to live, it is better to tell them what they are in Christ; once they understand who they are, how they should live will be largely self evident. So, we will apply that principle to the subject of prayer. If we understand the privilege of prayer, what we should do about it will be largely self-evident.

When my wife Barbara was seriously ill in hospital after a major spinal decompression operation, among the many letters and cards she received was one from a sweet 92 year-old West Indian member of our church; Violet closed her letter to Barbara with these words: 'Cheer up. God is with you, for I have committed you in his care—and he is a very good listener. Goodnight. Wish you have a very good rest. And God bless and keep you.' I have never forgotten that delightful phrase: 'He is a very good listener'. What a beautiful privilege that Violet understood so well: the sovereign God of eternity and infinity hears my prayer—and he is a very good listener.

None of us can be relied upon to listen attentively all the time. Wives complain to husbands, parents to children, teenagers to adults and teachers to pupils: 'You're not listening to me!' We turn on the radio to get the weather forecast, but our mind is so preoccupied that we hear without listening, and are none the wiser when the pips herald the news. We come to church and hear a sermon but we draw the blinds and drift back to the office, or to last week's holiday. Somebody reads instructions to us, but we don't understand them so we switch off, we're not listening. A thousand times in a day we are just too busy to listen. Tragically, a loved one talks to us about their fears or hopes, but we're not listening and they go away with an aching heart; a child pleads for our attention, for someone to show that they care, but their cause is trivial to us who have such important matters at hand, so we don't listen—and they wander off unloved. But God is always a good listener. No cause of ours is too trivial; there are never more important issues for him to deal with, and what is more, no one is ever ahead of us in a queue. He is never short on time or too busy. And still more encouraging in these days of recorded messages and protective secretaries is the fact that there is never a substitute for his personal attention. That is what 'access to the Father' unquestionably means.

The sovereign God of eternity and infinity hears my prayer—and he is a very good listener

Chapter 14

Prayer as access

Although the word 'access' is used sparingly in the New Testament and preached rarely from our pulpits, it is actually one of the big words of the Christian faith. In Romans 5:1–2, Paul linked it with justification, faith, peace, grace, joy, and glory—it could hardly be in better company. Elsewhere the apostle wrote of our: 'boldness and access with confidence' (Ephesians 3:12), and here in Ephesians 2:18 he confirms our 'access in one Spirit to the Father'. In the first century, the word was commonly used of the introduction of one person to another, and in the ancient world of inaccessible despots, access into the presence of a great king was fearful. An audience was gained only by waiting and trembling.

The reality of this is illustrated in the Bible story of Esther, who was a Jewish Queen married to the pagan Persian King, Ahasuerus. The King's prime minister, Haman, hatched a cruel plan to exterminate all Jews across the Persian empire, but Esther's uncle, Mordecai, heard of the conspiracy and informed his niece. She alone stood between the King and the massacre of the Jews. But no one, not even the Queen, would dare to approach the 'Great King' without an invitation. The Bible reflects the custom of the day in the following record: 'All the king's servants and the people of the king's provinces know that if any man or woman goes to the king inside the inner court without being called, there is but one law—to be put to death.' There could be only one exception to this, and that is if the king condescended to hold out his golden sceptre: 'so that he may live' (Esther 4:11). When the beautiful Queen Esther, dressed in her finest royal robes, entered the inner court of the king's palace we can hear the courtiers drawing their breath as they trembled for their queen; she was risking her life by entering, uninvited, into the presence of the Great King. And we can feel the relief and joy when the king 'held out to Esther the golden sceptre that was in his hand' (5:2). These cruel despots could act at whim, justly or unjustly, and the whole world stood in fear and awe.

If that power was true of earthly rulers, how much more awesome is the presence and power of the eternal Creator by whose word of command stars and planets came into being, oceans were filled with water, mountains rose, great and mighty beasts were created, and by whose wisdom all the laws of physics and the universe were planned? Ours is the God who puts up rulers and brings them down; who is so pure and holy that even the angels hide their faces from him, and when John the apostle saw such a vision of his glory on the island of Patmos he fell down as though dead, overwhelmed by the splendour of Christ and God (Revelation 1:17). This is the one whose presence made Mount Sinai tremble (Exodus 19:18), and whose glory filled the temple in Jerusalem (2 Chronicles 7:1); the God who will one day call everyone to account and before whom every mouth will be silent. Yet in Romans 5:2 Paul assured us that 'we have access ...' into the presence of this high and holy God.

In the early days of plastic money, the Access card was advertised by appealing to our desire for more and more—and immediately. We were promised that it would take the 'waiting out of wanting'. What was not advertised was that we could only gain access to what ultimately we would have to pay for; the day of reckoning would certainly come. But a far greater access is that which we have into the presence of God, and by turning our focus to 'things that are above' (Colossians 3:2), a prayerful spirit takes the wanting out of waiting for the things of this world. And this access is free to all, simply because none of us has the right currency to deposit against which we could draw the benefits. And at this point, all our banking illustrations fail, because none of us employs the services of a bank out of love for the manager. We bank only because of the benefits we hope to gain. But that is not the ultimate purpose of prayer. The decisive value of prayer is not what we achieve through it, but what we gain by it: an audience with the King of kings. That is of value for its own sake and is the highest value of prayer, though it is rarely thought of like this. Nothing brings more honour to God and more dignity to human nature than when a forgiven sinner approaches the Creator in prayer.

Paul loved to play with words, and one of his frequent puns is found in Romans 5:2 where he used two very similar sounding words to punch home his point. When he wrote 'we have' obtained access, the verb form he used

A prayerful spirit takes the wanting out of waiting for the things of this world

in the Greek is pronounced *eskaykamen*, and when in the same verse he wrote 'we stand', the verb form is *hestaykamen*. Unlike the English, there is a beautiful ring about these two words that would impress them on the minds of his hearers. We not only have access through the grace of prayer, but we can stand in this grace in the presence of our King; there is no grovelling here.

Old Testament access

In Hebrews 10:19, the apostle opens for us the incredible privilege of entering what he called 'the Most Holy Place' (*New International Version*), and added that we may enter it with confidence. That word confidence originally meant 'freedom or boldness in speech', though it was often used more generally than this. It referred to a confidence that leads to boldness in approaching someone or something. Have you ever found yourself caught in the experience of being in strange and intimidating surroundings? You ask yourself: should I be here? or: am I conspicuous as a newcomer? What do I do next? Perhaps it was a new school: what if I don't know the rules? Or a new office: what are the regulations here? Or a new club: am I following the correct etiquette?

A while back I was invited to preach in South Africa, and those who had invited me paid for me to travel on a Business Class ticket. This ticket allowed me to use some exclusive lounges, which was particularly helpful when I had six hours to lose between flights and a manuscript that I wished to read. But when I entered the Club World lounge, I was at first very hesitant. My ticket said I had a right to enter but I was unsure about the privilege, and when I first showed that ticket at the entrance I was afraid I would not be allowed in and that, to my terrible embarrassment, the nice lady at the reception would say: 'I'm sorry Sir, but you are not allowed in here'. But she didn't; in fact she welcomed me warmly. I had a right to be here; it was my place, and all the privileges of a Club World lounge were mine. Well, a few goes at this life and I was getting quite used to it: I soon learned to help myself freely to the food and drinks and I knew how to select a most comfortable armchair—complete with footrest—and with a fruit juice and nibbles settled down to my work.

But now see where Paul tells us we can go with boldness: 'the Most Holy

Place'. Sadly, that may not sound exciting, but in reality it is ten thousand times more of a privilege than the Business Class lounge of British Airways. The Jews would know what the writer meant by the phrase, though not many Gentiles would, therefore back in Hebrews 9:1–10 he had explained it all. So let me.

When Israel came out of Egypt in the time of Moses, they found themselves among nations all of whom already had priests and sacrifices. But Israel was to be different; they were not to worship in the way of the nations, and were not even to enquire how the nations worshipped (Deuteronomy 12:4,31). God himself would provide them with every aspect of their way of worship, even to the finest detail: the material to be used in the curtains, the clothes to be worn by the priests, the oil for lamps, construction of the altars and equipment—nothing was left to imagination or guesswork. The Israelites were not to worship anyhow, anywhere, anyway, but 'as I command you'. So, in Exodus and Leviticus we find the details of the Tabernacle. Let me give you an outline so that you have a picture in your mind.

At first Moses began with a small 'Tent of Meeting' (Exodus 33:7–11) but then God gave details of the Tabernacle, and six hundred years later the magnificent temple of Solomon followed the same general pattern. The whole Tabernacle area measured 150 feet by 75 feet and was surrounded by ten linen curtains. There was only one entrance, at the east end, and immediately just two objects confronted the worshipper: a great bronze altar for sacrifice and a large bronze basin which was a bowl of water for ceremonial washing. The message was at once clear: the priest could proceed no further in his worship of God without a sacrifice by shedding the blood of an animal, and a ritual washing away of sin.

At the far end of this outer court was the Tabernacle itself measuring 45 feet long by 15 feet wide by 15 feet high. This was known as the Holy Place, or literally in the Hebrew just one word meaning 'the holy'. Within this Holy Place there were two rooms; in the first room was a seven branched candle stand and a table with fresh bread laid on it—the significance of these need not bother us for our present purpose. Here the priests went about their daily business replenishing the oil in the stand and replacing fresh bread on the table; only the priests were allowed here. Dividing this room from the second room was a large, thick curtain of blue, purple and scarlet linen richly decorated. And behind this curtain was the 'Most Holy Place' or literally in the Hebrew 'the holy, holy'. The word holy was simply doubled in order to mean very holy, sacred, set apart. This holy, holy room represented the presence of God. Into this room only the High Priest was allowed, and only once a year on the great Day of Atonement (*yom kippur*). Here was the Ark—a box covered with gold and with two golden cherubim on the lid, which was called 'the atonement cover'. This Ark of the Covenant represented the immediate presence of God who had promised Moses: 'There I will meet with you ... and I will speak with you' (Exodus 25:22). The only other article in this room was the altar of incense.

No one came lightly into the presence of God; and if they did, they bore a terrible consequence

Imagine the awe and fear of that Holy Place. Into the outer court only Jews were allowed, and into the Tabernacle only priests were allowed for their daily ministry of replenishing the oil and replacing the bread, but into the Most Holy Place (the holy, holy) only the High Priest was allowed and then only once a year and only with the blood of sacrifice and incense from the altar. No one came lightly into the presence of God; and if they did, they bore a terrible consequence. Nadab and Abihu were two sons of Aaron the High Priest; once they carelessly offered what the Bible calls 'unauthorised fire' on the altar of incense—but only once. Precisely what they did wrong, we are not told, except that the LORD made it clear that it was something 'which he had not commanded them'. Suddenly fire came from heaven and 'they died before the LORD' (Leviticus 10:1–2). If this appears a drastic response to a minimal oversight, we have missed the whole point of the story. Just like a similarly severe judgement, shortly after the formation of the Christian church, that fell on Ananias and Sapphira for deceit (Acts 5:1–11), God intended to set a serious example to his people from the outset—one that that they would never forget: 'Among those who are near me I will be sanctified, and before all the people I will be glorified' (Leviticus 10:3). God had told his people that they must worship only in the way he instructed so that they would always approach him with reverence and awe; to come any other way would spell disaster.

Two more disobedient sons met a similar fate when they treated the Ark of the Covenant like a box of magic. Hophni and Phinehas were the sons of the old priest Eli, but unlike their father, they abused the priesthood; when the Philistines drew up battle lines against Israel, these two renegade priests carried the Ark with them into battle on the assumption that God would never allow it to fall into the hands of an enemy. But God will not be bribed by man, and the Ark was captured and Hophni and Phinehas were slaughtered on the field of battle (1 Samuel 4:1–11). The Philistines fared little better and were soon glad to rid themselves of the Ark, sending it back to Israel via the village of Beth-shemesh, where seventy men died after impertinently lifting the lid and peeping into the Ark (6:19). Finding it too hot to handle, the men of Beth-shemesh passed it on to Kiriath-jearim, where it stayed for more than half a century in the house of Abinadab.

Sadly, lessons forgotten must be repeated. When, half a millennium after Moses, King David brought the Ark of the Covenant from Kiriath-jearim to Jerusalem, it was placed on a new ox cart for the journey. The instructions had always been clear that the Ark was never to be handled and should only be carried between two poles on the shoulders of four priests; somebody, somewhere at sometime had overlooked this vital directive and had removed the poles; but there were no excuses, because the large rings in each corner of the Ark should have served as a reminder (Exodus 25:12). On its journey east to Jerusalem, the oxen stumbled, the cart wobbled and, fearful that the precious cargo might topple off, Uzzah the priest put out his hand to steady it. Suddenly Uzzah dropped dead to the ground beside the Ark of God and the whole procession came to a terrified halt. David complained to the Lord, but he knew the rules, and when, three months later, the journey was resumed it was being carried on the shoulders of the priests.

Why all these stories? On the principle that, 'Whatever was written in former days was written for our instruction' (Romans 15:4), they are there to teach us how holy God is, and how carefully we must come to him in worship. Through Christ we may come boldly and with confidence to God, but the trembling and fearfulness of the Old Testament worshippers are there to remind and warn us, and we should never lose that sense of awe and wonder expressed in so many of our hymns and by so few of our congregations. The questioning of God through Jeremiah has lost none of its power today: 'Do you not fear me? declares the LORD; do you not tremble before me?' (Jeremiah 5:22). Whilst something wonderful has happened to change the way we come, nothing has happened to change the awesome holiness of God and therefore the care with which we must approach him.

We should never lose

that sense of awe and

wonder expressed in

so many of our

hymns and by so few

of our congregations

I like the word 'celebration' that has been minted in the past few decades to describe Christian worship, but there is a danger: too often we are encouraged to approach God as if we were one big happy family celebrating mum and dad's golden wedding. Of course there is joy and gladness in worship, but when did we last tremble in his presence? And when congregations today are encouraged from the front to become, as someone has commented, 'all matey with the Almighty' we have these accounts to remind us what God thinks of such careless and trivial attitudes. The results may not always be precisely what they were three millennia ago, but tragic results there certainly will be. When Isaiah saw the Lord Jesus Christ in the temple he heard angels crying, 'Holy, holy, holy'(Isaiah 6). It is rare for Hebrew to add to the doubling for emphasis, but if the Tabernacle was 'holy' and the inner sanctuary 'holy, holy', then the presence of Jesus is 'holy, holy, holy'. That should all speak for itself.

But there is something more for us to consider in this great privilege of prayer. The apostle tells us that we come 'by the blood of Jesus, by the new and living way that he opened for us through the curtain, that is, through his flesh' (see Hebrews 10:19–20). This strange language will be clear if we keep in mind that earlier picture of the Tabernacle. Do you recall the layout of the Tabernacle? With one eye on Hebrews 10:20–22 I want to take you on a short but significant journey. Remember, there is only one entrance to the Tabernacle and the first thing we meet is a great bronze altar. Over the centuries thousands of animals have been killed there. Why? To show how serious sin is and what is the cost of forgiveness.

Now it is the great Day of Atonement which happens only once every year. The High Priest enters the outer court of the Tabernacle and walks slowly to the bronze altar where he sacrifices a bullock, takes some blood in a bowl and live coals from the altar, pauses to wash at the great bronze basin, and moves on to the Tabernacle itself. Through the entrance and into the first room, he passes the lampstand and the table of bread and then, cautiously and with fear, through the blue, purple and scarlet curtain. No one has been here for a whole year. There has been no dusting, sweeping, or polishing of the gold, and the stain of the sprinkled blood from last year is still visible. The High Priest places some of the coals on the altar of incense and sprinkles the blood once on the Ark of the Covenant, and seven times in front of it. All the time the incense is rising towards heaven. And this is just for his own sins.

The High Priest now returns to the great altar of Burnt Offering and sacrifices a goat—then he repeats all that he has done before, though this time for the sins of the nation. But he has not quite finished. A second goat is waiting beside the altar; on this one he lays his hands, confesses the sins of the whole nation over it, and sends it off into the desert. This animal is known as the 'scapegoat'. The Hebrew word is *azazel*, which even today Hebrew scholars are at a loss to know its true translation and so we have settled for the word William Tyndale introduced in 1530.

How ridiculous. Could one goat die for the sins of a whole nation, and could another carry the nation's sins far away into the desert? Of course not, neither is possible. But they both present for us a picture of the Son of God who can and did; for as Paul expresssed it so simply: 'This is an illustration for the present time' (Hebrews 9:9 NIV). We can now understand what lies behind the picture of the 'hearts sprinkled clean' and the 'bodies washed with pure water' in Hebrews 10:22. These are all references to the great altar, the basin of water, and the blood sprinkled on the Ark in the Most Holy Place. And this is how we are to understand the death of Christ on Calvary. He was a sacrifice in our place and our High Priest to present that sacrifice to God: 'He himself bore our sins in his body on the tree' (1 Peter 2:24). That single word 'himself' is intended and is emphatic; there is no substitute for him because he was a substitute for us.

But isn't this all very offensive? Imagine tens of thousands of animals sacrificed over hundreds of years—the noise and blood, the stench, flies and dirt. Animal lovers recoil and theologians retreat. It is surely all so primitive and even barbaric; it has no place in the thinking of Christianity. Why not just offerings of fresh baked bread, oil and wine? That would be all very homely, neat and tidy—very civilised. But that is precisely the point. If this offends us, how much more offensive was it that God's holy, pure, blameless Son should die such a cruel, mocking death and in full gaze of a jeering crowd? In his letter to the Hebrews, the apostle deliberately referred to the blood of the sacrifices a dozen times and to the blood of Christ seven times—which is only one less than in all his other letters combined.

But this emphasis upon the 'blood' is so offensive to many and to avoid it they say, 'It was not like that' or 'It was not Jesus who died'. Cults and religions across the world deny the manner of the death of the Son of God, or that he died at all; Islam teaches that it was Barabbas who died, not Christ. But the reality is that he died that way to show how vile our sin really is, how terrible in the sight of a holy God, and how utterly and perfectly God will forgive when his Son has paid the price. How else will God get across to us the seriousness of sin? Capital punishment was introduced to show the seriousness of the sin of murder—nothing greater could be handed out to those guilty of treating the life of a human being so casually; even our modern substitution of life imprisonment is considered the worst penalty that we can impose for such a serious crime. In which case, how much more does the death of the Son of God reveal the seriousness of sin? How more vividly than the brutal death of his Son could God impress upon us that sin does matter and that its consequences are fearful—both in this life and in the next?

We take sin too lightly. Will a shrug, or an apology, or a little penance do to wash away our sin? No, they will not do. Then will a few tears, or signing a card or joining the church cover over my rebellion against God? No, they will not. Nothing but the blood of Jesus will make amends for my sin. The guilty conscience that we hope no one will uncover, a distant past that we are afraid one day will return to hound us, a long covered secret that inescapably haunts us, all these can be entirely forgiven and for ever. Christ can cleanse our conscience from dead works like these (Hebrews 9:14). Because he is our scapegoat.

Just as the scapegoat disappeared over the horizon and Israel knew that their sin was taken away for ever, so forgiveness is full and complete when we trust only in Christ. The pictures God uses to express what he does with our forgiven sin are impressive: he will plunge them into the ocean—remove them as far as the east is from the west—grind them into the dust—dissolve them like the morning mist on a summer day—wipe them from his memory—remove them as far as the infinity of space—turn his back on them—and erase them from the record of our life.

Here we are

encouraged to come

to him not as eternal

creator, sovereign lord

or omnipotent God—

but as our Father!

Access to whom?

We have now arrived back at our starting point: 'Through him we both have access in one Spirit to the Father' (Ephesians 2:18). Similarly Hebrews 10:22 encourages us to 'draw near to God'. The God of power who created the universe, the God of purity who is utterly holy, invites us to come to him in prayer confidently and with full assurance of faith. But here we are encouraged to come to him not as eternal creator, sovereign lord or omnipotent God—but as our Father!

Many prayers are exclusively Christ centred and in some congregations you can hear the constant 'Dear Jesus' mantra, which is only marginally better than those prayers that are not even offered in the name of Christ and could just as easily be a prayer to Allah, the Great Architect, Mother Earth or Vishnu. When the apostle referred to Christ always making intercession for us through his resurrection, he surely did not have in mind our Lord perpetually on his knees ferrying the requests of his people and unloading them to the Father. No, it is his very presence in heaven that is our intercession; the fact that he died and rose from the dead and is now seated with the Father is the guarantee that all for whom he died are eternally secure, and in that sense 'he always lives to make intercession for them' (Hebrews 7:25). Our Lord himself made the pattern very clear to his disciples: 'In that day you will ask in my name, and I do not say to you that I will ask the Father on your behalf; for the Father himself loves you …' (John 16:26–27).

The 'throne of grace' (Hebrews 4:16) is a picture of both the Father and the Son seated in glory, surrounded by the adoring angels and saints, and ready to respond to the prayers of those still battling on earth. Because of this it is quite true that our prayers do come to Christ just as they come to the Father, but there would be no access to the Father apart from the Son—and we must forget no part of that statement. I don't say that we cannot pray to Christ or that we should not pray to Christ, only that we need not pray to him, and that in the New Testament we are not encouraged to pray to him. Christ is not our prayer carrying mediator, but our heaven opening mediator. He died so that we could gain access to the Father.

Christ is not our prayer carrying mediator, but our heaven opening mediator

And what a privilege to call him 'Father'! In an age when as many families fall apart as stay together, when leadership in the home is despised or ignored and when countless children sob themselves to sleep at night wondering when and how the burning row downstairs will ever end, the idea of God as Father has lost much of its lustre. But it need not. This is just the time to reassert its magnificent meaning.

There is something so reassuring in the word 'father'. Properly understood it carries all the associations of leadership and love, protection and provision, warmth and affection. A good father cares and takes an interest, listens to the anxieties and concerns of his children, and encourages and rebukes then. He gives advice and warns of danger, and he picks up the weak ones when they fall. A good father commands respect but dispels fear. We live in a society, that for all its hard-nosed scientific materialism, is besotted with the paranormal. Psychic phenomena, occult practices, spiritism, astrology and the New Age (ancient Hinduism in new clothes), all the way down to ghosts and ghouls and things that go bump in the night, are growth industries—and they all bring fear. Ours is a world of fear: the fear of war, of terrorism, of poverty, of heartbreak and death, of the unseen and the unknown. Nothing has changed since the century in which Paul was writing when he encouraged the Christians in Rome: 'All who are led by the Spirit of God are sons of God. For you did not receive the spirit of slavery to fall back into fear, but you have received the Spirit of adoption as sons, by whom we cry, "Abba! Father!"' (Romans 8:14–15). What a fantastic statement that is!

Genealogies may not matter much today, but in Bible times they were essential. Your parentage, and particularly your father, was your passport into society and into the future. To be able to trace your line of descent back to a great man was more important than the fortune you left when you died. So, when Paul wrote to a mixed congregation of converted bankers and lawyers, soldiers and slaves, Gentiles and Jews, he encouraged them with a reminder of their true parentage. This theme of adoption runs like a silver thread through the New Testament. John informs his readers: 'To all who did receive him, who believed in his name, he gave the right to become children of God' (John 1:12). Paul, writing to the Ephesians, encouraged them that this was something God wants for us, plans for us, and finds great pleasure in: 'He predestined us for adoption through Jesus Christ, according to the purpose of his will' (Ephesians 1:5). And to the Galatians we were redeemed: 'So that we might receive adoption as sons' (Galatians 4:5). Paul gladly uses the common legal term for adoption and typically hijacks it for his own use. All who have been chosen by God to become part of his family may confidently count themselves as friends and brothers and sisters of Jesus and sons and daughters of the Father. Jesus is not ashamed to call them brothers (Hebrews 2:11).

Paul even runs ahead of himself and looks forward to the time when it will be more *evident* that we are the children of God than it is now. He is clearly excited as he thinks of that day when: 'The creation itself will be set free from its bondage to decay and obtain the freedom of the glory of the children of God'; meanwhile: 'We ourselves … groan inwardly as we wait eagerly for adoption as sons, the redemption of our bodies' (Romans 8:23). As children, we will inherit everything that the father has planned and prepared for us (Romans 8:17).

But why does Paul preserve that little Aramaic word *abba* in Romans 8:15? Why did he not use the common Greek word for 'father' which is *pater*? There can be surely only one reason: ever since Christ himself used the word 'abba' to address his Father in the garden of Gethsemane, it had become a very precious word for Christians; never could they forget the intimacy of that occasion when their Lord, in his emotional and spiritual agony before the cross, prayed 'Abba, Father, all things are possible for you' (Mark 14:36). When we use this same word to approach God in prayer, we are humbly asserting our right of access no less than that of his only Son, and our privilege of access with the status of his children. Whether or not the word abba carries the child-like familiarity that has often been ascribed to it—and this has been more recently questioned—it is certainly a word of high status and firm relationship. There are no half measures with God: all who are born again by the Holy Spirit are children of God—with all the privileges that implies. Therefore, as Martin Luther once commented, the word 'abba' is more eloquent than 'the most eloquent rhetoricians that ever were in the world.' Why, therefore, is it as hard to bring saints to prayer as it is to bring sinners to the cross?

Our right and privilege is to pray: not in grovelling fear or awesome dread, but in bold assurance and joyful confidence

We must live securely in this relationship. Paul encourages us to come to God: 'Praying at all times in the Spirit with all prayer and supplication' (Ephesians 6:18). If 'all prayer' means 'all kinds of prayer', then we may come with adoration and praise, with thanksgiving and gratitude, with intercession and petition; we may come when our heart is bursting with love and devotion, and when it is clouded with fear and anxiety; we may come in the odd moments of peace and through the long hours of pain; we may come in frustration and failure, as well as in anticipation and achievement; we may come when we feel like prayer and when we do not. But our right and privilege is to pray: not in grovelling fear or awesome dread, but in bold assurance and joyful confidence.

Every prayer is an expression of our consciousness that we are living in the light of the great privilege of being God's children and therefore have not simply a duty but a delight to approach him; and it is an expression of the certainty that he who is a good listener will hear us. Our God is awesomely powerful, blindingly holy, fearfully just and utterly other than us; but he is also a loving, caring Father to all his people, and he invites them to talk with him—that is the magnificent grace of prayer.

> THERE IS AN EYE THAT NEVER SLEEPS
> beneath the wing of night;
> there is an ear that never shuts
> when sink the beams of light.
>
> 2 There is an arm that never tires
> when human strength gives way;
> there is a love which never fails
> when earthly loves decay.
>
> 3 That eye is fixed on angel throngs,
> that arm upholds the sky,
> that ear is filled with heavenly songs,
> that love is throned on high.
>
> 4 But there's a power which we can wield
> when mortal aid is vain,
> that eye, that arm, that love to reach,
> that listening ear to gain.

Chapter 14

5 That power is prayer, which soars on high
through Jesus to the throne,
and moves the hand which moves the world,
to bring salvation down.

JOHN A WALLACE 1802–70
Praise! 613

Rejected grace

'You have fallen away from grace' Galatians 5:4

In the opening chapter of this book we said that grace is the most beautiful word in the Bible and a hallmark of Christianity. No world religion has an equivalent word so rich in meaning and so profound in its value.

Grace is God's kindness and care over the whole of creation and his control over all the events of this world—that is his universal and sovereign grace. Grace is God's law that teaches us the best way to live, and it is his undeserved love by which he reckons the righteousness of Jesus Christ to our account, covers over all our sin, and never again counts our transgressions against us—that is justifying grace. Grace is the willingness of his Son to lay aside his glory and become a man—that is incarnate grace; and it is his persistent authority that wins the affection and response of our heart and then pardons us—that is invincible and forgiving grace. His grace assures us that we are secure for ever—that is eternal grace, and that he has a perfect plan for our lives whoever we are—and that is purposeful grace. When we are weak, he provides sufficient grace and at the moment of our conversion he brings us into the church which is community grace. His sanctifying grace supplies all that we need to conform us more to the likeness of Christ, his prayerful grace assures us of the glorious privilege of access to the Father, and his ultimate grace will finally bring us safely into his heavenly kingdom.

In fact, we have claimed that every approach of God to us, and every word of God to this world, is grace. Whatever God says to humanity is grace. Not just his promises but his warnings also. When God warned Adam and Eve: 'In the day you eat of that fruit you will die', and when he cautioned Israel in the wilderness that those who did not obey his laws must be 'cut off' from the nation, and when our Lord alerted Judas: 'Woe to that man by whom the Son of Man is betrayed', and when the writer to the Hebrews counsels, 'How shall we escape if we neglect such a great salvation'—that is all grace. God does not *have* to speak to us. The fact that he says anything at all is his undeserved kindness.

Every challenge of the gospel, every plea to the sinner to repent, every presentation of the message of Jesus Christ is grace. Every moving of the Holy Spirit in the conscience, every quickening of the pulse under the hammer of the word of God, this too is grace.

But not all who receive God's grace benefit from it. Some hear and reject, others simply turn away and neglect it. There are tragically millions who can marvel at the grandeur of magnificent scenery, the immensity of the universe around us, or the incredible mechanism of our world, and walk away mumbling about 'blind chance'. Nothing can be more terrible than to hear and then reject or neglect God's grace in whatever form it comes to us—and nothing is more certain than that this happens regularly in evangelical churches.

Not all who receive God's grace benefit from it

There are millions across the world who have only an outline of God's grace: they can see love and beauty in the world around them—what Paul refers to in Romans 1:20 as 'his eternal power and divine nature'—but it leads them nowhere. Millions more, from their perspective in a Calcutta slum or a Filipino squatter camp perched on a rubbish tip, can see far less of God's grace. But among a congregation of those transformed by this very grace are those who, though involved in the worship of the Creator and listening to what this God has revealed in his word, are nevertheless deaf to the meaning of grace. Simply to be among such a community is grace; and yet many despise it and neglect it, or inwardly scoff at it and finally reject it. Yet still, in his grace, God allows time to repent. In a million pictures, through a thousand circumstances and a hundred voices he points to himself; but still many do not—will not— look and listen. But grace is magnified in that while we were Christ-rejecting sinners Christ died for us, and even though we go on rejecting, if God has set his invincible love upon us then finally he will conquer our stubborn mind and will.

But the fearful thing is to provoke grace by assuming that it will always be available. When Paul wrote to the church at Corinth he knew by their lifestyle that there were some in the church who had never responded positively to the grace of God and he urged them: 'We appeal to you not to receive the grace of God in vain' (2 Corinthians 6:1). In other words, just by being connected with the Christian congregation at Corinth they had all received some measure of grace, but some had turned it into a wasted benefit. Grace is not always available. It is only too possible to fall away from a grace that is so close; to allow the hope of peace with God to slip from our hand at the very moment when we almost have it within our grasp. Some spend a whole lifetime struggling with faith when all the time the Saviour is so close.

Our national poet William Cowper, whom we met in chapter nine, was never certain of his personal salvation; even though he had no doubt that Christ died to save, it always seemed to be beyond his own reach. In what is considered to be one of his most moving short poems *The Castaway*, Cowper pictured a sailor swept overboard in a storm. His shipmates threw casks, ropes and even the hen coop into the sea in a vain attempt to keep him afloat; sometimes with hope but mostly in despair he struggled in the water. To save herself in such a storm, the ship could not turn or stop, and the drowning mariner watched as the crew sailed on:

> 'Yet bitter felt it still to die
> Deserted, and his friends so nigh.'

In a pitiful expression of his own spiritual state, the poet compared the sailor's plight with his own, in which he felt overwhelmed by the loss of a salvation he could not grasp:

> 'No voice divine the storm allay'd.
> No light propitious shone;
> When, snatch'd from all effectual aid,
> We perish'd, each alone:
> But I beneath a rougher sea,
> And whelm'd in deeper gulphs than he.'

With friends so close who are secure in Christ, many will die alone and overwhelmed by their unbelief.

Nothing could be more urgent than that we are careful not to lose what is so clearly within our grasp. This is why the New Testament is full of challenges to check out where we stand with God; we may be fooling others, even ourselves, but never can we deceive God. Perhaps nobody knows where we stand, but we do. Deep inside, privately, silently, many know that they are rejecting God's grace that has come to them in all its varied forms.

Some hear the word of grace and reject it.

Peter wrote about scoffers who mocked the Christian confidence in the second coming of Christ. They deliberately rejected the word of God, ridiculed the very idea of eternal grace and laughed at the warning of the Flood in the time of Noah: 'Forsaking the right way, they have gone astray', is how Peter described them in 2 Peter 2:15; this means that they must have known the truth at one time, because they were forsaking a path they once walked. They made a conscious decision to reject the word of God and the message of his grace, and having done so, they set out to oppose the truth.

The tragedy of some is that they once benefited by the very grace they have now rejected. Peter wrote of these in 2 Peter 2:20–22. Some had clearly been changed by their contact with the gospel of Christ. They had presumably listened to the message, come to a knowledge of 'our Lord and Saviour Jesus Christ' and had been impressed by the purity of his life and the moral standards of Christianity—which contrasted so beautifully with those of the world. They made a decision to follow this 'way of righteousness', and consequently tidied up their life. In the words of Peter they even: 'escaped the defilements of the world.' But it was all short-lived. They had

Nothing could be more urgent than that we are careful not to lose what is so clearly within our grasp

followed a code and to some extent the historical Jesus, but there was clearly no true repentance or new birth; the entanglement of the world was too great and, in Peter's vivid description borrowed from the biblical proverb, like a dog they returned to their own vomit.

There are many in our evangelical churches who have learned the word of God from infancy and all through Sunday School and the youth group. Perhaps they responded positively at an early age, and to a degree it preserved them from many snares and temptations as a teenager. They did not get into the wrong set and they never joined a gang; clubbing and the drug scene was not for them. All around them was the example of those who followed 'the way of righteousness', and they could see that it was a better way than that of their peer group in the world around them. In other words they enjoyed—though not always consciously—the grace of Christian parents and grandparents, youth leaders and friends, all of whom prayed and were saying, 'Come this way and we will do you good.' But tragically, at the end it did them no good. They rejected a young life surrounded by grace and, to use Peter's own analogy, like a washed pig they return to wallow in the mud.

Often when I travel the country and find myself sharing a meal with Christian parents whose children have long left home, it is only natural to enquire about the family. Once we have passed the preliminaries about universities and degrees, successful professions or trades, happy (or unhappy) families, and the pleasure of grandchildren, sadly I can too often anticipate the response when I enquire about their spiritual state. Voices become lower and more serious, faces tighten and eyes moisten. I learn that they all once made a profession of faith, some were even baptised and worked in the Sunday School or youth group, or on the audio desk, perhaps even in evangelism. But now? They go nowhere to worship God; their parents are prayerful, of course, and hopeful, and some of the children are friendly towards the gospel, whilst others are firmly opposed. It may seem unkind and extreme to compare them to Peter's dog or pig, but in reality that is just what they are: they have returned to a world without Christ and have abandoned the 'way of righteousness'.

To reject such an early life of grace is terrifying in its consequences.

Others hear but simply neglect it

Not all make a conscious decision to reject God's grace. They may attend church regularly, or occasionally, and are perpetually 'interested' and 'thinking about it'. The one thing they have certainly not done is to consciously reject the message. When asked what they are doing with it, the answer has to be: 'Not a lot at present; but I probably will.' That is their great self-deceit, they feel sure they will respond positively one day. But they probably won't; many of them never do. I have known people leave church in tears having been so challenged by what they have heard, which would be encouraging if it were not for the fact that they have left church in tears many time before—over many years.

To reject such an early life of grace is terrifying in its consequences

One of the saddest complaints of Paul in his letters concerns a man called Demas. Somewhere around the year AD 62 Paul wrote from house arrest in Rome to the church at Colossae. The final greetings came from Luke, the beloved physician, and Demas, both of whom Paul described as 'my fellow workers' (Colossians 4:14 and Philemon 24). Two years later, when Paul expected his execution at any time, he wrote sadly to Timothy that 'Demas, in love with this present world, has deserted me and gone to Thessalonica' (2 Timothy 4:10). Demas must have neglected all the signs of backsliding in his own life. He did not wake up one morning and decide to reject the gospel—it rarely happens that way. But little by little he neglected all that he knew of the grace of God until he slipped away to Thessalonica to live without the pressure of being known as a Christian. Perhaps Demas still called himself a Christian. But all the evidence had gone. And without the evidence there can be no assurance.

This is exactly what Paul warned the Corinthians against: 'Working together with him, then, we appeal to you not to receive the grace of God in vain' (2 Corinthians 6:1). That is what happened to Demas: the grace of God in vain. It is no use unless you follow through. You know what you must do but you keep putting off your response. On the Day of Judgement no one can hope to tell God they were close—you don't score goals after the final whistle is blown.

Sometimes we cover our neglect with pious excuses. 'I may not be one of the elect', is a frequent complaint. I have known some people spend half their life worrying over this: 'What if I am not one of the chosen? Then there is no hope for me.' To which I can only reply, 'Yes, you are quite right; and all the time you excuse yourself from commitment to Christ with that sort of reasoning, you never will be one of the elect!' Some may not like the theology of that, but the reality is only too apparent.

Some hear the word of grace and then confuse it

Grace and numeracy have a lot in common! There are always some who add, subtract or multiply—with grace as the only constant.

Paul wrote to the church at Galatia because he was concerned for their *addition* to the message of grace. When he warned them that they had 'fallen away from grace' (Galatians 5:4), it was because they were adding to the message of unearned and undeserved grace by demanding obedience to some aspects of the Jewish ceremonial law. They were adding to the freedom of salvation by faith through grace alone, and attempting to be justified by observing the law—admittedly not very much of the law, but law nevertheless. There is still a vast swathe of so called Christendom that believes the only way to heaven is by the death of Christ plus good works. They may be our own good works, like charity and kindness, or they may be the good works of the 'super saints' that we can trade to make up our deficiencies; those works of 'supererogation' that we considered in

On the Day of Judgement no one can hope to tell God they were close—you don't score goals after the final whistle is blown

chapter ten. Either way, if we think we can add anything by way of our works then we have spoiled grace.

Imagine that you present me with a valuable painting. You suggest that I hang it in a prominent place in my lounge, and you explain its value because it was painted by Harmens Van Rijn Rembrandt, the Dutch Renaissance master. I duly follow your instructions, but when you visit me next you discover me in front of the picture busy with my palette and paints. In response to your none-too-polite enquiry what I think I am doing, I comment that I considered the bottom right hand corner to be a little too dark so I thought I would lighten it—but only a little. Your reply will be immediate and urgent: 'Leave it alone. Don't touch it. That is the work of the master and if you try to improve on it, you will only devalue it.' The lesson is plain: to add to the work of the Master, that he perfectly completed on Calvary, will completely ruin it. However little you may add by way of your own effort, it can only devalue all that he has done for you.

To add to the work of the Master, that he perfectly completed on Calvary, will completely ruin it

On the other hand, when Paul warned Timothy of false teachers in the church at Ephesus, his concern was not addition but *subtraction*. Hymenaeus and Philetus were representative of those who were claiming that the resurrection was already past (2 Timothy 2:17–18). Exactly what they were trying to say Paul did not make clear, but he commented that they were 'upsetting the faith of some'. They were denying a fundamental truth of the Christian message and robbing the young converts of their great expectation of the resurrection to come. Whether these two men could rightly be called Christians Paul did not say, but they were clearly weak in grace because Paul urged Timothy to be 'strengthened by the grace that is in Christ Jesus' (2:1). The apostle went on to point out that they have been ensnared by Satan and that if Timothy boldly and faithfully instructs them: 'God may perhaps grant them repentance leading to a knowledge of the truth' (2:25–26).

There are so many today who whittle down the truth of Christianity by denying what they find hard to believe, or what does not sit comfortably with a pseudo-scientific fraternity that maintains science has all truth locked in place. The virgin conception of Christ, the supernatural combining of human and divine natures in one person, the miracles of his ministry, his death as a substitute on behalf of sinners, the literal, physical resurrection of Christ, his ascension back into heaven and his promise to return one day in glory—all these are beyond a full explanation. But to deny any one of them is to destroy grace by subtraction.

However, as great a danger is that of *multiplication*. Jude wrote of those who: 'Pervert the grace of our God into sensuality and deny our only Master and Lord, Jesus Christ' (Jude 4). These people were not denying the word of God, so in that sense they were not subtracting from the truth, instead they were 'perverting' the truth, and that word means to change or transpose. They did this by interpreting the truth in such way that they were able to justify their own lusts and pleasures. They were twisting the truth to make it say what they wanted, in order to give authority for their immoral conduct. Many today are eager to justify their behaviour from Scripture, but in order to do so they have to distort the truth to provide an excuse for them to satisfy their own preferences. The Bible can be used to prove anything we wish—providing we ignore its plain teaching, its consistent message, and the context of the passage we are exploiting.

It is tragic to hear of Christians today trying to justify from Scripture their gross materialism, their immoral conduct in co-habitation (or worse), their adultery to escape a sad marriage, their homosexual relationships, and their eagerness to marry an unbeliever. Even shady business dealings, dishonest tax returns, and unlicensed software on our computers can be easily justified once we choose to separate one part of Scripture from another and stir its clarity into the muddy swirl of our own inclinations. It is possible to provide a long list of issues over which Bible Christians had no quarrel for centuries, but all of a sudden some discovered a new way of interpreting texts—coincidentally just after the world of political correctness had come to those same conclusions.

Multiplying grace is what Paul had in mind in Romans 6:1. He anticipated that some might claim that once we have received free and unlimited grace we can go on sinning so that more and more grace will be needed to forgive! It may seem incredible that anyone should argue like this, but Paul thought they might, and his response was to conclude that such a line of thought betrays that they have never really found new life and forgiveness in Christ.

A young man once sat in my study and quoted my own theology to me. He had been disciplined over immoral conduct for which he was totally unrepentant, and had no interest in abandoning. He had been an active member of the church and yet I told him that right now I doubted his salvation, and so should he. Immediately he reminded me that I had often preached that we can never lose our salvation—once a Christian, always a Christian. I agreed, but pointed out that he had not been listening to something else I repeatedly preached: the single clear evidence we have that we are Christians is the consistency of our lives; as James reminded his readers, the only way that you can see that a person is justified is 'by works, and not by faith alone' (James 2:24). No one can see another person's faith, they can only see its result in action. I told my young friend that at this precise moment there was no evidence of his salvation, and that that should make him very afraid. In reality he was using the grace of eternal salvation as an excuse to multiply sin.

The result of rejected grace

There are at least two passages in the New Testament that cause a great deal of debate among some Christians and a lot of anxiety among others. In Hebrews 6:4–6 the apostle wrote, 'It is impossible to restore again to repentance those who have once been enlightened, who have tasted the heavenly gift, and have shared in the Holy Spirit, and have tasted the goodness of the word of God and the powers of the age to come, if they then fall away, since they are crucifying once again the Son of God to their own harm, and holding him up to contempt'.

Who are these? They are the very people we have been describing. Those who one way or another, and for one reason or another, have abandoned the grace they once knew and even professed to experience. They are often people who sit around us in church every Sunday. These people are inside, not outside; or at least they were inside and some are now outside; and if there are any still on the inside they are heading for outside! They have experienced so much. They knew what it was to have an understanding of the message of Christ, they experienced times when the Spirit of God was real and present, and convicting them of sin. They perhaps even went through a time of repentance and they loved to listen to the word of God. But then, all that once was so dear to them they trod under foot and rejected the Christ whom they claimed had died for them. They never really found salvation, though it looked very much like it, and in fact for a time they believed that they had received forgiveness. That is frightening.

Some years ago a man showed me around a church that had once been the scene of a great spiritual revival. In fact, he had been present at the time and could talk animatedly about the large crowds, with people gathering outside and looking in at the windows, and about the powerful preaching; he knew that the whole village had been affected by the work of the Spirit and many lives had been radically changed. Sadly, as he talked, it was clear that he knew nothing personally of the experience of new birth and conversion. He had 'shared in the Holy Spirit', had 'tasted the goodness of the word of God', and had even experienced something of the 'powers of the age to come', but it had all left no life-changing mark on his life. That is what the apostle described in Hebrews 6:4–5.

There is another statement, in Hebrews 10:26–29 that warns us of this same danger: 'If we go on sinning deliberately after receiving the knowledge of the truth, there no longer remains a sacrifice for sins, but a fearful expectation of judgement, and a fury of fire that will consume the adversaries … How much worse punishment, do you think, will be deserved by the one who has spurned the Son of God, and has profaned the blood of the covenant by which he was sanctified, and has outraged the Spirit of grace?'

Some say that this shows you can lose your salvation if you backslide. But that flies in the face of all the Scriptures that promise us that nothing in all creation can separate us from the love of God (Romans 8:31–39 and John 10:28 for example). Others think it is a hypothetical case with Paul saying, 'Of course this cannot really happen, but what if it could …' But that flies in the face of logic. Paul is not so stupid as to give us a warning of a danger that was entirely imagined and not real. This is for real. It refers to those who, having received a knowledge of the truth then go out and trample on all the privileges that they have received.

But the apostle referred to 'the blood of the covenant by which he was sanctified'. What is that if it is not conversion? Perhaps it is similar to the encouragement of Paul in 1 Corinthians 7:14 that unconverted partners in a marriage are 'made holy' (some translations have 'sanctified') by the believing partner. In other words a life can be made more clean or holy as a result of contact with Christians—or in this case, 'the blood of the covenant'. Unquestionably those who listen regularly to the message of Christ dying for sinners, will be affected by such an example of grace and will often wish to live in a better way. Both John Bunyan and John Newton record times before their true conversion when they prayed regularly, fasted for long periods and read their Bible daily; in fact they gave everyone the impression that they were serious-minded Christians. In reality they were nothing of the kind. This self-deceit is repeated all too often among those who are deeply moved by the example of Christ or the ceremonies of the church.

Paul is not so stupid as to give us a warning of a danger that was entirely imagined and not real

Alternatively, a better translation of this phrase may be: 'by which [there is] sanctification'. In other words, if you abandon Christ there is no other sacrifice for sin. Where else will you go? I once spent years trying to help a young man come to faith in Christ. He read everything I gave him and met with me often to talk about the Christian faith, but somehow he just could not trust. One day I took a chance. I hoped I had judged my man accurately, so I suggested that perhaps Christianity was not for him and that he might do well to try another religion. His immediate reply was what I had hoped for: 'Oh I could never do that, because I know there is no other way of salvation but through Jesus Christ'. He came to faith soon afterwards. Had he at that point turned his back on Christ and looked elsewhere, where else would he have found salvation?

The terrifying prospect is that for anyone who rejects Christ there is nothing to look forward to except what Paul calls, 'a fury of fire that will consume the adversaries'. Whatever else that terrible phrase means, it must refer to the hot anger of God. It is so much harder to win someone back to Christ once they have known the truth and rejected it, and that should be an awful warning not to let go the grace that we have.

John Newton learnt this lesson in a frighteningly tragic way during his final voyage as a captain. On Sunday 21 October 1753 in a light breeze, Newton's crew of twenty-seven weighed anchor and steered their little ship called the *African* across the Atlantic. On this journey John took with him a young man named Job Lewis. He had met him seemingly by chance on the quayside at Liverpool, and when the owner of Lewis's ship went bankrupt, John offered to take him on board. An entry on the ship's muster roll refers to 'Captain Job Lewis, Volunteer and Captain's Commander.' Explaining his apparent care to Mary, Newton wrote simply: 'There are other reasons for my concern, which I need not mention to you.' Those reasons could be found on board *H.M.S. Harwich,* nine years earlier, where Newton, newly converted to unbelief and free living, perverted the mind of the impressionable young midshipman to the same ugly trend. Lewis had been discharged from the *Harwich* a few days before Newton, but now he was as careless as Newton had once been. With a sense of grief the older and wiser Newton hoped to lead Job Lewis to a better way of life. His intention was more commendable than his judgement.

Job Lewis was the greatest trial to Newton. His blasphemy and loose morality was a mirror of John's early life, and constantly he felt an accusing finger pointing in his own direction. Job ridiculed the services Newton held for his crew on Sunday, worked hard to undo the captain's influence, frequently reminded John that it was he who had first infected his mind with ideas of personal freedom, and was generally a pain to Newton all through the voyage. At last, on the African coast, Newton purchased a small boat called the *Racehorse,* fitted it for trade, set up Lewis as captain and provided him with a crew. Job Lewis went on board on 18 January and a month later he was dead. He died of his excessively immoral life of wine and women and, according to those around him, left this world in rage and despair: 'Pronouncing his own fatal doom before he expired, without any appearance that he either hoped or asked for mercy.' It is a man like this that Peter compares to a dog returning to eat its own vomit.

What is this fearful expectation of judgement and fiery indignation?

I do not wish to appear dramatic or extravagant, but there will be something more terrible about the judgement of God for those who once sat so close to the truth. This is very clear in Scripture.

There will be

something more

terrible about the

judgement of God for

those who once sat so

close to the truth

We cannot escape if we turn away from the one who has spoken to us by his Spirit through the word (Hebrews 12:25). There is no escape. In Revelation 6:15–16 we have a vivid picture of world leaders calling on the mountains to hide them from the anger of Christ who comes as their judge. But there will be no hiding place for anyone—least of all for those who treated the cross as a thing of contempt. In a plain and unambiguous statement the apostle warned, 'It is appointed for man to die once, and after that comes judgement' (Hebrews 9:27). Nothing could be clearer: both death and judgement are inevitable. But more than this, our Lord himself warned that those who come closest to the truth will be judged more strictly. To those who rejected his message and miracles, Jesus warned that it would be more bearable on the day of judgement for the citizens of Sodom and Gomorrah, than for those who, having heard his word and seen his work then reject him (Matthew 10:15; 11:23–24)). Just how more unbearable it will be, he does not tell us, but we have his word for it.

All such people will be utterly without excuse. God will say, as he said to Israel nearly three millenniums ago: 'What more was there to do ... that I have not done?' (Isaiah 5:4. See also Romans 1:20). We may think, 'Well, judgement is a long way off, I can leave it for now.' But we do not know how far off it is. Not one of us has a guarantee of seeing tomorrow's sunrise. And punishment deferred may be all the more severe. Imagine seeing so clearly what you know you could have grasped, and loved ones—a husband or wife, a mother or father, a child or friends with whom you enjoyed so much here—entering heaven without you and you are locked out for ever. So near, yet so far. If I may turn just a little to the agonised prayer of Christ recorded in Matthew 23:37, it will be a terrible thing for many who experienced so much of his grace to hear him say: 'O friend, O sinner, you who ignore my word, reject my cross and neglect my grace! how often I would have gathered you as a hen gathers her brood under her wings, and you would not!'.

In his classic *Pilgrim's Progress* written in the seventeenth century, John Bunyan described Christian entering heaven to a great welcome and fanfare of the angels. Christian and Hopeful were safely over the river of death and securely in the Celestial City. At this point Bunyan draws attention to another man coming up to the river side: his name was Ignorance. However, he got over the river without half the difficulty the other two men met with because he took advantage of the offer of a ferryman by the name of Vain-Hope. Ignorance came alone to the gate of the celestial city and began to knock for entrance; he was fully confident that he would gain admittance immediately. However, he was asked where he came from and what his business was, and Ignorance replied, 'I ate and drank in the presence of the King, and he has taught in our streets.' When asked for his certificate, that they might go in and show it to the King, Ignorance fumbled for a moment, but found none. Let Bunyan himself conclude the story: 'So they told the King, but he would not come down to see him, but commanded the two shining ones, that conducted Christian and Hopeful to the City, to go out, and take Ignorance, and bind him hand and foot, and have him away. Then they took him up, and carried him through the air, to the door that I saw in the side of the hill, and put him

Punishment deferred may be all the more severe

in there.' Finally Bunyan adds these terrible words: 'Then I saw that there was a way to hell, even from the gates of heaven, as well as from the City of Destruction.'

No one will then say, 'It's unfair', because God is a righteous Judge. It will be a terrifying thing to fall into the hands of God on the wrong side of grace. We may now follow our pleasure, but we will have a fearful eternity to regret allowing God's glorious grace to slip from our experience. If we trade with sin we will bank judgement; but if we receive grace freely we will enjoy all eternity with our Friend and Saviour—and with the community of God's redeemed. So many are so close to grace, but are rejecting it and they know they are. Yet Christ is only a word away and we can call on him at any time and receive his free, undeserved and unlimited grace. For now is the day of salvation. Tomorrow may be an eternity too late.

WHEN YOU, MY RIGHTEOUS JUDGE, SHALL COME
to fetch your ransomed people home,
shall I among them stand?
Shall such a sinful child as I,
who sometimes am afraid to die,
be found at your right hand?

2 I love to meet among them now,
before your gracious feet to bow,
though vilest of them all;
but can I bear this piercing thought:
what if my name should be left out,
when you for them shall call?

3 Prevent, prevent it by your grace;
and be, dear Lord, my hiding-place
in this, the gospel day!
Your pardoning voice, O let me hear,
to still my unbelieving fear,
nor let me fall, I pray!

4 Let me among your saints be found
when all shall hear the trumpet sound,
to see your smiling face;
then loudest of the throng I'll sing,
and all the courts of heaven will ring
with shouts of sovereign grace.

LADY HUNTINGDON'S HYMN BOOK 1774
Praise! 963 © in this version Praise Trust

Chapter 16

Ultimate grace

'An eternal weight of glory beyond all comparison'
2 Corinthians 4:17

I spent two days working on a sermon on heaven but it defeated me and I gave up. The subject was far too big for me to grasp and everything I planned to say was either wishful thinking without evidence or inadequate for what I thought heaven must be. Whenever I deal with this subject, I feel like someone writing a travel guide for a city he has never visited, of which he has read only sketchy records from previous travellers—only one of whom had ever been there—and has little more to guide him than rumours of its magnificent splendour that defies human imagination and language!

In my attempt to write this travel guide, I have searched Paul's letters and cannot find a better definition of the ultimate grace of God than his simple statement: 'An eternal weight of glory beyond all comparison'. In the space of just four words in Paul's Greek he offers us a definition of his final destination and his supreme hope in this world of suffering. And if ever there was a church that made Paul long for heaven, it was this one at Corinth! The church was in a mess morally, spiritually and socially, and Paul's letters and visits had too often been rudely rejected. Finally the Corinthians came to their senses, repented of their sin, and put matters right. Here in chapter four Paul describes his ministry: he refuses to be discouraged, will never tamper with the truth however unpopular it may be, and will only ever preach Christ—and not to enhance his own reputation. In fact, Paul admits that there would be little point in him trying to promote his own reputation because he is acutely aware that God has wisely entrusted the magnificent gospel to men like himself who are nothing better than jars of clay (2 Corinthians 4:7)—what one preacher fittingly compares to plastic bags! This is God's deliberate policy so that the honour will belong to God alone. In fact, to rub this in, Paul reviews some of his suffering for the sake of the gospel (vs 8–10). Lilias Trotter, a pioneer missionary to North Africa, commented towards the end of her life in 1926 on a valuable lesson she had learned: 'Years ago it was a joy to think that God needed me; now it is a great joy to know that he doesn't need me.'

However, Paul will never give up or lose heart even though his body is getting daily weaker. In fact, as his outward body wastes away, his inner spirit is growing stronger and stronger. More than this, he has learnt to see his anxiety and suffering as a 'slight, momentary affliction' (v 17). However gruelling the march, however disappointing the news, however painful the suffering, he will remind himself that it is just for a moment by comparison with what lies ahead. All that he can see and feel now is temporary and passing; but more important than this is the fact that it is preparing him for: 'An eternal weight of glory beyond all comparison.' This was no new thought for Paul. He lived constantly in the light of the future, and declared the same thing to the Christians at Rome: 'I consider that the sufferings of this present time are not worth comparing with the glory that is to be revealed to us' (Romans 8:18).

But what is this 'eternal weight of glory beyond comparison'?

The beginning of that short phrase presents us with no problem. Whatever it is, it is 'eternal'. That means that it is everlasting, never ceasing, without end. In fact it means without beginning or end—and we know nothing in this world that deserves this description. Some scientists may just be changing their minds on that. Recently the theory has been put forward of a never ending universe—without beginning or end. Apparently, the universe is a continuous cycle of total self destruction out of which a new universe is born ready to destroy itself in order to make way for the next—that really is something to look forward to!

So, our description of heaven as eternal is already 'beyond comparison'. Growing old, wasting away and death are all irresistible ingredients of this life here. In Romans 8:23 Paul describes the whole of creation 'groaning' under the burden of disease, decay, violence and death, and longing for the very day that Paul refers to here in 2 Corinthians 4:17. In terms of this life on earth, and our investment in it, we are all ultimate and inevitable losers.

A while back I visited the National Waterways Museum in Gloucester, England. It provides a fascinating history of Britain's five thousand mile canal system. For one hundred years from the mid eighteenth to nineteenth centuries canal construction was big business, and thousands bought shares in this growth industry. To help us understand this we were issued, along with our entry ticket to the museum, with a bond of £100 worth of shares which we could invest in one canal, and as we progressed round the museum we could trade our shares in other canals. We were told that £100 in 1790 was equivalent to £25,000 today, so I set out to enjoy my newly acquired wealth. We bought in 1790 and could trade in 1810, 1840, 1880 and the final value was recorded in 1947. Of my £100 I *lost* just over £96 by 1947! Today, every investment carries a warning that it may go down as well as up. Canals occasionally had short-term gains, but none of them were good long-term investments. By the end of the nineteenth century it was better to switch an investment to the railways that were putting the canal trade out of business.

In terms of this life on earth, and our investment in it, we are all ultimate and inevitable losers

Nothing changes! The massive slide on the shares market after 11 September 2001, accelerated by the revelation less than a year later of dubious accounting among major companies, may have left some investors wishing they had a few shares in canals! There will never be a secure investment in this world. Everything is rapidly passing. Interestingly, the reason why I lost my money at the National Waterways Museum is that, out of loyalty to a local canal, I chose to invest in the Basingstoke Canal Company. In fact I knew that this canal never made money and was short-lived as a commercial route. All history was against me and I knew it—but still I invested. What a fool. Yet billions of people choose to invest all their hopes and ambitions, all their time and energy, and all their gifts and abilities in this life alone—even though all history and experience screams that nothing ever lasts. This is why Paul, wise man that he was, kept his eyes on eternity and encouraged the young Christians to do the same: 'Set your minds on things that are above, not on things that are on the earth' (Colossians 3:2).

If the word 'eternal' is not difficult to understand, the end of our short phrase in 2 Corinthians 4:17 is just as easy to grasp. This eternal weight of glory is 'beyond all comparison'. The word that Paul uses gives us our word 'hyperbole'—something that is greatly exaggerated. In 1 Corinthians 2:9 Paul describes the gospel as something no one could have imagined—not kings, nor rulers, nor prophets: '"What no eye has seen, nor ear heard, nor the heart of man imagined, what God has prepared for those who love him"—these things God has revealed to us through the Spirit.' If that is true of the gospel of Jesus Christ how much more is God's ultimate grace for us unimaginable. It is beyond explanation because there is nothing to compare to it. No words can describe it and no imagination can excel it. Human language will inevitably fall short because our finest poetry, our strongest comparisons and our most dramatic pictures will fail completely to explain heaven to us. This may not be a very positive conclusion, because it means that what we are about to do is to explain that which is unbelievably wonderful, unimaginably glorious, and wholly indescribable. It is beyond hyperbole.

Our finest poetry, our strongest comparisons and our most dramatic pictures will fail completely to explain heaven to us

In other words, I am about to write that travel guide for a city I have never visited, of which I have read only sketchy excerpts from previous travellers—only one of whom has ever been there, and I have little more to guide me than rumours of its magnificent splendour that defies human imagination and language! We are about to describe the indescribable, explain the inexplicable and keep a steady eye on the invisible—that doesn't look too hopeful as a final chapter in a book.

So, what is this 'weight of glory' that Paul squeezes between 'eternal' and 'beyond all comparison'?

You may notice Paul's use of 'glory' in this chapter. In verse 4 his message is the gospel of the 'glory of Christ'; in verse 6 Jesus Christ reveals to us the 'glory of God', and in verse 15 the salvation of more and more people is also for the 'glory of God'. Glory is a common word in the New Testament—used 167 times in all. Paul uses it about eighty-five times if you include the letter to the Hebrews among Paul's letters—which I do. Originally the word meant the worth or value of something and eventually it evolved to stand for an opinion or estimate, and hence an assessment of someone's character. It referred to all that a person is. The Greek word is *doxa*, and we use it in our word 'doxology' to refer to a short song of praise to God. However, the word glory is mainly used in the New Testament to refer to God the Father or the Son, and here are some examples of its use:

Understanding the word 'glory' will take us a long way into heaven

Jesus Christ is the glory of God—2 Corinthians 4:4, 6

We see the glory of Christ and are being transformed from one degree of glory to another—2 Corinthians 3:18

When Christ appears we will be with him in glory—Colossians 3:4

Hell means to be excluded from God's glory—2 Corinthians 1:9

Christ's purpose was to bring many sons to glory—Hebrews 2:10

Peter uses the word and he tells us that, 'glory will be revealed', we will 'receive a crown of glory' and we are 'called to his eternal glory'—1 Peter 5:1, 4, 10

For his part, Jude encourages us that we will be presented, 'blameless before the presence of his glory with great joy'—Jude 24

It will be no surprise to find that the word appears often in the last book of the Bible, and it occurs in all the songs of heaven—Revelation 4:9, 11; 5:12–13; 7:12; 19:1, 7

Finally heaven is made bright with the glory of God—Revelation 21:23

It seems that understanding the word 'glory' will take us a long way into heaven.

Heaven by negatives

Listen to any sermon or read any book on heaven and there is a high chance that you will learn easily as much about what heaven is not as what it is. Too often heaven is described by negatives: in heaven there is no sin, no pain, no death, no tears and so on. We are all well aware what we will *not* be like in heaven. The Bible itself speaks in this way, though briefly: there will never be need for the sun to shine there, and nothing unclean, detestable or false will enter there; never again will there be hunger, thirst, darkness, scorching heat, pain, tears or death (Revelation 7:16–17; 21:4, 23, 27; 22:5). It is easy to talk about what heaven is not because there are so many things that some would like to offload in the next world: from rheumatism to rats, from famine to football, and from murder to mobiles. However, the true glory of heaven is not what it is not, but what it is.

It will not do either, to begin our search in terms of the restoration of the pre-Fall condition of the human race. When God completed his creation of the heavens and the earth, he pronounced them 'very good' (Genesis 1:31), but that perfection was in a different quality from heaven itself. There was a heaven before the heavens, a paradise before Eden, and fellowship with God among the angels long before he walked in the garden with Adam and Eve. And even in the reference to the 'cool of the day', there is at least a hint of the heat of the day—which will certainly not be true of heaven itself (Revelation 7:16; 21:23; 22:5).

Equally, it is unhelpful to begin our search for heaven in terms of all that we enjoy best here and would like to enjoy perfectly for ever. That will mean that our hope of heaven may become little more than a reflection of our earthly priorities; and since we know that heaven is 'beyond comparison' it will be a massive limitation if we can think of it only as an extension of the best that we have here. This is the trap into which world religions have fallen. Islam describes heaven in terms of the sensual pleasures of men enjoying hundreds of pure maidens, and Mormonism has invented a special service for eternal marriage union. It is for this precise reason that our Lord took the most beautiful relationship that he created for men and women and shattered our illusion: 'In the resurrection they neither marry nor are given in marriage, but are like angels in heaven' (Matthew 22:30). We can all understand what the first part of that sentence means, but what on earth are angels like?

However, if we must not begin our description of heaven as the opposite of the worst on earth, or even the best of earth made better, where *do* we begin?

The hyperbole of heaven

If the word 'glory' is the single word that best defines heaven, it seems a little odd that Paul writes of the *weight* of glory; and the more so when we learn that the word 'weight' (*baros*) refers to a heaviness, burden or trouble; it was used of something oppressive—a heavy load. In the first century we find it in the context of taxation! Surely a word like that is best suited to the suffering Paul has described in vs 8–10. But perhaps that is just why he uses it here. We would think of all his suffering as *baros*, a heavy weight; but Paul called it a temporary lightweight—'slight momentary'—by comparison with something that is substantial. For Paul, glory is the heavyweight of reality.

Heaven is to be described best of all by the character of God himself … all that God is, heaven is

If our definition of 'glory' is correct, then 'an eternal weight of glory' is a summary of all that God is. We can therefore best describe heaven as the one place where the full character of God—and that alone—is perpetually revealed and enjoyed. If God is to be revealed 'to us' (Romans 8:18), and if when Christ appears we will appear 'with him in glory' (Colossians 3:4), and if his purpose in saving us was to 'bring us to God' (Hebrews 2:7 and 1 Peter 5:10) so that we will be presented 'into the presence of his glory with great joy' (Jude 24), and if it is the 'glory of God' that gives heaven all its brightness (Revelation 21:23), then clearly heaven is to be described best of all by the character of God himself. In other words: all that God is, heaven is. We will see all that God is, and we will enjoy a transformation to be like him—and that is glory. This would make Paul's conclusion that heaven is 'beyond comparison' a massive understatement! But still he is determined to keep his eyes on that which is unseen (2 Corinthians 4:18); Paul wants to maintain twenty-twenty vision of the invisible.

Heaven is not to be described by what we are like, still less by what we like, but by what God himself is like. All that God is will be enjoyed by all that we become. How far we can grasp this will reveal how fully our minds are set on 'things above' (Colossians 3:2). Heaven is filled with the glory of God (Revelation 15:8), and it is this glory that gives heaven its light (21:23). Struggling to find some words that will describe the perfect splendour of heaven, the apostle John claims that the glory of God, which is the radiance of heaven, is 'like a most rare jewel, like a jasper, clear as crystal' (21:11). If glory is the worth or character of someone, when it is used of God it must be all that God is in the fullness of his character: God is pure and perfect, he is all knowing and all wise, he is the all powerful Creator and Sustainer, and he is loving and compassionate. The glory of God is all that we could ever describe him to be—and infinitely more besides.

But we have a problem. To attempt a portrayal of the character of God will be doomed to failure. John Blanchard, in his book, *Does God Believe in Atheists?* declares 'in a nutshell' fourteen descriptions of God, but John would never pretend that he has made the first—let alone the last—comment on the subject. The fullness of God will always defy man's imagination, understanding and language. However, for our subject, what we may look for are those aspects of God that are reflected in his creation—including us. The fact that he is unique, self existing and self eternal, must, by definition, belong to him alone and will never be ours—not even in heaven; God *is* eternal whereas we *receive* eternal life. However, since the human race was created 'in the image and likeness of God' (Genesis 1:26), we should look for those characteristics of God that are reflected in his creation; and according to Paul, his 'eternal power and divine nature' are clearly seen in the world around us (Romans 1:20). It will be the re-creating of these qualities in us—in all their eternal beauty—that will be the true 'glory' of heaven. Perhaps this is what C S Lewis meant when he described us as being 'more human than human' in heaven.

Heaven is never portrayed in the Bible as a full stop on all that we are here, but a continuation in glory. Eternal life is not something that begins when we die, it is the possession of all true believers now. Even though she claimed to believe it, I doubt whether Martha fully understood our Lord when he promised, 'Whoever believes in me, though he die, yet shall he live, and everyone who lives and believes in me shall never die' (John 11:25–26), but *we* should understand it. According to the apostle John, when we see Christ in the full glory of his heavenly character, we will be transformed to be like him; this is our ultimate destiny and it will be the fulfilment of our present adoption as sons of God (1 John 3:2). Paul glories in the same fact: 'We shall all be changed' (1 Corinthians 15:51–52). However, the continuation is only on the basis of an unimaginable transformation; that is why I said earlier that heaven is not simply an extension of the best here. It is beyond comparison with anything that we know. And this is why we should not describe heaven solely in terms of a 'far better than here' state.

It is my purpose to explain the inexplicable without once stating what heaven is not

The guarantee that heaven is so incomparably different from anything that we know here, is not primarily the small glimpses that we gather from the travel directory found in the Bible, but our guarantee is the character of God. So, what do we know about God that will help us to understand what it will be like for us to be changed into his glory? From here on, it is my purpose to explain the inexplicable without once stating what heaven is not.

Heaven is purity and holiness, goodness and love

That is what God is. Here on earth we are never to think of God as like us—though pure; on the contrary we are like him—though polluted. It was Sarah Edwards who claimed that to live with her husband Jonathan, the notable American preacher in the eighteenth century, was like living with Jesus. I am sure Sarah was sincere in her adoration of her husband, but she must have been wide of reality. Every thought, every word, every intention, every action and reaction from God is only, and can only ever be, wholesome and holy. In heaven, all relationships will be transparent and honest; they will be pure and eternal.

When Paul encouraged the Colossians with the reminder that the Father has 'qualified you to share in the inheritance of the saints in light' (Colossians 1:12) he was not talking about watts, kilowatts, megawatts, halogen bulbs or candle power, he was referring to the completeness and purity of everything: holiness, joy, the knowledge of God, the love of God and the worship of God. All relationships will be God centred and pure. In a world of physical, moral, social and spiritual graffiti, it is hard to imagine a place where just everything is pure and clean and wholly dedicated to reflect the glory of God. The call of the seraphim that Isaiah heard in the temple: 'Holy, holy, holy is the LORD of hosts.' (Isaiah 6:3) was a summary of everything about heaven. The most holy spot on earth for Israel was the room behind the curtain in the Tabernacle. The word 'holy' means sacred and set apart as clean for God, and so the Tabernacle was called the 'holy' place and the room behind the curtain where the High Priest could enter only once a year was called the 'holy, holy' place; but heaven was the 'holy, holy, holy' place. There is nothing and nowhere more pure, clean and full of the presence of God.

To help us grasp this, I want us for a moment to forget the picture of heaven in terms of crystal rivers, a rainbow covered throne, jewel studied walls and the tree of life. I want you to see it in the light of Paul's remarkable statement in Ephesians 1:14 in which he tells us that the Holy Spirit: 'is the guarantee of our inheritance until we acquire possession of it, to the praise of his glory.' The Holy Spirit in the life of the Christian is a deposit which guarantees the final possession of our future inheritance. I plan to buy a house and arrange with the lending company that I will repay by instalments until the house is finally mine. Normally they will require a deposit as evidence that I will be able to keep up the payments; but the deposit has to be in the same currency as the final payment. They will not be impressed if I plead that I do not have five thousand pounds but that the children's guinea pigs have recently produced a fine litter—and the promise of more to follow—and will they do instead! The Holy Spirit is the same currency now that we will enjoy when heaven becomes ours. What is the work of the Spirit here? He is the one who creates in us a passion for God and for holiness—he makes God real to us; he creates in us not only an awareness of eternity but an eager longing for it. In other words the Spirit begins to equip us now for what we will receive then. This is precisely what Paul meant when he prayed for the Ephesians: 'Having the eyes of your hearts enlightened that you may know the hope to which he has called you, [and] what are the riches of his glorious inheritance in the saints.'

In other words, every longing desire we have now for purity and holiness, goodness and love will be fulfilled totally and eternally in heaven—but only because these are all part of the character of God into whose likeness we will be transformed. All our activity and relationships in heaven will be open, honest, rich and full—and as pure as God himself is pure; everything that we do and say and think will please him—and us—perfectly, because we will be changed into the likeness of Christ (1 John 3:2). This clearly refers to our physical—if we may still use that word—body and not only our spiritual being. Paul reminded the Philippians that our lowly body will be transformed 'to be like his glorious body' (3:21); this was one of his great themes in 1 Corinthians 15:35–49 where the apostle intrigues us with the promise of 'the image of the man of heaven'. To be like Christ in every respect save only his deity, is part of this unimaginable transformation that will set us free to be pure in every thought, desire and action.

Heaven is communication and appreciation

When we refer to God as a person, we are not applying to him an attribute that we recognise in the human race. On the contrary, *our* personhood is derived from and is a reflection of our Creator. When the Triune God declared, 'Let us make man in our image, after our likeness' (Genesis 1:26), this was not God talking to himself but it was a revelation of the God he is, and at the same time a revelation of what we are like *because* of what he is like. Remember, he is not like us, but we are like him.

God is a God of communication. There is communication in heaven between the three persons of the Godhead, revealed in that little phrase 'Let us make man in our image' (Genesis 1:26). But there is constant communication between God and the angels who are his agents (Hebrews 1:7,14) and whose focus is upon the Son (1:6). The last book of the Bible is filled with activity and communication between the inhabitants of heaven. Paul longed for the Christians at Ephesus to increase in their 'knowledge of him' (Ephesians 1:17); that must surely be the deep desire of every truly Christian heart and mind—that we may know God. When we see Christ in the full glory of his wonderful character we shall be free to worship him as we always knew we must and wanted to. It was for this we were created in the first place, and it was this that was so tragically lost soon after Creation.

The best of all relationships in Heaven will be centred around the Lord who died for us. When John saw into Heaven itself, he saw 'a Lamb standing, as though it had been slain' (Revelation 5:6); that mysterious and puzzling picture—apart from the even more bizarre description that follows—helps us to understand that these are accounts not of something that we will *literally* see in heaven, but they are explanations of all that the Lamb will mean to us when we see him as he is. We will have a perfect relationship with the one whose wisdom and knowledge will excite us more that ever we understood here, yet we will never forget the deadly cost that purchased this privilege. We will appreciate him so perfectly in heaven. When the Bible tells us that we will 'see him' as he is (1 John 3:2), we will do much more than gaze at his splendour—a splendour as bright as the sun itself (Revelation 1:16)—we will enjoy the

Heaven is far more than staring, as crowds do at royalty, but sharing, as a wife who sees her husband again after a long absence

richness of friendship with him. Heaven is far more than staring, as crowds do at royalty, but sharing, as a wife who sees her husband again after a long absence. And we will be transformed into the same pure holiness (Matthew 13:43).

Perhaps it is significant that when Paul spent the last remaining days of his earthly life in a Roman prison and penned his final instructions to his own faithful legionaries for the gospel, he introduced a word that he had rarely used before in his letters. It was the word that we call 'epiphany', and it means an unveiling; it was a common word used in the first century of the gods when they supposedly came to help men on earth, and Paul knew that many of the kings of the Seleucid (Syrian) dynasty had added *Theos Epiphanes* (God made manifest) to their titles; as he often did, Paul turned a common word to his own use. Four times to Timothy and once to Titus he used the word 'epiphany', because the glorious expectation of seeing Christ in all his unveiled beauty captured his soul in those closing days before the executioner's sword fell. Paul wrote of 'the appearing of our Lord Jesus Christ' (1 Timothy 6:14), and those who 'have loved his appearing' (2 Timothy 4:8), and those who are 'waiting for ... the appearing of the glory of our great God and Saviour Jesus Christ' (Titus 2:13). To see Christ in all his unveiled glory, excited Paul's imagination more than anything else could.

When Paul contrasted the trembling fear of the terrified nation gathered at Sinai with the new assembly of those who are 'enrolled in heaven', he did not downgrade or dismiss the awesome holiness of God—that has not changed. But he tumbled over himself with a description of the new covenant people who can appreciate all that is true of God among 'the assembly of the firstborn' (Hebrews 12:18–24). Here we have a glorious mix of the 'innumerable angels ... God, the judge of all ... the spirits of the righteous made perfect and to Jesus, the mediator of a new covenant.' What an assembly!

What makes the human race uniquely human is that we are a reflection of our Creator. When he declared that all he had made was 'very good', it must mean that God took a great delight in what he had made. We can hardly imagine that God remained passively distant from the incredible intricacy and beauty of his universe. He found pleasure both in creating and in the result of his creation. 'Very good' is not the dispassionate comment of the teacher at the end of the student's essay, it is the enthusiastic commitment of the parents admiring their newborn baby. And God passed this ability to communicate and appreciate to the human race. Our capacity to talk and value far surpasses anything in the animal kingdom.

We may marvel at the bee that returns to the hive loaded with nectar and does a little dance to show his buddies how far and in what direction they need to fly to pick up the goodies, but the human race has far more sophisticated ways of providing directions! Your dog woofs down his dog nuts day after day and seems perfectly satisfied, but few people would be content with shreddies for every meal, day in, day out. The richness of communication and appreciation are unique to the human race.

The complexity of human language and our enjoyment of a vast array of beauty through the senses of sight, sound, smell, touch and taste must surely reflect something of God himself. It is not without reason that heaven is described in terms of all that is most dazzling and beautiful here. It is a place of music and song and of sweet smelling incense (Revelation 5:8), where the gentle hand of the Father brings joy to the face of his children (Revelation 7:17) and where a banquet is laid for all his friends (Revelation 19:9).

The best here will be surpassed in heaven by a thousand hyperboles

When God created a world with intriguing and colourful fish deep in the oceans, and insects, flowers, birds and animals that would still enthral the human race thousands of years on from Eden, this was surely because he is a God of beauty and order—and a God who appreciates and communicates beauty and order. He wrote these two characteristics into the genetic coding of all men and women, and in the new heaven and new hearth he will allow that reflection of himself full reign. We will have an eternity to communicate and appreciate. The best here will be surpassed in heaven by a thousand hyperboles. The restored beauty of our present creation that is liberated and obtains 'the freedom of the glory of the children of God' (Romans 8:21) is part of the unimaginable wonder of the new earth.

Heaven is relationships renewed

What made that moment of the abandonment of Christ on the cross so terrible was not only his experience of hell as the Father turned his face away from his sin-loaded Son, but the fact that this was the first and only occasion when there had been even a moment of breach in the otherwise perfect bond of the Father, Son and Holy Spirit. We are accustomed to the best of our relationships turning sour sooner or later. Even if they do not end in a row, there is the fleeting irritation, passing hard thought, momentary cross word—we can enjoy the aftermath of reconciliation, but always there is the memory of the breach. And finally there is the inevitable bitter separation of death. Yet from all eternity the relationship between the Father, Son and Spirit was one of constant and secure harmony. The only thing that ever came between the Father and Son was our sin. And the purpose of that breach was to bring about the reconciliation of our broken relationship with the Father.

When Adam and Eve were created, part of the 'image and likeness' of God was exactly at this level. At first the relationship between the husband and wife in the garden was a perfect reflection of relationships in heaven; and each evening it was strengthened by the calm and peace of God 'walking with them' in the cool of the day. The 'sound' of the approach of the Lord was the most delightful part of their whole experience. In fact, their own relationship together as compatible companions was a beautiful reflection of the relationship of their heavenly Creator with them and, more than this, it was a reflection of the perfect harmony in heaven.

The human race was created for community and every reference to heaven is about community: a banquet, a people, a great choir, a city. But we also have here the ability to communicate and associate at a fundamentally deeper level than anything else in creation. One of the greatest enjoyments of life is just to be with those whom you love and trust. Constant babble is not the only or even the best way for communication; silent company in the presence of a scene of majestic and awesome splendour is infinitely better than the incessant chatter of a chimpanzee. It must surely be this human enjoyment of true relationships that led Paul to encourage the Thessalonians with the promise that when Christ comes again, he will 'bring with him those who have fallen asleep' and that those who are alive will be caught up 'together with them' to 'meet the Lord' (1 Thessalonians 4:14–17). This passage is full of deliberate references to relationships— even the word 'meet' was used of the official welcome given on the arrival of an important public figure. Paul wanted to reassure the Christians who had recently experienced death among their members, that there would be a glorious and welcome reunion.

If relationship is a hall mark of the Triune God, and if this is reflected in his perfect creation pattern for men and women, then heaven is a re-creation of relationships to what they were always intended to be. Whilst a great joy of heaven will be the expression of our love and worship of the God who is all in all (1 Corinthians 15:28), there is more beyond that for the occupation for our time. The creation and re-creation of relationships on earth is simply a reflection of that which is far better in heaven.

Around the year AD 30, a proud young lawyer, Saul of Tarsus, gave his word for the stoning of Stephen to begin. He watched dispassionately until the lifeless body of the first Christian martyr lay soaked in blood on the desert floor. Thirty four years later that same Saul from Tarsus, but now a recipient of grace, knelt in the prison yard as the Roman sword severed his own neck. Now picture Stephen and Paul enjoying friendship together in that Kingdom where peace and joy, love and trust reign for ever. That is ultimate grace.

Somewhere in the year 1751 John Newton anchored his 100 ton 'Snow' off the coast of New Guinea and began trading for slaves. A man, separated from his wife and child, was herded below into the stinking hold of the 120 foot vessel; he never saw his family again. Let's imagine—for we know that this happened to thousands of African slaves—that this man survived the cruel journey to the West Indies, was sold onto a plantation, and ended his life a few years later in 1760 under the barbaric conditions of a pitiless estate manager. However, before his death, worn out by poor food and incessant labour, our man had found Christ from one of the many slaves who had been taught the gospel by a compassionate Moravian missionary—and he therefore died with a certain hope of heaven. What he did not know was that the man who tore him away from his family and sold him in the Jamaican slave market was also a Christian! But John Newton had only been converted for two years, had not yet met a gospel preacher and had no Christian understanding of the horror of the slave trade. When he did, he became one of the most powerful advocates for its abolition. John died in 1807. Imagine the reunion of these two men in heaven! That too is ultimate grace.

But do you find that hard to imagine? Then let me help you. Not long ago someone handed me an article culled from a magazine. Around the picture of two smiling men, one with his hand on the shoulder of the other, was their story. Tom Kelly had been a sniper with the Irish Republican Army and James Tate had been an Ulster Volunteer Force commander. Two men on opposite sides of a bitter and bloody divide—sworn enemies. Both wound up in the Long Kesh prison, and were there in 1974 when trouble broke out in the jail; given an opportunity each would have gladly killed the other. Their story coincides when, on release from prison they eventually came to faith in Christ. Today, Tom Kelly and James Tate work side by side for peace and reconciliation. A little more of the image of God has been restored in the lives of these two men. But what reunions will ultimate grace reveal!

Let me be personal. I have no quarrel with our Lord's declared plan that there will be no husbands and wives in heaven, but second to seeing the Lord himself face to face I have two more things that I long for in heaven. The first is to walk over and sit beside my Barbara and talk with her again like we used to; she is no longer my wife because a few years ago she passed from death into life and was released from every obligation to this world. That will be fine by me because I believe relationships in heaven will be richer and fuller than the best we ever enjoyed here.

But there is something else for which I look forward to heaven. I would like to meet all those who played a part in my salvation from the time of the apostles onward. Someone, a legionary or merchant, brought the message of Christian hope to this wild part of the Roman Empire and shared it with a Briton. It was passed on through the fall of Rome and into the Anglo Saxon kingdom under Alfred: neighbour to neighbour, friend to friend, merchant to merchant, parent to child; in the hovel, in the forest, in the field, in the university. It was still there in the hearts of my spiritual forefathers through the dark ages of ignorance following the Norman conquest; someone passed it on to a friend and perhaps died for it. But all through the Reformation, the Civil War, the Tudors and Stuarts and Hanovers and into the time of Victoria and through two terrible world wars, my spiritual ancestors were passing on the same message—until someone shared the gospel with me more than nineteen hundred years after it all began. That is the real apostolic succession, and that is my true 'family tree'. I cannot research it here, but I will have eternity to meet them all and to hear their stories.

I used to think that the most God-honouring way to explain heaven was that we would spend all our time adoring the person of Christ. I do not think like this any more. After all, we do not honour God here only when we are bowed in prayer, singing a great hymn or listening thoughtfully to a Christ centred sermon; we can honour God equally in our Christian relationships, our creative work and our admiration of his creation. Why should heaven be different? What a glorious privilege to know the saints from every tribe and culture and language, and to hear their personal stories of grace. Will that not be among the most Christ-honouring things we can do with eternity?

Remember, we have arrived at these conclusions because relationship is a characteristic of God, and heaven is the full enjoyment of all that God is.

Heaven is wisdom and knowledge

That God is all-knowing and all-wise should be uncontested among true Christians. Knowledge does not guarantee wisdom, but wisdom guarantees the right use of knowledge. God knows the past, present and the future—and all perfectly. His knowledge is unbounded and his wisdom ensures that his knowledge is always applied for our ultimate benefit. He always acts and behaves in such a way that no other action or behaviour could have been better. All his decisions are based upon perfect wisdom and unlimited knowledge.

Human enquiry and the thirst for knowledge is a reflection of God. The animal world never explores much beyond its own immediate environment. Lions from Africa do not trek into the arctic, nor do polar bears show a passion to swim to India. Even the birds that migrate long distances are not intrepid explorers; on the contrary, they each keep to a clearly defined route, and the British swallow will return year after year to the barn in which it was born—amazing, but hardly adventurous since it is bound by a built-in tradition. Animals may stumble across answers, but they never ask questions. Mankind, on the other hand, has a passion to know and to explore. He will climb the highest mountain simply because it is there and because he longs to see from the top. When it was thought that the earth was flat, men circumnavigated the world and risked falling off the edge. We send men into space, land them on the moon and now we are reaching for Mars. Always and relentlessly the human race is pushing frontiers.

On the door of heaven hangs a notice which reads, 'Enquire within', for that is where all the answers will be found: full, satisfying, perfect and complete answers

None of this is the result of the Fall into sin, it is the result of creation in the likeness of God. The Fall has seriously damaged our wisdom, so that much of our knowledge is turned into ill use and we abuse our discoveries. There is no end to man's philosophies of ethics and religion as he longs to find answers to the great mysteries of life. The world, that Dick Stroeve in Somerset Maugham's *The Moon and Sixpence* referred to as, 'Hard and cruel. We came, none knows where, we go, none knows whither', is full of unanswered questions, like the problem of pain and suffering, sin and evil. There are so many questions that we cannot answer now. I have written two books on the subject of suffering, and I have hardly scratched the surface of an answer. But on the door of heaven hangs a notice which reads, 'Enquire within', for that is where all the answers will be found: full, satisfying, perfect and complete answers. Answers to ethnic cleansings, cruel holocausts, grotesque murders, painful diseases, devastating disasters and unfavourable circumstances—an explanation for the millennia of misery that God has allowed.

Here on earth we accept by faith that the infinitely powerful and caring God is, as the hymn writer Samuel Medley expressed it: 'too wise to err, too good to be unkind.' Heaven, on the other hand, will be understanding why all things were as they were—internationally as well as personally. There *are* answers to all the mysteries of life and death. Faith believes that, but heaven will reveal it. When we know even as we are now known (1 John 3:2) we shall have a perfect and intelligent understanding of all mysteries. Here in this life there will always be 'secrets that belong to the Lord', but in heaven all those secrets are in the open. Only when we walk the new earth with the innumerable company of the saints, will we know the ultimate fulfilment of the promise that, 'The earth will be filled with the knowledge of the glory of the LORD as the waters cover the sea' (Habakkuk 2:14 and Isaiah 11:9).

And if heaven will be when the Lord's people talk together and share their stories of the grace of God, might it not be also that heaven will fill in the gaps of the gospel story? John assured us that there were 'many other things that Jesus did' and that if they were to be written down 'the world itself could not contain the books that would be written' (John 21:25). It must therefore have been desperately hard for John to keep his short Gospel record to a manageable length! But with eternity stretching before us, there will be 'time' enough to tell every story Jesus told, and review every body that he healed and every life that was transformed. And that will bring honour to Christ like nothing else can. I have always wished that I could listen in to the Bible study that Jesus gave on the road to Emmaus, when 'beginning with Moses and all the Prophets, he interpreted to them in all the Scriptures the things concerning himself' (Luke 24:27); perhaps in heaven I will.

When the hymn writer longed to see 'The king in all his glory' and added three verses later as an apparent amendment: 'I will not gaze at glory but on my king of grace', she need not have troubled to correct herself. All the glory of heaven belongs to the Father and the Son, and the glory and person of Christ are one and the same. Our gaze will be with a mind filled with the knowledge of all that our Saviour is.

Heaven is discovery and construction

Will the arrival of heaven when 'we know even as we are now known' suddenly kill our passion for discovery, curtail our search for knowledge and eclipse even the wisdom we gained here through Christ? How would a few billion brain glutted zombies reflect the glory of God?

If my starting point is right that heaven is 'an eternal weight of glory'—

which is the full revelation of the character of God—and that his purpose for us is that we will share that same glory, then we need not imagine heaven as a place of static inaction where all that can ever be done is instantly achieved. On the contrary heaven is a place of vibrant life and action, of discovery and—perhaps—even of creating power. This is what God is like so, if my understanding of heaven is correct, this is what we will be like also. Like our Creator himself, we are not only capable of appreciating beauty, but we have the outstanding ability to create it. Will that Creator-like gift really come to an end in heaven, or will it be re-created as an exact reflection of the one who made us?

Thank God the universe of science fiction is not our final odyssey

This world with its kaleidoscope of colours, sounds, sights, scent, taste and touch, is not only a reflection of the character of God but it would all be unimaginable if we did not actually experience it here. If you had only ever lived on the moon you could never imagine this earth. The evidence of this is seen in the fact that the galaxies and planets invented by our science fiction writers are dull and uninteresting by comparison. Oh they may be vast and mysterious, but they are boringly bland. The set for one will pretty much do for the set of another. Thank God the universe of science fiction is not our final odyssey.

Our God has imagination, together with creative power and enjoyment of it. He is an infallible engineer and a wise architect; he is the most perfect artist and the most exquisite musician. This is all part of the glory of his character. And if we are to be like him, will we not share in this glory and therefore go on creating beauty and order? What if there is still a universe of amazement to discover? Or universes beyond universes? What if the creating glory of God did not stop at this little ball in space that we call Earth? What if we have not yet tiptoed into the outskirts of his infinity or hardly begun to understand 'what God has prepared for those who trust in him' (Isaiah 64:4; 1 Corinthians 2:9)? Will the inventiveness and imagination of mankind cease when we no longer see through a glass darkly? Will we be less than human in heaven—or more human than human?

At one time the coins of Spain depicted the two great Herculean pillars guarding the entrance to the Mediterranean: Mt Ceuta on the North African coast, and Gibraltar at the southern tip of Spain. Because it was thought that to sail into the Atlantic would court certain destruction, underneath were inscribed the words: *Ne Plus Ultra* (no more beyond). Then, in 1492 Christopher Columbus, an Italian sailor in a Spanish ship, discovered the coast of America and the word 'Ne' was struck off the coins. There was 'more beyond'—much more. In every imaginable and unimaginable way, heaven is *plus ultra* for the Christian.

Will our God-reflecting passion for discovery, exploration and creation be given full scope in a new heavens and new earth?

When Peter tantalisingly referred to the day that this present world and universe will be 'burned up and dissolved' (2 Peter 3:10), he simply wrote of 'new heavens and a new earth in which righteousness dwells' (v 13). That may not look much of a description, but a little thought reveals far more than we first imagined. Peter might have left his promise at the dissolution of our heavens and earth, but he deliberately wrote of a replacement of what we already have. In other words there will be some form of continuity that will enable us to recognise an earth and heavens. Who really knows what this earth was like before sin ravaged what was originally 'very good'? And who knows whether the vast universe, which is now so coldly inhospitable, may not have been a beautiful place of inviting wonders? Will our God-reflecting passion for discovery, exploration and creation be given full scope in a new heavens and new earth?

Ultimate ultimacy!

Heaven is a new everything of which there can be nothing better. Time, as we know it, will be measured into eternity; we will have a new body, new relationships, a new appreciation of the Father and the Son, a new experience of joy, a new life, new values—and the list is as endless and as unimaginable as God himself.

The word 'heavens', relating to the skies and space above us, occurs on just over twenty occasions in the New Testament, whereas 'heaven' as the kingdom belonging to God appears more than three hundred times. Only once is the phrase 'new heaven' used in the singular (Revelation 21:1) and only once in the plural (2 Peter 3:13) where it refers to the skies above us. So we are not to think of a new heaven being created—the idea of heaven passing away like this earth would be hardly appropriate unless we assume that heaven is somehow also tainted by the Fall! The picture that follows the 'new heaven and the new earth' is that of 'The holy city, new Jerusalem, coming down out of heaven from God, prepared as a bride adorned for her husband' (Revelation 21:2). What is this? As with so much in the final book of the Bible, we are wise to take it as a picture of something that could never be wholly described in human language or concepts. Jerusalem was the place of God's earthly dwelling and where he especially met with his own people. Here then is an assurance that when the new heavens and new earth are created, heaven and earth will become one and God will be among his people. There will be no commuting from the new earth to heaven! What the Spirit is emphatic to reveal to us is that the new earth—in a size, shape, form and timescale that is not revealed to us—will be the dwelling place of God among his people.

Everything that we have discovered about heaven, we discovered by reference to the character of God himself: purity, holiness, goodness, love, communication and appreciation, relationship, wisdom and knowledge, discovery and construction.

At the start of this chapter I made the assertion that I could not find a better *definition* of heaven than Paul's four Greek words *huperbolayn aionos baros doxa*—'beyond comparison an eternal weight of glory'. But John provides the best *description* of heaven when he heard a loud voice from heaven anticipating the end of all things with the claim: 'God himself will be with them' (Revelation 21:3). But to find the shortest description of heaven I would have to turn to the Old Testament. There is so much in that complex and mysterious book of the prophet Ezekiel that I do not understand, but there is at least one part in the Hebrew that I have no problem with—except that it also is beyond comparison. Heaven is summed up in the final two words of the book: *Yaweh shamah*—'the Lord is there'. It is precisely that which makes heaven 'an eternal weight of glory beyond comparison'.

What is deliciously attractive for those who will arrive in heaven from a weary life of hard labour, cruel persecution or painful suffering is the promise that 'there remains a Sabbath rest for the people of God'. A long break is all the more pleasurable after a period of hard work. C S Lewis referred to heaven in the simple expression: 'Term is over, the holidays have begun'. Even more delightful was the comment of the three year old grandchild of a friend of mine. After church one Sunday she declared in a toddler's loud whisper: 'Now, the plan is to go home'. How magnificently profound—after the service, the plan is to go home.

AWAY WITH OUR SORROW AND FEAR!
We soon shall recover our home,
the city of saints shall appear,
the day of eternity come.
From earth we shall quickly remove,
and mount to our native abode,
the house of our Father above,
the palace of angels and God.

2 Our mourning is come to its end,
when, raised by the life-giving word,
we see the new city descend,
adorned as a bride for her Lord;
the city so holy and clean,
no sorrow can breathe in the air;
no gloom of affliction or sin,
no shadow of evil is there.

3 By faith we already behold
that lovely Jerusalem here;
her walls are of jasper and gold,
her buildings as crystal are clear.
Immovably founded in grace,
she stands as she ever has stood,
her builder she brightly displays,
and flames with the glory of God.

4 No need of the sun in that day,
which never is followed by night,
the splendours of Jesus display
a pure and a permanent light:
the Lamb is their light and their sun,
and with his reflection they shine,
with Jesus inseparably one,
and bright in his radiance divine.

5 The saints in his presence receive
their great and eternal reward;
in Jesus, in heaven they live,
they reign in the smile of their Lord:
the flame of the holiest love
is kindled on seeing his face;
this all their enjoyment above:
on Jesus's beauty to gaze.

CHARLES WESLEY 1707–88
Praise! 966

Index of Scripture references

Genesis

1:26	321, 324
1:27	20
1:31	25, 319
3	31
3:9	7
6:8	6
17:1	130
28:15	229
43–50	165
50:16–17	166
50:17	166
50:20	50

Exodus

19:6,17–19	268
19:16	58
19:18	283
20	90, 268
21:28–30	156
25:12	287
25:22	286
32:19	51
33:7–11	285
34:6–7	6
34:29–35	117

Leviticus

10:1–2	286
10:3	287
11	68
11:33–34	68
11:45	130
19:18	78, 83
20:12, 14	65

Numbers

12:12	88
14:18–19	6
14:33	206
18:15–17	156

Deuteronomy

1:7	62
4:5–8	22, 74
4:6–8	65, 268
6:5	90
7:6–11	268
11	61
12:4,31	285
22	69
22:6–7	69
22:8	69
25:4	67
27	61
28	61, 63
28:1–14	63
28:15–68	63
30:6	144
31:6	227
31:12–13	75
32:47	62

Joshua

1:5	229
7:1–5, 24–26	204

8:35	62	**Nehemiah**	
22:20	204	9:17	6
24:19–27	158		
		Esther	
1 Samuel		4:11	282
4:1–11	287	5:2	282
6:19	287		
15:11	51	**Job**	
20:34	51	3:16	88
		3:20–21	224
2 Samuel		7:4	227
6:3–7	65	9:4,12	47
12:14	74	14:14–17	152
24	152	36:10	159
		38:4	27
1 Kings		38–41	27
21:26	62		
		Psalm	
2 Kings		1:5–6	172
19:25, 27–28	45	6:8–10	172
2 Kings 19:35–37	45	7:6	172
2 Kings 21:11	62	14:1	26
2 Kings 24:4	159	23:1	220
		25:16	6
1 Chronicles		31:9	6
17:16–17	17	32:1–2	105, 152
		32:3–4	152
2 Chronicles		32:8	208
7:1	283	34:19	228
7:14	158	36:6	33
16:9	227	40:5	29
20:7	220	41:9	131
		46:6	205
Ezra		51:1	6
6:22	32	73:24–25	70

77:19	32, 137	16:33	46
78:38	139	27:8	247
85:10–11	6		
86:15	224	**Ecclesiastes**	
103:8	6, 224	3:11	20
103:8–12	153	6:3	88
103:10	19	7:14	46
103:13	220		
111:4	224	**Isaiah**	
112:4	224	1:18	153
118:6	227	5:4	310
119	69, 82	6	288
119:9–16	86	6:3	19, 323
Psalm:119:11	82	6:3, 10	114
119:18	85	9:1	125
119:20, 40	82	9:2	125
119:34, 69	82	9:6	114
119:45	22, 70	11:9	333
119:47	85	26:8–9	67
119:47–48	22	26:10	39
119:105	64	31:34	153
139:1–4	44	38:17	153
139:2–5	32	40:1–3	229
139:14	29	40:12–14	30
145:8	6, 224	43:1–3	228
145:9–10	30	43:25	152
145:5–16	30	44:22	153
		44:28	46
Proverbs		49:4	257
3:34	12	51:6	185
6:25	73	63:9	224
6:27	73	64:4	335
7:25	73	66:13	220
10:12	172		
16:4	46		

Index of Scripture references

Jeremiah

1:5	135
5:22	288
6:19	82
9:13	82
9:23–24	38
15:19	158
16:11	82
23:23–24	44
26:4	82
29:11	208
31:32	220
31:33	69, 82
44:10	82

Lamentations

3:22–23	5

Ezekiel

14:6	158
18:30	158

Daniel

3:18	228
4:35	47
7:13–14	112

Hosea

6:6	5
8:7	204
13:12	152

Joel

2:13	6

Jonah

3:1–10	159
3:4	75
4:2	6

Micah

5:2	124
7:19	153

Habakkuk

2:14	333
3:17–19	229

Matthew

1:6	125
2:23	125
3:2	159
3:15	76
4:12–16	125
4:17	159
5	77
5:7	170
5:13–16	34
5:16	37
5:17	9, 76, 78
5:18	76
5:19	76
5:27–28	73
5:44	171
5:45	30
6:12	165
6:14–15	165
7:6	170
9:13	83
9:36	51, 169, 225

10:15	310	28:20	229
10:22	184		
10:29–30	47	**Mark**	
10:40	91	3:5	51
11:18–19	123	6:12	159
11:23–24	310	6:53	125
11:29	270	14:36	294
12:18–21	143		
12:31	188	**Luke**	
13:43	325	1:30	8
14:14	169	2:40, 52	8
14:34	125	4:22	8
15:32	169	4:29	125
16:18	234	4:30	119
18	164, 165, 170	5:1	125
18:15–20	167	6:27–28, 35–36	171
18:15–35	167	6:27–35	171
18:21–35	164	6:35	20
18:23–35	167	6:35–36	172
18:27	170	9:22	121
18:33	170	9:51	181
19:17	76	10:16	91
21:11	124	13	57
22	91	13:4–5	57
22:20	117	13:11	189
22:30	319	15:7	203
22:34–46	90	15:10	203
22:37–39	131	17	165
22:37–40	79	17:3–4	165
22:40	76	22:53	157
23:23	69, 77	23:33–34	170
23:37	311	23:34	173
26:65	123	24:27	333
26:67	213		
27:16–26	155		

John

1:9	20
1:12	293
1:14–17	8, 9
1:29	16
3:3	143
3:8	143
3:16	177
3:27	134
6:44	132, 133
8:11	80
8:48	123
8:59	119
9:24	123
10:28	307
10:28–29	184, 187
10:39	119
11:25–26	322
11:44	144
12:40–41	114
12:44–45	91
13:20	91
13:34	79
14:1–3	231
14:9	223
14:15, 21	76
14:16, 26	179
14:23	255
15:10	76
15:21	91
15:26	179
16:8	179
16:7	179, 257
16:26–27	292
17:23	274
19:12	123
19:19	124
1:14	9, 121
20:25	155
21:25	333

Acts

2:23	45
2:38	160
2:47	13
3:19	160
5:1–11	286
5:31	160
7:58	149
7:60	173
8:1–3	149
9:15	137, 199
9:16	218
9:26	275
10	218
11:18	160
13:24	160
13:48	143
14:3	7
15:36–40	218
16:6–10	233
17:25	19
17:26	134
17:27	21, 116
17:27–28	21
17:30–31	160
19:4	160
20:21	160
20:24	7
20:29	218

20:30	218
21:27–36	150
22:4–5	197
24:27	13
25:3,9	13
26:5	91
26:11	89, 149, 197
26:14	140
26:20	160

Romans

1:7	12
1:18	98, 133
1:19–20	23
1:20	23, 25, 298, 310, 321
1:21	133
1:24–27	133
1:32	133
2:4	40, 160, 171, 272
2:12	98
2:14–15	23, 24, 64
2:20	74
3:10, 23	98
3:20	98
3:31	72
4:4	98
4:5	99
4:7–8	105
4:15	64
4:25	96, 106
5:1–2	282
5:2	283
5:8	223
5:18	95
6:1	305

6:1–2	185
6:4	185, 243
6:4–8	243
6:5	243
6:6	185, 243
6:7, 12–14	185
6:14	80, 81
6:17	13, 81, 94
6:18	81
6:19	261
7–8	81
7:6	66
7:12	7, 61, 72
7:12, 14	66, 74
7:13	7
7:13–25	97
7:14	133
7:15–19	154
8:3	74
8:5–8	132
8:7	133
8:14–15	293
8:15	294
8:17	294
8:18	315, 320
8:19–22	31
8:21	327
8:23	294, 315
8:26	180
8:28	140, 202, 208
8:29	262
8:29–30	133
8:30	103
8:31–39	187, 307
8:37	219

9:17	45
9:23	110
11:33	30, 42, 48, 200
11:33–36	47
12:6	253
13:8–10	78
13:9	78, 83
15	10
15:4	66, 72, 207, 287
16:1–2	237
16:3–5	238
16:5	237
16:7	238
16:10	237
16:12	237
16:13	238
16:20	12

1 Corinthians

1:2	261
1:3	12, 94
1:8	100
1:13	109
1:30	104, 261
2:9	317, 335
2:14	132
3:13	258
5	166
5:1	166
5:5, 13	166
7:14	308
7:19	72
9:8–11	67
10:6–10	82
10:11	83

10:13	220
13	171
15	106
15:9	10
15:10	11, 87, 93, 219
15:14, 17	106, 189
15:28	329
15:35–49	324
15:51–52	322
15:52	58
16:19	238
16:23	12

2 Corinthians

1:2	12
1:4	175
1:4, 9	206
1:5–6	235
1:8	206
1:8–10	233
1:9	318
2:5–11	166
2:13	177
2:14	177, 201, 219
2:17	181
3:1–2	37
3:18	318
4:4	117, 133
4:4, 6	318
4:7	314
4:8	206
4:8–9	219
4:8–10	314
4:17	314, 315, 317
4:18	321

5:6–8	167	2:16	98
5:7	167	2:20	177
5:10	167	3:2	109
5:21	100, 104, 105	3:10	102
6:1	299, 302	3:13	75, 97, 101, 102
6:4–10	214	3:21	84
7:5	186	3:24	65
7:9	160	4:5	293
7:9–11	265	5:4	297, 303
7:9–13	167	5:14	78
8	109	5:16, 25	67, 145
8:1–7	253	6:10	253
8:2–5	110	6:16	67
8:6–7	14		
8:9	109	**Ephesians**	
8:12	127	1:1	193
9:8	211, 214	1:1, 15, 18	195
10:2, 10	217	1:4	100, 133
11:15	39	1:4–5	266
11:23	213	1:5	293
11:23–27	214	1:5, 11	133
11:23–33	213	1:7	266
11:28–29	215	1:7–8	155
12:7	213	1:8	266
12:9	11, 213	1:13	266
12:11	10, 219	1:14	323
13:14	12	1:15–16	236
		1:17	325
Galatians		1:18	110, 324
1:13	88, 149	1:21	202
1:15	93, 129	2	241
1:15–16	132, 133	2:1	13, 132, 133
1:23	89	2:1, 4, 5	266
2:11–21	218	2:5	243
2:14	218	2:5–6	243

Index of Scripture references

2:6	243	4:29	253
2:7	4	4:31	51, 244
2:8	7, 129, 183	4:32	163
2:8–9	107	5:2	157
2:12	6, 241, 242, 255	5:25	163
2:13	241	6:17	145
2:14	242	6:18	294
2:18	280, 282, 291	6:20	209
2:19	195, 242, 243, 247, 250	6:21	251
2:19–21	247, 266		
2:19–22	243	**Philippians**	
2:21	243, 254	1:3–5	236
2:21, 22	255	1:6	139
2:22	243, 254	1:7	242
3	199	1:12	208
3:1	275	1:12–14	209
3:6	244, 266	1:15	269
3:7	199	1:15–18	217
3:8	10, 11, 193, 195, 199, 200	1:20	198
3:9	200	1:23–24	233
3:12	282	1:27	209
3:16–19	260	2:3	270
3:18	243, 244	2:6	117, 118, 270
3:20	260	2:19–20, 25–26	217
4	265, 267, 269	2:21	217
4:1	265, 275	2:25–30	237
4:1–3	260	2:27	218
4:2	88	3:6	83, 91
4:2–3	268, 269	3:12, 15	262
4:3	275	3:13–14	147
4:4–6	277	3:21	324
4:7	241, 253	4:2	269
4:9	88	4:2–3	218
4:16	244	4:4	219
4:26	51	4:11	208

4:11–13	219	2:13	175
4:13	210, 219, 232	3:6	175
4:19	110	4:3	264
		4:9	175

Colossians

		4:12	37
1:3–4	236	4:14–17	328
1:7	237	4:16	58
1:12	323		
1:16	110		

2 Thessalonians

		1:3	175
2:9	114	1:3–4	236
2:13	155	1:4	175
2:13–14	154	2:1–12	182
2:14	85	2:16	175, 178
2:15	186	2:16–17	176
2:19	275		
2:20–21	109		

1 Timothy

		1:2	12
3:1, 3–4	243	1:5–11	83
3:2	283, 316, 321	1:6–7	83
3:4	318, 320	1:8	66, 72
3:12–15	273	1:9	83
3:13	163	1:9–10	83, 147
3:14	275	1:12	13
4:3	209	1:13	148
4:6	14	1:14	11, 147
4:7	237, 251	1:15	11, 148
4:9	237	2:5	179
4:10	237	3:7	37
4:10–11	217	3:7	179
4:14	237, 302	4:2	23, 64
4:15	238	4:4	31

1 Thessalonians

		4:10	33
1:2–3	236	6:14	326
1:3	175		
1:8–9	175		

Index of Scripture references

2 Timothy

1:2	12
1:3	13
1:7	199
1:9	11, 133, 199, 232
1:12	11
1:15	217
1:16–18	237
2:1	304
2:14	217
2:17	217
2:17–18	304
2:19	134
2:25	160
2:25–26	304
3:16	72
3:16–17	66, 81, 232
4:8	326
4:10	217, 302
4:11	237
4:14	217
4:17	227
4:18	227
4:20	208, 218

Titus

1:4	12
2:11–12	264
2:12	269
2:13	326
3:15	12

Philemon

1–2	251
2	244

8–20	237
10	209
15	251
24	302

Hebrews

1:3	40, 116, 117, 126
1:6	324
1:7,14	324
2:7	320
2:9	12
2:10	318
2:11	293
2:16–17	226
4:13	44
4:15	121, 223
4:15–16	225
4:16	292
6:4–5	307
6:4–6	306
7:25	188, 189, 292
9:1–10	285
9:9	289
9:14	291
9:27	310
10	258
10:4	100
10:19	284
10:19–20	288
10:20–22	289
10:22	289, 291
10:24–25	256
10:25	257
10:26–29	307
11:1	227

11:13 — 206
12:1, 22 — 238
12:14 — 261
12:18–24 — 326
12:25 — 310
12:28 — 233
13:5–6 — 227
13:25 — 12

James
2:24 — 264, 306
4:6 — 12

1 Peter
1:2 — 12
1:4 — 250
1:12 — 200, 203
1:15 — 130
2:21 — 162
2:23 — 173, 272
2:24 — 102, 290
3:18 — 101
4:10 — 253
4:12–16 — 37
5:1, 4, 10 — 318
5:10 — 39, 320
5:12 — 12, 40

2 Peter
1:2 — 12
1:3 — 145, 232
1:4 — 143
2:15 — 300
2:19 — 133
2:20–22 — 300

3:4 — 39
3:10 — 335
3:13 — 335, 336
3:18 — 12, 278

1 John
2:1 — 178
2:2 — 96
3:2 — 322, 324, 325, 333
3:20 — 190

2 John
3 — 12

Jude
2 — 12
4 — 12, 305
24 — 318, 320

Revelation
1:4 — 12
1:16 — 325
1:17 — 283
4:9, 11 — 318
5:6 — 325
5:8 — 327
5:11–12 — 112
5:12–13 — 318
6:12–14 — 58
6:15–16 — 310
7:12 — 318
7:16 — 319
7:16–17 — 319
7:17 — 327
13:8 — 133

Index of Scripture references

15:8	321	21:3	337
17:8	133	21:4, 23, 27	319
19:1, 7	318	21:11	321
19:9	327	21:23	318, 319, 320, 321
21:1	336	22:5	319
21:1–5	39	22:13	126
21:2	336	22:21	12